IMPERIAL POWER

AND REGIONAL TRADE

THE CARIBBEAN BASIN INITIATIVE

ABIGAIL B. BAKAN

DAVID COX

COLIN LEYS

EDITORS

Wilfrid Laurier University Press
WLU

Canadian Cataloguing in Publication Data

Main entry under title:
Imperial power and regional trade : the Caribbean
    Basin Initiative

Includes bibliographical references and index.
ISBN 0-88920-220-6

1. United States – Relations – Caribbean Area.
2. Caribbean Area – Relations – United States.
I. Bakan, Abigail B. (Abigail Bess), 1954-   .
II. Cox, David, 1937-   .   III. Leys, Colin, 1931-   .

HF1456.5.C27I56 1993   337.73-0729   C92-094902-9

Copyright © 1993

Wilfrid Laurier University Press
Waterloo, Ontario, Canada
N2L 3C5

Cover design by Connolly Design Inc.

Cover illustration by Jack Lefcourt

Printed in Canada

Imperial Power and Regional Trade: The Caribbean Basin Initiative has been produced from a manuscript supplied in electronic form by the editors.

Contents

List of Tables

Preface

The research reported in this volume was carried out between 1984 and 1989 under the auspices of the Programme (now Group) for the Study of National and International Development (SNID) of Queen's University, Kingston, Ontario, as part of a larger project on "Sovereignty and Security," funded by the Donner Canadian Foundation and directed by David Cox and Colin Leys. The larger project sought to explore the implications for the other countries of the hemisphere, and not least Canada, of the assertion of US hegemony by the Reagan administration from 1980 onwards. The Caribbean Basin Initiative was an eminent example of this assertion of US power. It was a policy that directly affected the Caribbean nations and their hard-won and still precarious regional organization, and indirectly affected other industrial powers with significant interests in the Caribbean, notably Canada and Britain.

Abigail Bakan joined the project in 1986. With the assistance of Godwin Friday she was chiefly responsible for reducing the individual research reports (not all of which are included in this volume) to a publishable form and recruited an additional paper (Chapter 8, by Fauzya Moore) on the impact of the CBI on Caribbean regional integration.

When the research reports were in draft, they were presented to a group of Caribbean and Canadian diplomats, and Caribbean, Canadian, American, and British academic specialists at a workshop held in Kingston, Ontario, in May 1989. The editors and authors would like to express their appreciation of the valuable contributions made by the participants at that workshop, although responsibility for errors of fact and for the judgments contained in the book naturally belongs to the authors alone. Here it might be noted that the economic report card on the CBI has changed very little from the time of the completion of the main research in mid-1989.

Thanks are also due to a series of SNID research assistants, especially Usha Thakur and Judith Soares, and to Mrs. Bernice Gallagher and Mrs. Shirley Fraser of the Department of Political Studies at Queen's, for invaluable practical help at various stages of the project.

This book has been published with the help of a grant from the Social Science Federation of Canada, using funds provided by the Social Sciences and Humanities Research Council of Canada.

1

The CBI: An Overview

1 Introduction

The election of Ronald Reagan as president of the United States in November 1980 opened a new chapter in international relations, albeit one which had many familiar features to the small states of the Caribbean. Under Reagan the US shifted towards a more overt use of its immense economic and military power and increasingly tended to discount alliance-based, consensual politics, confronting adversaries and allies alike with stark choices. In spite of dramatic apparent successes, such as the collapse of the Eastern Bloc communist regimes at the end of the 1980s, the long-run ability of even a sole superpower to achieve its foreign policy goals remains limited, as the Persian Gulf crisis has painfully demonstrated. It is also evident that new centres of economic power are rapidly emerging in Europe and South East Asia which could increasingly call into question the economic foundation of the US's unique military superiority. Nonetheless, the Reagan years threw into sharp relief the absolute and growing disparity of power between the US and even its larger allies. As for its smaller neighbours, allied or not, the effects of the US's decision to use its power decisively to assert its hegemony in the Western hemisphere were immediate and far-reaching. Their sovereignty was called in question, not simply in terms of their ability to protect their domain, but even in terms of their formal legal equality.

The Caribbean Basin Initiative was one of the earliest expressions of the "new reality" in American foreign policy-making. Presented as an Economic Recovery Act, and indeed forcefully pressing the small Caribbean island states to reorient their trade towards the US, the CBI was nonetheless a building block in the construction of a new North American trade bloc under US hegemony. From the standpoint of the US, the 1989 free trade agreement with Canada, the soon-to-be-concluded agreement with Mexico, and the continental free trade system urged on the South American states by President Bush in December 1990 are logical extensions of the policy which began with the CBI.

Notes for Chapter 1 are on pp. 217-18.

The experience of the Caribbean region under this policy thus has a relevance far beyond the Caribbean, and it is this experience which is recorded and analyzed in the chapters that follow.

These chapters suggest that, with greater or lesser degrees of reluctance, Caribbean governments and opinion leaders have felt obliged to co-operate in implementing the CBI policies, even when these appear not to serve the best interests of their countries or the region.

2   The CBI: Its Fundamental Features

The Caribbean Basin Initiative (CBI) was officially unveiled by US President Ronald Reagan at the Organization of American States (OAS) meeting in February 1982. For the most part, it was enthusiastically received by regional leaders.[1] As a major US initiative, it seemed to promise a welcome change from the customary concentration on military aid to the countries of the region. In his OAS address, President Reagan explained:

> [t]his economic proposal is as unprecedented as today's crisis in the Caribbean. . . . It represents a farsighted act by our own people at a time of considerable economic difficulty at home. . . . This commitment makes unmistakably clear our determination to help our neighbors grow strong.[2]

This promise has thus far been unfulfilled. Assessments of the CBI have ranged from a "modest success," a view held primarily by its most influential proponents, to an unmitigated failure.[3]

The CBI comprises three basic parts: (i) bilateral aid; (ii) tax incentives for certain US businesses' activities in the Caribbean; and (iii) concessionary trade arrangements. The latter is generally regarded as the most important aspect of the program and deserves most attention. What ultimately emerged from Congress in the summer of 1983 as the Caribbean Basin Economic Recovery Act was not exactly what the program's originators in the Reagan administration had intended. Despite the confident rhetoric of President Reagan and others associated with the program, compromises had to be struck along the way in order to win sufficient support for the legislation in Congress. The effect was to dilute the final legislation as domestic interests sought to ensure that they were not injured by the program. The Act took effect on January 1, 1984.

3   The CBI Package

Twenty-seven countries were made theoretically eligible to participate in the CBI.[4] To benefit, however, each country had to reflect and be granted beneficiary status by the president, providing certain conditions were met.[5] These conditions clearly indicated the political parameters of the policy initiative. No country designated "Communist" could be included in the program.[6] Also excluded were any country that (a) expropriated or utilized property controlled by US citizens without adequate compensation; (b) provided preferential treatment to commodities from a developed country other than the US, to the detriment of US commerce; (c) failed to satisfy Washington that it was co-operating adequately in the combatting of narcotics trafficking;[7] (d) violated US copyright laws governing broadcast material; (e) nullified or abrogated contracts with, or awards made to, US citizens; and, finally, had no extradition treaty with the US.[8]

There are also several discretionary criteria which may be considered in granting a country beneficiary status. They are summarized by the US Department of Commerce as follows:

> [a]n expressed desire by the country to be designated; [e]conomic conditions in the country; [t]he extent to which the country is prepared to provide equitable and reasonable access to its markets and basic commodity resources; [t]he degree to which such country uses export subsidies, or imposes export performance requirements and local content requirements; [t]he degree to which the trade policies of the country as related to other CBI beneficiaries are contributing to the revitalization of the region; [t]he degree to which a country is undertaking self-help measures to promote its own economic development; [t]he degree to which workers in such a country are afforded reasonable working conditions; [t]he extent to which such country prohibits its nationals from engaging in the broadcast of copyrighted material belonging to U.S. copyright owners without their express consent; [and] the extent to which such country protects the intellectual property rights, including patents and trademarks, of foreign nationals.[9]

As first proposed by the administration, the CBI would have provided duty-free entry for virtually all Caribbean Basin products, with the exception of textiles and apparel, for 12 years; supplemental aid for the region, amounting to US$350 million for the program's inaugural year; tax credits for US firms that locate production facilities in the region; and duty-free entry for sugar produced in the Caribbean, up to 110 per cent of existing imports.

The Congress did approve what it termed "emergency support" for the region of US$355 million, marginally surpassing the administration's original $350 million request. Moreover, in keeping with the label "emergency support," this aid was approved in August 1982, a full year before the rest of the program won congressional approval. Congress also voted in favour of a 12-year program as requested by the Reagan administration, designating September 30, 1995, as the termination date.

But with regard to the duty-free trade component of the program, Congress voted to exclude a considerably wider range of products than textiles and apparel as proposed by the Reagan administration. The additional excluded categories of products were petroleum and petroleum products; canned tuna; footwear; luggage; handbags; flat goods; leather, rubber, and plastic gloves; leather wearing apparel; and watches and watch parts containing material made in a "Communist" country. Furthermore, though Caribbean sugar was granted duty-free status, it remained subject to non-tariff barriers such as import fees and unilaterally imposed quotas. Of the other commodities excluded, textiles and leather goods are perhaps the most significant, as they are produced in some quantity in the region and would be the manufactured products most likely to bring immediate benefits to regional producers.

To be granted duty-free access to the US market, eligible products must be grown or manufactured in one or more of the beneficiary countries and exported directly to the United States, and at least 35 per cent of their value must be added in the beneficiary country. There is, however, a provision that up to 15 per cent of this may be attributable to materials made in the United States. Materials made in Puerto Rico and the US Virgin Islands may also contribute towards the stipulated 35 per cent of the value added. There is a further eligibility requirement, the "substantial transformation" clause, which states that in order to qualify for duty exemption, commodities which contain materials that originate outside the CBI countries must satisfy US Customs authorities that the final product is "new and different" from its non-CBI components. The stated purpose of this, and of the value-added requirement, is to discourage superficial activities such as mixing, labelling, and packaging (from which little benefit accrues to the region) and encourage more substantial manufacturing.

Another important feature is that the CBI does not rule out the exclusion of Caribbean exports to the US by means of quotas, as it specifically permits the US government (officially the president) to impose quotas unilaterally on any commodity imported duty-free under the program. Use of this provision would normally be made after it had been determined, or at least forcefully argued, that the unrestricted importation of a particular product was causing injury to US domestic producers. The provision has already been applied in the cases of ethanol and steel.

From the outset, then, it was apparent that political considerations were paramount in the trade component, as well as the military component, of the legislative package.

4 United States Hegemony and the Caribbean Basin

Since the unilateral proclamation of the Monroe Doctrine nearly two centuries ago, the United States has made clear its intention to maintain its hegemony in the Caribbean Basin. The means have changed over time to suit prevailing domestic political conditions and objectives, ranging from outright military intervention to more subtle forms. The CBI is one of the most recent expressions of this: an ostensibly economic package designed to address political concerns which the US administration of the day felt could no longer be ignored.

The stated aim of the CBI was to bolster the economies of the Caribbean and Central American countries. By introducing it the Reagan administration sought to demonstrate that it took the welfare of the people of these countries seriously and was prepared to promote it with more than the customary military aid, if not entirely without it. The political character of the program, however, was obvious. The CBI followed in the wake of the Nicaraguan and Grenadian revolutions, and the growing rejection of US hegemony throughout the region.

The United States has consolidated its dominance in the Latin American and Caribbean region since the turn of the century. This process has involved military invasion or occupation of territory no less than 80 times. Furthermore, US direct economic investment, especially in the larger economies of Latin America such as Mexico, Brazil, Argentina, and Venezuela, is a critical element of US global power.

The small countries of Central America and the Caribbean are a vulnerable link in this structure, not because they are economically important to the United States, but for two other reasons. First, the region that the United States has dubbed the "Caribbean Basin" is of great strategic interest to the US. Second, resistance to American control — from the guerrilla resistance movement in El Salvador, to the Sandinista Revolution in Nicaragua, the New Jewel Movement regime in Grenada, and the obstinacy of dictators of largely US creation, such as Manuel Noriega in Panama — has constantly led recent American policy-makers to fear a threat to US hegemony. The traditional antidote, tried and tested throughout the years, is a show of US strength, backed up by the threat and sometimes the reality of military repression.[10] The CBI, accompanied as it was by very large increases of US military aid and force commitments in the region, was in this sense a traditional US policy response, but with a significant new twist — the attempt to redirect Caribbean trade and economic links away from regional multilateral relations (and away from traditional links to other industrial powers such as Canada and the UK) towards bilateral ties to the US, under the auspices of "free trade."

5 Subsequent Developments in the CBI

The CBI program has evolved considerably since it was first announced in 1982 and even since the legislation took effect in 1984. In the wake of poor performance during its first two years of operation (1984-86), the program received stringent criticism from various sources, particularly business and government leaders in the beneficiary countries. The exclusion of textiles, garments, and the other products mentioned above from the duty-free treatment was strongly challenged, and persistent pressure was brought to bear on the administration and Congress to modify the legislation. It was not without some success.

In February 1986, the Caribbean Basin Special Access Programme for Apparel was introduced under the framework of the CBI. This provides for more favourable treatment for Caribbean Basin apparel and textiles under three types of agreements. The first is Specific Limits (SLs) "which are absolute quotas either negotiated or unilaterally imposed and which increase by a certain percentage annually."[11] The second type is Guaranteed Access Levels (GALs). It is reserved for garments assembled in beneficiary countries from materials manufactured and cut in the United States. For such products exported to the United States, customs duty is charged only on the value added in the beneficiary country. A request from a beneficiary country for an increase in the guaranteed access level for its apparel in the US market is "automatically enacted" unless the US government rejects it within 30 days. Furthermore, if the requesting country can demonstrate that the size of the increase it has specified corresponds to its existing idle capacity, or its projected additional capacity due to come on stream, the US is prepared to guarantee access "for virtually all production capability of apparel and other made up articles (such as bed linens or soft side luggage)" eligible under this aspect of the program.[12] The third component, Designated Consultation Levels (DCLs), allows negotiated levels of apparel articles to enter the United States. These articles are exempt from any US content requirements but not from customs duty. They may, however, be accorded more favourable treatment than similar articles from countries not included in the CBI. These measures were intended to boost the garment industry in the beneficiary countries to provide immediate benefit under the program, while at the same time not jeopardizing the interests of US domestic garment producers.

There was a second addition to the program. In 1986, Section 936 of the US Internal Revenue Code was revised to permit funds generated in Puerto Rico under that section of the US tax code to be invested in CBI beneficiary countries. To be eligible to use these funds, however, the beneficiary country must first sign a Tax Information Exchange Agreement with the United States. Furthermore, the funds are available primarily to establish branch plants for companies which have existing operations in Puerto Rico. It is the desire of Puerto Rican authorities that the branch-plant investments utilizing these funds concentrate on low-wage, labour-intensive activities which complement manufacturing located in Puerto Rico.

The CBI was originally scheduled to run for only 12 years, with September 30, 1995, as its intended expiry date. However, from the outset, the governments and business leaders of the beneficiary countries argued that such a limitation would cripple the program, because entrepreneurs would be extremely reluctant to undertake sizeable investments, particularly in manufacturing — the type of investment most needed — within the context of such a short-term development program. Interested agencies persistently lobbied Washington to have the duration of the duty-free provision of the program extended so that it would become "a permanent feature of U.S. international trade policy."[13] Other objectives included:

> making enhancement of the region's tourism sector a major objective and instrument of the CBI; providing preferential trade access for categories of products currently excluded from the CBI; exempting CBI-origin products from the cumulation rule in cases of alleged dumping and illegal subsidization; [and] providing freer U.S. market access for the region's sugar producers.[14]

During 1989, the Caribbean Basin Economic Expansion Act of 1989 — HR 1233 (more commonly known as CBI II) worked its way through the labyrinthine legislative process of the US House of Representatives. Before passing the bill on to the House Rules Committee in late June 1989, the House Ways and Means Committee made significant amendments to it. One of these was to reject the administration's requests for a 50 per cent reduction of duty on imports of leather footwear, petroleum, and petroleum products, and canned tuna fish for CBI beneficiary countries. The administration's proposal to grant duty-free status to Caribbean Basin textiles and apparel which are either not available or in short supply in the US was also rejected. The Committee chose instead to establish a statutory list of foreign fabrics that would be eligible for duty exemption under the GAL component of the Special Access Programme for apparel. The requests regarding sugar imports fared somewhat better, as a guaranteed minimum import quota, set at the 1989 level of 371 000 tons, was established. This measure protects Carribean Basin producers from any further unilateral reduction of quotas in the future, even if the US were to lower its quotas worldwide, while CBI producers can still benefit from any rise in US global quotas. The Committee also voted to relax the rules of origin for ethanol in order to boost exports to the US. Finally, the duty-free allowance granted to US residents returning from CBI countries has been raised from US$400 to $600.

After interminable delays, CBI II was also passed in the US Senate, on April 26, 1990, with only minor differences from the House version. The final stage of the legislation, the resolution of these differences in a joint House-Senate Conference Committee, took over a year to complete, eventually becoming law in August 1990.

Though these improvements are important, in terms of the overall effect of the CBI they are, in truth, marginal. The pattern of a trade package designed first and foremost to protect the interests of the United States, and only secondarily to promote those of the Caribbean region, has not been altered by the amendments.

The picture with regard to the economic performance of the CBI has also changed rather little since the main research reported in this volume was done. According to the latest available *Annual Report on the Impact of the Caribbean Basin Economic Recovery Act on US Industries and Consumers* (i.e., for 1988) prepared by the United States International Trade Commission, US total imports from CBI beneficiary countries rose in value only marginally, from US$6.0 billion to US$6.1 billion, between 1987 and 1988. Traditional exports from these countries continued to decline. Coffee exports, for example, fell by $215 million over that period, and petroleum by $318 million. On the other hand, textile and apparel exports to the US rose by $350 million, helping to offset declines in other areas. The more up to date *Report by the US Department of State on the Caribbean Basin Initiative*, issued in November 1989 and including data on the period up to June 1989, shows that a similar trend continued up to that point. So-called non-traditional CBI-eligible exports, principally textiles and apparels, continued to perform better than traditional exports, registering an increase of 90.8 per cent between 1983 and June 1989. It is important to note, however, that the increase was very unevenly distributed among the beneficiary countries and that it was not enough to offset the declines in other exports. Total US imports from CBI beneficiaries over this period declined by over 27 per cent while US exports to these countries rose by 80 per cent. As a result of this, US trade surplus with the region increased. Between 1987 and 1988, for example, the US trade surplus with the region rose from US$629 million to US$1.4 billion.

The study which follows is divided into two parts. The first part considers the Caribbean Basin Initiative from the perspective of the industrialized countries most involved in the economic and political life of the region; the second part considers it from the perspective of the region itself. Devanand Ramnarine's "The Philosophy and Development Prospects of the CBI" (Chapter 2) analyzes the context of the CBI and its origins in the Reagan administration's concern to reassert US hegemony in the region. This is followed by an examination of the responses to the CBI of Britain and Canada—the anglophone Caribbean's two largest trading partners and sources of aid, prior to the CBI. In Chapter 3 Colin Leys discusses the scope and limits of Britain's complicity in the assertion of US hegemony represented by the CBI, while in Chapter 4 Catherine Hyett examines the rationale behind Canada's apparently enthusiastic "mini-CBI," Caribcan. Part II opens with an analysis, also by Ramnarine, of the problematic nature of the development model implicit in the CBI. In Chapter 6 Hyett compares and contrasts the experience of Jamaica, Barbados, and the Eastern Caribbean states, stressing the differential impact of the CBI on the receiving countries; while in Chapter 7 Godwin Friday does the same for Trinidad. The volume concludes with a study by Fauzya Moore of the dislocating impact of CBI on regional economic integration.

Taken as a whole, the research reported in this volume suggests the prospect of a growing credibility gap between the claims made for the US initiative, and the reality of its economic results. It seems unlikely, therefore, that the CBI's political consequences—its significant contribution to the weakening of regional co-operation and to the strengthening of US hegemony in the Caribbean—will continue for long unchallenged.

2

The Political Logic of the CBI

Devanand J. Ramnarine

1 Introduction

The Reagan administration came into office in 1981 amidst a gathering recession in the US and capitalist world economy, and after a series of reversals in parts of the world where US influence and hegemony had been viewed as normal. The "Reagan Doctrine" was meant to address both of these problems. Its economic component rested on principles designed to reinvigorate the capitalist world economy under continued US leadership, at the expense of the agenda of global economic restructuring which developing countries were advocating in the 1970s. The political aspect of the doctrine consisted of a vigorous reassertion of the cold-war perspective on international politics, which provided the framework for unprecedented US military expansion. A more decisive US military superiority over the Soviet Union could, by the logic of "nuclear blackmail," frighten the Soviet Union away from areas of the Third World where the US chose to intervene.

This worldview was transplanted into the conflict-ridden Caribbean Basin. A White Paper on "Communist intervention" in El Salvador, a Special Report on Cuban activities in the region, and a clever reversal of the human rights policy of the former administration paved the way for more widespread US intervention. This came in the form of a three-tiered strategy of "rolling back" the status quo in "unfriendly countries," "drawing the line" against further challenges to US hegemony, and extending comprehensive support to friendly governments of the region.

The implementation of a militarist and confrontational policy in the Caribbean Basin, however, elicited apprehension at home and abroad of imminent direct US intervention and precipitated a crisis of legitimacy in the administration's Caribbean Basin policy. It was in this context that the Caribbean Basin Initiative was formulated. Its political

---

Notes for Chapter 2 are on pp. 218-27.

logic was twofold: it perpetuated the administration's "hard line" approach to the region, while simultaneously resolving the obstacle of congressional opposition.

The CBI was presented as a multilateral economic strategy that could address instabilities in the region at their socioeconomic source, while promoting US interests there. This convinced the majority in Congress that the administration had embarked on a profoundly new and different policy toward the Caribbean Basin.

When divested of its elaborate disguise, however, the CBI represented a continuity with the basic three-tiered approach of the administration to US hegemonic problems in the region. The political logic of the CBI, from its initial conceptualization to its final legislative form, was consistent. Three significant phases in the development of the CBI are highlighted below. First, there was an officially sanctioned but privately executed policy aimed at fashioning Jamaica, under its conservative, pro-US government, into a model of development that could present a compelling alternative to Cuban development. Second, the Reagan administration attempted to generalize this strategy for the rest of the region but as an *official* (rather than private) and *multilateral* (rather than bilateral) approach. This, however, ran into Mexican objections over the political and ideological interpretation of multilateralism. Finally, the administration produced its own regional initiative which, after some congressional amendments, became the present version of the CBI. Our examination of several important features of the CBI will demonstrate that, with support from Congress, the administration successfully infused into the program its political perspective on the region.

2   The Reagan Doctrine and the Caribbean Basin

The Reagan administration's solution to the world economic crisis consisted in what has been appropriately termed the "locomotive theory of recovery."[1] A revitalized US economy would pull along the economies of other developed countries which would, in turn, pull the developing countries along.[2] This process was to be energized and sustained through the dismantling of trade barriers between countries.[3]

The dominant issues in the North-South dialogue—reform of international institutions, realignment of the global division of labour, equalization of terms of trade—were thus effectively derailed. Ironically, developing countries were now required to implement far-reaching reforms themselves to help resolve the problems of the world economy. To lure these countries into opening their markets, the US offered the "carrot" of reciprocal trade concessions through an expanded General System of Preferences (GSP); the "stick," however, was that official lending, already conditional on internal adjustment policies, now became conditional on the adoption of certain trade policies as well.[4] But more sobering than the reversal of the global agenda at the expense of developing countries was the bitter reality that developed countries were not prepared to observe their own stipulated *quid pro quo*. Protectionist sentiment had increased in the US Congress, and new restrictions had been imposed on the US General System of Preferences program which had negative consequences for the newly industrializing countries.[5] With regard to credit to developing countries, US assistance had declined,[6] and shifted in emphasis from development aid, which had traditionally constituted up to 75 per cent of the external capital of low-income countries, to balance of payments assistance.[7] At the same time, international lending institutions had been unable to fill this void.[8] Private banks were apprehensive that the debt might not be repayable, and developing countries were therefore pressed to divert scarce resources to debt servicing rather than development.[9] The philosophy of development implied in this approach was given expression in the CBI and endorsed by the US Congress.[10]

Important political events under the Carter administration—the overthrow of a US ally, the Shah of Iran, as well as of the friendly Caribbean Basin dictators, Grenada's Eric Gairy and Nicaragua's Anastasio Somoza, the passage of the treaty which promised an end to US sovereignty over the Panama Canal, and the thawing of the cold war disposition toward Cuba—were interpreted by the new Reagan administration as steps in an unwarranted surrender of US global supremacy to communist expansionism. The Reagan administration launched a sustained ideological offensive against the Soviet Union, portraying it as a Goliath "Evil Empire" bent on consuming a God-fearing West on its way towards global domination.[11] Not only was the *ideology* of Soviet expansionism emphasized, but also the conviction that it was fast becoming a reality, that both the means and ends involved were immoral, and that the Soviets were exporting their version of social change to other countries.[12]

The anti-communist offensive was faithfully reproduced in the Caribbean Basin. The ideological basis for a military and confrontational policy was first prepared with the publication of the White Paper on El Salvador, which purported to demonstrate that "communist interference in El Salvador" had made that country a "textbook case of indirect armed aggression."[13] A supplement to this report claimed "definitive evidence of the clandestine military support given by the Soviet Union and their Marxist allies to the Marxist-Leninist guerrillas now fighting to overthrow the established Government of El Salvador."[14] Accordingly, most of the widespread killings in that country were blamed on leftist guerrillas of the Farabundo Marti National Liberation Front (FMLN), and the Salvadoran government was vindicated as a neutral force with broad-based support trying to stem the violence. On specific points such as these, the White Paper was clearly in error.[15] Indeed, overall the White Paper was revealed to be a fabrication. Important documents disproving its claims were conveniently omitted from the public compilation, certain documents were altered, and there was no documentation to support the alleged role of the Soviet Union and the Palestine Liberation Organization in El Salvador.[16] The White Paper did, however, serve a major political/ideological function: it refocussed the debate from whether there was "communist interference" in the Caribbean Basin to how widespread this interference actually was. The administration exploited this apprehension to appropriate more military aid for El Salvador and to "punish" Nicaragua, which was implicated in the White Paper.

A decision was taken to send $25 million in military aid to El Salvador and to increase US military advisers there from 19 to 55, under the added rationale that the US itself was threatened and should act in accordance with the principles of the Monroe Doctrine.[17] Soon, US personnel were actually piloting helicopters on military missions against the guerrillas.[18]

With regard to Nicaragua, the administration publicly committed itself to a diplomatic solution. By March 1981, Secretary Schultz reported that there was "some moderation in the flow of arms" from Nicaragua to El Salvador and that the Nicaraguan government assured the US that it would abstain from the Salvadoran conflict.[19] But actual events indicated that this was hardly the issue in US-Nicaraguan relations. The US was not prepared to live with a Sandinista government and was, in fact, committed to a policy of "rollback" by the tactic of "war not defined as war" or "low intensity conflict." The 1986 "US Army Operational Concept for Low Intensity Conflict" described this tactic as "the proactive, thoughtful, energetic, innovative, and synergistic application of comprehensive political, social, economic and psychological efforts."[20] The first act was to cancel the remaining economic aid to Nicaragua.[21] While the president was empowered to do this if it were determined that a recipient country was supporting violence in another country, the document explaining the decision noted that in Nicaragua this was not the case: "We have found no hard evidence of arms movements through Nicaragua during the past few weeks."[22] The document then noted that "Important US security interests are at stake . . . in the region" and proceeded to reveal the real policy toward Nicaragua: "We . . . want to continue to assist moderate forces in Nicaragua which are resisting Marxist domination, working toward a democratic alternative and keeping alive the private sector."[23]

US economic war was expanded through efforts to cut off multilateral aid from international financial institutions, invariably through the use of technical economic arguments.[24] By late 1981, economic warfare was supplemented by a CIA covert operation. Counter-revolutionary forces or "Contras" were united, expanded, trained on US soil, and financed. But, as they became notorious for corruption, ineptitude, and the slaughter of civilians, the CIA resorted to foreign operatives to mine harbours and destroy other vital economic infrastructure in Nicaragua.[25]

The Reagan administration completed its cold-war picture of the Caribbean Basin with a comprehensive country-by-country special report on "Cuba's Renewed Support for Violence in Latin America."[26] The gist of the report was that in return for Soviet aid, Cuba had renewed its campaign of the 1960s to promote "armed insurgencies" in areas where the USSR faced constraints. At the diplomatic level, Cuba was said to be championing "the notion of a 'natural alliance' between the Soviet bloc and the Third World," altogether enabling Moscow to maintain a "low profile" in the hemisphere, which was necessary for cultivating "state-to-state relations and economic ties" with countries in the region. The covert insurrectionary activities, the report claimed, were being co-ordinated by the America Department of the Cuban Communist Party through diplomatic missions, particularly the embassy in Mexico City. These activities included military training for groups from El Salvador, Nicaragua, Guatemala, Costa Rica, Honduras, Grenada, the Dominican Republic, Guyana, Jamaica, Haiti, and the South American countries of Colombia, Uruguay, and Chile.[27]

Although the administration had a clear policy of supporting friends and punishing opponents in the region, there was nevertheless one obstacle. This was the legislative requirement that the human rights performance of recipient countries be a condition for bilateral aid. To pass assistance for El Salvador, the administration had already issued fraudulent presidential certifications that the government of that country was making progress on human rights. To continue to do this would prove embarrassing, especially since Congress was already alert to this tactic.[28] The solution to this problem consisted in overriding the moralism of human rights in favour of a "higher" moralism of anti-communism and US national security interests.

The major proponent of this new strategy was Jeanne Kirkpatrick.[29] She criticized the Carter administration for what she deemed a philosophy of history based on the inevitability that the Third World would modernize. The result, she argued, was a deterministic approach to foreign policy. When the administration sought to "assist change" by insisting on human rights, it did so only selectively, with the result that friendly, anti-communist or right-wing regimes were forced to liberalize, thus diluting their power. Eventually, the US abandoned them in the face of insurgencies, while the revolutionary autocracies of communist regimes with similar human rights abuses were allowed to prosper.

Kirkpatrick challenged the Carter administration's philosophy of history and the foreign policy which it produced. First, she argued, events are shaped not by "forces" but by people, whose identity she unambiguously disclosed with the rhetorical question: "So what if the 'deep historical forces' at work . . . look a lot like Russians and Cubans?"[30] Following this alternative philosophy, Kirkpatrick indicated her foreign policy preference with the nostalgic observation that "Where once upon a time an American President might have sent marines to assure the protection of American strategic interests, there is no room for force in this world of progress and self-determination."[31]

Second, the Carter administration had fallen victim to a number of fallacious assumptions about friendly regimes faced with insurgency. These were the belief that a democratic alternative existed; the fatalistic conclusion that the status quo could not persist; and the view that "any change, including the establishment of a government headed by self-styled Marxist revolutionaries, was preferable to the present government."[32] Against these "fallacious assumptions," Kirkpatrick argued that the requisite "political culture" and constitution did not exist for democracy to take root and that "[d]ecades, if not centuries, are normally required for people to acquire the necessary disciplines and habits."[33] Further, the status quo could have liberalized had the Carter administration advised a policy of gradual "contestation and participation" instead of urging the replacement of the autocrat. In fact, in doing the latter, the administration brought the crisis to a head since "[w]ithout him [the autocrat] the organized life of society will collapse like an arch from which the keystone has been removed."[34]

Lastly, Kirkpatrick deplored the view that a traditional autocracy is worse than its revolutionary alternative: "Although . . . there is no evidence of a revolutionary 'socialist' or Communist society being democratized, right-wing autocracies do sometimes evolve into democracies."[35] In a now-familiar passage, she added the virtue of social order to the superior guarantees of traditional autocrats:

> Traditional autocrats leave in place existing allocations of wealth, power, status and other resources which in most traditional societies favour an affluent few and maintain masses in poverty. . . . They do not disturb the habitual rhythms of work and leisure, habitual places of residence, habitual patterns of residence, habitual patterns of family and personal relations. Because the miseries of traditional life are familiar, they are bearable to ordinary people who, growing up

in society, learn to cope, as children born to untouchables in India acquire the skills and attitudes necessary for survival in the miserable roles they are destined to fill.[36]

To these attributes of democratic potential and social order, Kirkpatrick added the strategic merit of traditional authoritarian regimes. They are "more compatible to US interests," a foreign-policy imperative which, in her view, the Carter administration ignored as it lost the Panama Canal "to a swaggering Latin Dictator of Castroist bent" and presided over the "dramatic extension of Soviet power in the Horn of Africa, Afghanistan, Southern Africa and the Caribbean."[37]

In reality, the policy of the Carter administration bore little resemblance to the benign characterization offered by Kirkpatrick. Furthermore, beyond her evident medieval political morality and candid insolence for the underprivileged sectors of society is the glaring contradiction and selectivity of her arguments. She at once condemns the deterministic philosophy of history and counsels it in accounting for the miseries of traditional life (i.e., the role of destiny, which exonerates autocrats from responsibility for miseries), a contradiction born of her enthusiasm to celebrate the virtues of traditional autocrats.

But flawed and disconcerting though the Kirkpatrick thesis is, its clever combination of a "higher" morality of anti-communism with a patriotic appeal to national interests became a familiar part of the foreign-policy lexicon and lent a timely intellectual rationalization to the administration's policy of supporting brutal right-wing regimes and supplanting revolutionary governments and movements in the Caribbean Basin. By the end of 1981, however, this policy generated its own problems, and US policy towards the Caribbean Basin began to flounder in a crisis of legitimacy which assumed both domestic and international dimensions.

Three issues were central to this crisis. First, serious doubts emerged about the administration's cold-war interpretation of conflicts in the Caribbean Basin, particularly Central America. Former ambassador to El Salvador Robert White advanced the increasingly popular view that the "insurgent movement" in El Salvador arose from "fifty years of injustice" and would exist "whether the Soviet Union or Cuba was lending assistance or not."[38] In April 1981, following the publication of the White Paper, 62 per cent of respondents to a *CBS-New York Times* poll agreed that the Soviet Union and Cuba were involved in the Salvadoran war. However, this declined one year later, according to a *Los Angeles Times* poll, to 45 per cent.[39]

The second aspect of the legitimacy crisis was the prevailing feeling that the administration's policy was in disarray. While to informed observers it was clear that the administration was committed to military solutions, its mixed rhetoric of confrontation and diplomacy could not but elicit confusion. Senator Glenn captured this when he rhetorically asked Secretary Haig: "I do not say this tongue-in-cheek, but do we have a Central American policy?"[40] Between March and October 1981, public approval of the president's handling of El Salvador fell from 36 to 22 per cent, and by March 1982, US Central American policy in general elicited an approval/disapproval rate of 33 per cent/49 per cent.[41]

But by far the most troubling issue for the administration was the lingering fear in Congress and among the public at large that US involvement in Central America was gradually being escalated into a Vietnam-like situation and that the administration was deliberately concealing this intent. It was believed, for instance, that the US actually persuaded the Salvadoran government that it needed military aid.[42] In late February 1981, Secretary Haig responded vigorously to reports of US plans to send more military advisers to El Salvador with the assurance that "there is no intention, there's been no discussion of it and there's been no consideration of it."[43] Barely one week later, however, came the decision to do so. At the same time, repeated assurances that the US would not pursue a Vietnam-like involvement were matched by occasional reminders that no options were being ruled out, including actions against Cuba, the alleged source of instability.[44]

Congressional response focussed on three issues. First, interference in El Salvador was seen as inappropriate. Representative Leach, a Republican, remarked that "we are partially considered in the eyes of the world to have intervened in a colonialist fashion. We have identified [with the Salvadoran government] to the point of being pointed out as complicitous of human rights violations."[45] The second concern was that the administration was violating the War Powers Act by not consulting with Congress prior to sending US personnel into situations of hostility, and that this was a ploy to keep Congress from knowing the true motive for and measure of US involvement in El Salvador.[46] Third, the Vietnam parallel was becoming so plausible that even the "ultra-right" Republican Congressman, Jack Kemp, was asking the administration for an assurance that it would not "send troops or military personnel or in any way risk a Vietnam-type experience for the United States."[47]

The administration tended to respond to critics by questioning their "patriotic" and "anti-communist" credentials[48] and by suggesting that there were other issues of more importance for Americans to consider.[49] But public apprehension remained high, with 65 per cent of respondents to an ABC-Washington Post poll agreeing that "the war in El Salvador is much like the war in Vietnam."[50]

International opinion was equally disconcerting to the Reagan administration. Already during the Carter administration, Mexico and the Andean Pact nations gave recognition to the Sandinista struggle in Nicaragua; Panama and Costa Rica actually assisted the Sandinistas; and the OAS had called for the "immediate and definitive replacement of the Somoza regime."[51] During the initial period of the Reagan administration, the Mexican government and Social Democrats in Europe and Latin America expressed support for the insurgents in El Salvador.[52] The Socialist International, the international confederation of Social Democratic parties, declared in opposition to the Reagan administration that the conflict was rooted in "unjust economic and social structures," urged an end to foreign interference, and called for a negotiated solution.[53] More significantly, a Franco-Mexican Declaration of August 1981 affirmed, *inter alia*, the legitimacy of the Salvadoran insurgency, the right of the Salvadoran people to initiate their own process of political settlement, and the need for other countries to restrict their interest to the framework allowed by the United Nations.[54] The West German government might have followed suit had US influence not been exerted.[55]

With regard to post-revolutionary Nicaragua, Mexican President Lopez-Portillo, during his visit to Washington in June 1981, urged President Reagan: "I really must insist that you understand clearly that Mexico has a special experience in Latin America."[56] In his visit to Managua in February 1982, the Mexican president continued this defiance of the US by extolling Nicaragua as "the path and model of liberation," and a "source of pride to Mexico" and pledged "Mexico will always be at your side."[57] He further declared, in a refutation of the position of the US, that "Central American and even Caribbean revolutions are above all the struggles of the poor and oppressed people to live better and with freedom" and warned "An intervention . . . would represent a gigantic historical error . . . and provoke . . . the resurgence of deep anti-US feeling in the best men of all Latin America."[58] In September 1982, the Mexican and Venezuelan presidents reminded their US counterpart that their countries, "tied to the region geographically, cannot be detached from the problems that may occur there" and, in a clear objection to US support for the Contras in Nicaragua, urged an end to the "support, organization and positioning of Somocist ex-Guardsmen."[59]

Several European governments continued to differ with the US in their policies toward the Sandinista government. As the Reagan administration escalated its economic war against Nicaragua, Western European and Scandinavian countries increased their economic assistance from $63 million in 1980 to $87 million in 1983.[60] The EEC Commission has since 1979 provided $32 million in aid to Nicaragua, and France defied US pressures in continuing to fulfill a 1981 arms contract with the Sandinista government.[61] True to its familiar cold-war rhetoric, the Reagan administration responded to this generalized legitimacy crisis by attributing it to "[a] determined propaganda campaign."[62]

3   The CBI in the Context of the Legitimacy Crisis

The presentation of the CBI as an economic, and particularly a trade-oriented, private sector-based initiative, the emphasis on multilateralism rather than bilateralism, and the portrayal of the CBI as a program designed to respond to the interests of the US even as it served the Caribbean Basin had the effect of convincing most members of Congress that the administration had abandoned its militaristic and confrontational posture. While the congressional commentary presented here reflects only the majority opinion of members who responded to the CBI, minority opinion, or dissenting views, focussed largely on specific elements of the program such as the potential effects on certain US producers of trade provisions, or the need for human rights stipulations on CBI eligibility. Invariably, even dissenters supported the general policy thrust that the CBI was thought to represent.

The elements of the CBI were first disclosed by President Reagan in his address to the Organization of American States (OAS), in February 1982. This speech was seminal, and almost every official comment on the CBI thereafter either reiterated or elaborated on elements contained therein. From a historical perspective on US policy towards the region, the president acknowledged that, "at times we have behaved arrogantly and impatiently toward our neighbors," but explained this in terms of the misinterpretation of the "good intentions" of the US. The appearance of "paternalism" was due to the "very size" of the US. He then proceeded to articulate a link between the political instability of the region and its deteriorating economic health. The "economic disaster," he argued, was "shaking even the most established democracies" and providing "a fresh opening to the enemies of freedom, national independence, and peaceful development."[63] The CBI represented a response "as unprecedented as today's crisis in the Caribbean Basin" and a "commitment [which] makes unmistakably clear our determination to help our neighbors grow strong."[64] In short, the president identified the economic adversities of the region as the cause of political instability which, in turn, facilitated intervention by the "enemies of freedom," or "communism." This analysis represented a significant revision of the administration's prior insistence that communist intervention was the source of political conflicts, in favour of an admission that internal factors were the primary determinants.

To members of Congress who had persistently advocated this perspective and denounced the administration's strident cold-war or anticommunist interpretation of, and confrontational solutions to, the region's political problems, this revision represented a welcome basis for forging a new foreign policy consensus between the executive and legislative branches of government. Representative Fowler spoke for the majority of the members of the House when he noted:

> It is my opinion . . . that the principal problems in Central America are economic and political rather than military, and are primarily domestic in origin rather than foreign dominated. I am pleased that the President has at least rhetorically acknowledged that there is truth in these propositions. But the administration's primary reliance on military solutions to the turmoil in the region has risked widening the conflict and made it more difficult for the United States to be credible in its support of regional negotiations. Indeed, in those areas where this has not been the case I have supported the administration's policy, specifically as original co-sponsor of the Caribbean Basin Initiative for promoting economic growth.[65]

On the day of the President's OAS address, House Majority Leader Jim Wright commended him for "his vision and understanding of the fundamental problems of poverty and landlessness throughout much of Latin America . . . which, when they grow to the point of despair, provide fertile breeding grounds for dictatorships of both the right and the left."[66] Even those amongst the minority in Congress who expressed objections to specific provisions of the CBI as formulated by the administration and passed by Congress were moved to vote for its passage for the same reason. Representative Garcia noted that "the present course of action of the White House has been less than positive. This administration has emphasized military not economic solutions," but still supported the bill "as a symbolic stand against the administration's policy of increased militarization of the Caribbean Basin."[67] The response in the Senate was similar. Senator Dodd, perhaps the most steadfast critic of the administration's Caribbean Basin policy, noted that,

> in terms of the various options available, the CBI represented the best hedge we have against the kind of tragedy we see in El Salvador, we saw in Nicaragua, that we are seeing in Guatemala, [and] . . . may yet see in Costa Rica before the year is out. The best hedge against totalitarianism, against the Marxists, the Leninists, is to have a country that is economically sound.[68]

A second point emphasized by the administration was the comprehensive nature of the CBI, in that it integrated trade concessions with investment incentives and financial assistance. In his message of transmittal of the CBI to Congress, the president explained that "the actions in trade, aid and investment are interrelated. Each supports the other, so that together they comprise a real spur toward the entrepreneurial dynamism which the area so badly needs."[69] Representative Barnes applauded the "series of mutually reinforcing provisions in the aid, trade and investment areas" and concluded that "the proposal is the first truly comprehensive effort on the part of the United States in many years to provide a long-term response to the economic difficulties affecting our neighbors."[70] The Senate response was equally positive. Senator Percy captured the sentiments of members in his observation that:

> The Caribbean Basin Initiative is the single most important program the administration has suggested for Latin America. It represents the most comprehensive economic cooperation package since the Kennedy administration's Alliance for Progress 20 years ago.[71]

A third emphasis in the presentation of the CBI was that, with trade as its "centerpiece," it represented a departure from traditional US economic programs which stressed financial assistance. The president explained that the CBI would enable the Caribbean Basin "to make use of the magic of the marketplace, the market of the Americas, to earn their own way toward self-sustaining growth" and supported this approach with the observation that "all of the countries that have succeeded in their development over the past 30 years have done so on the strength of market-oriented policies and vigorous participation in the international economy."[72] Elsewhere, the president described the CBI as "based on the same principles and practices which are uniquely American and which have worked in the past."[73]

This aspect of the CBI was also lauded by members of Congress. Representative Conable urged his colleagues to take note that:

> It [the CBI] is a program that represents a departure from foreign aid and a new focus on assistance based on free market principles. It will help demonstrate that a market-oriented economic foundation for a country, whether large or small, can insure for it a better and more secure future.[74]

Representative Moore argued that the CBI would succeed where other programs had failed, with the added advantage of reinforcing the dignity of beneficiaries:

> Where we have gone wrong over the years is in giving a demeaning handout to a country who [sic] looked to us for the secret of our own success. That secret is the engine of our own progress our free market, free enterprise system. That is precisely what this bill begins to set in motion.[75]

Another "secret of American success" which the administration emphasized in the CBI, was the role of the private sector. In his message to Congress, the president pointed out:

> A key principle of the program is to encourage a more productive, competitive and dynamic private sector and thereby provide the jobs, goods and services which the people of the Basin need for a better life for themselves and their children. *All the elements of this program are designed to help establish the conditions under which a free and competitive private sector can flourish.*[76]

In his address to the OAS, the president noted that this strategy was already succeeding in Jamaica:

> One early sign is positive. After a decade of falling income and exceptionally high unemployment, Jamaica's new leadership is reducing bureaucracy, dismantling unworkable controls, and attracting new investments. . . . Jamaica is making freedom work.[77]

Congress avidly supported this aspect of the CBI. In the various Committee reports which represented stages in the development of Congress' version of the CBI, however, a "sense of the Committee" observation was recorded — at the prompting of a few members of Congress who felt that the requisite infrastructure for private-sector activity was underdeveloped in many countries of the region — to the effect that some attention should also be paid to the public sector. This was, however, a non-binding recommendation which failed to win inclusion in the final bill.[78]

A fourth emphasis in the administration's presentation was that the CBI represented a cost-effective alternative to options that might be necessary in the future. The president argued that "The energy, the time, and the treasure we dedicate to assisting the development of our neighbors now, can help to prevent much larger expenditures of treasure."[79] The CBI was placed in the context of "two different futures which are possible for the Caribbean area." One was "the establishment or restoration of moderate, constitutional governments with economic growth and improved living standards" and the other, "further expansion of political violence from the extreme left and the extreme right, resulting in the imposition of dictatorships and, inevitably, more economic decline and human suffering."[80] Secretary of State Schultz warned of a third possibility: mass emigration from the Caribbean Basin to the US. He defended the first "alternative" (*sic*), embodied in the CBI, and which he called "democratic development," as

> a forward looking effort to boost both development and stability . . . because it can help ease delicate social and political transitions before they create security problems of an international dimen-

sion . . . a program to get ahead of history instead of countering its unwelcome effects.[81]

In contrast, he referred to "the Cuban and now Nicaraguan models" as "clear demonstrations of political repression and economic failure."[82]

This argument appealed to a Congress which was wary of future massive foreign assistance expenditures and eager to avoid US military intervention in the region. Representative Conable urged that the implementation of the CBI "means lesser demands on US resources for defense and assistance in the Caribbean."[83] In a fervent plea to the House, Representative Michel urged that his colleagues: "join us in this bipartisan effort to have our nation do something beneficial in the Caribbean now, *so that we will not be forced to do something painful later.*"[84]

A fifth theme in the presentation of the CBI was its "multilateral" nature. In his address to the OAS, President Reagan identified this as a crucial aspect of the CBI:

> We will work closely with Mexico, Canada, and Venezuela, all of whom have already begun substantial and innovative programs of their own, to encourage stronger international efforts to co-ordinate our own development measures with their vital contributions, and with other potential donors like Colombia. We will also encourage our European, Japanese, and other Asian allies, as well as multilateral development institutions, to increase their assistance to the region.[85]

Asserting the multilateral nature of the CBI, the administration claimed that the program was formulated after close consultation with the potential beneficiaries. Ambassador Robert J. Ryan, Director of Regional Economic Policy when the CBI was formulated, noted that the initiative

> has been developed through careful consultations with both government and private sector leaders in the Caribbean Basin countries. It reflects not only our analysis of their needs, but more importantly their own priorities and assessments of their needs and their capacity to address their problems.[86]

The idea of a multilaterally formulated CBI was seen by many in Congress as an appropriate testimony to hemispheric co-operation. Said Representative Broomfield:

> I am pleased that the United States, in developing the Caribbean Basin Initiative, has coordinated its approach with other donor countries in the region. I am speaking of Canada, Mexico, Venezuela and Colombia. . . . This spirit of cooperation demonstrates that the good neighbor policy still exists, that others in the hemisphere are pre-

pared to work in harmony with us in achieving common goals, and that the definition of an American border is broader than is often thought.[87]

The final theme in the presentation of the CBI was that it offered reciprocal benefits to the participants. The economic development of the region would promote stability which was vital to US interests. President Reagan expressed this as follows:

> The Caribbean region is a vital strategic and commercial artery for the United States. Nearly half our trade, two-thirds of our imported oil and over half our imported strategic minerals pass through the Panama Canal and the Gulf of Mexico. Make no mistake: The well-being and security of our neighbors in this region are in our own vital interest.[88]

The president then proceeded to emphasize the communist-inspired threats to US interests in the region. This constituted the larger portion of his OAS address and was distinguished by a dramatic sense of urgency. Lars Schoultz, a keen observer of US politics, vividly recalls this shift in focus and delivery in the president's speech:

> quite suddenly, there was a shift in focus, and the world price of oil and the demand for sugar and coffee became irrelevant to an explanation of instability. The president had begun to discuss Communism. It was more than a change in subject; it was a change in mood. When the word "Communism" is inserted into the context of instability in Latin America, the effect on many policy makers is not unlike that of turning up the speed of a model train. These officials may be chugging along, talking leisurely about the adverse impact of declining world prices for sugar or yawning their way through a discussion of Latin political culture. Then someone mentions Communism, and the speed picks up. Words come faster, delivered with much more conviction. Adjectives become more colorful; conditional verbs are replaced by straightforward declarations. The discussion hurtles along. Latin America slips off the side track and onto the main line.[89]

Consonant with this sudden change of focus, the President identified "Cuba and its Soviet backers" as representing a "dark future"[90] for the region. Predictably, Nicaragua was also implicated in this scheme. "For almost two years," the president noted, "Nicaragua has served as a platform for covert military action. Through Nicaragua, arms are being smuggled to guerrillas in El Salvador and Guatemala."[91] The president proceeded to list human rights violations of the Sandinista government against the Miskito Indians, free trade unions, the media, etc. In contrast, he pointed to the "unprecedented land reform" undertaken by the Salvadoran government and its conciliatory call to the guerrillas "to join in the democratic process." He condemned the "determined propaganda campaign" aimed at misleading "many in Europe and certainly many in the United States as to the true nature of the conflict in El Salvador."[92]

The CBI was portrayed as a guarantee against the Cuban-Nicaraguan path that militated against US and hemispheric security. In urging quick passage of the CBI, the president warned:

> If we don't act now the dangers will grow. New Cubas will arise, and the cost of insuring our security to the south will escalate. . . . Our program, like the crisis itself, is unprecedented. . . . *I wouldn't propose this program if I were not convinced that it is in our own vital national interest.*[93]

The president and officials of the administration consistently mentioned the strategic significance of the Caribbean Basin for US security and the need to preserve the region from hostile forces. The Caribbean Basin was viewed as a crucial conduit for the movement of troops and war equipment in the event of an outbreak of hostilities involving the US or its allies. Moreover, its proximity to the US was seen as directly significant to US physical security. These considerations also dictated a policy of "strategic denial" to the Soviet Union of influence in the region. The details of US security bases and installations in the region were not, however, elaborated in the administration's presentation of the CBI, though these are widely known and may be briefly outlined.[94]

The Bahamas and surrounding area is the location of the Atlantic Undersea Test and Evaluation Centre (AUTEC), a test facility for US anti-submarine warfare (ASW) equipment, as well as two offshore facilities for the US navy's Sound Surveillance System (SOSUS) anti-submarine program, a global network of hydrophones that relay information via satellite to the US. Puerto Rico, the Grand Turks, Antigua, and Barbados are also locations for SOSUS.[95] The US has a network of bases in Barbados, Jamaica, St. Lucia, and Trinidad and Tobago for testing missiles, as well as a naval base and gunnery in Puerto Rico. The naval base at Guantanamo in Cuba is the site for frequent US manoeuvres, though it is more important as a political symbol than a strategic facility.[96] The Panama Canal has been historically regarded as vital to US security interests. It has become less functional with the introduction of big carriers but is still important in the US policy of strategic denial. The Canal Zone houses four schools for the training of Latin American military personnel and has the Jungle Operations Training Centre, the only US jungle warfare training facility. In view of the imminent loss of many of the US's rights in the Canal Zone, Honduras has also become important in US strategic planning.[97]

Finally, the president expressed his commitment to defend the region against the "enemies" of freedom. He indicated that he would ask Congress "to provide increased security assistance to help friendly countries hold off those who would destroy their chance for economic and social progress and political democracy" and, referring to the US commitment to "reciprocal defense responsibilities" under the 1947 Rio Treaty, he warned: "Let our friends and our adversaries understand that we will do whatever is prudent and necessary to ensure the peace and security of the Caribbean area."[98]

Later, the administration extended the list of US vital interests in the region to include the safeguarding of export markets and investments and to stemming the tide of illegal immigration from the region to the US. Secretary of State Schultz pointed out the economic significance of the region for the US:

> The health of the Caribbean economies also affects our economy. The area is now a $7 billion market for US exports. Thousands of American jobs were lost when our exports to the region fell $150 million last year as income in the region declined. A large portion of the debt of Caribbean countries is owed to banks in this country. At the end of 1981, US direct investment in the region was approximately $8 billion.[99]

With regard to illegal immigration to the US, the secretary identified the Caribbean Basin as the "second largest place of origin" due to its proximity. Former US Trade Representative William E. Brock, credited with formulating the administration's version of the CBI,[100] estimated that "illegal immigration from the Caribbean within the last 3 years imposed a financial and structural burden on the US economy, which, if quantified, would amount to well in excess of $1 billion."[101]

The congressional debate on the CBI reflects at least an equal preoccupation with US national interests and foreign-policy concerns. That most members of Congress now found agreeable the hitherto objectionable "security" and "cold war" rhetoric of the administration may appear ironic. But it became palatable in several respects. First, despite a conspicuous emphasis on themes such as communist infiltration and US vital security interests, the fact that these were articulated in the context of the unveiling of an economic initiative tended to give the impression of balance to the administration's policy. Second, the president's open declaration that he would persist in militarily aiding countries of the region may have caused less anguish because he justified it in terms of the need to provide a "security shield" for the process of economic development which the CBI would initiate. Third, the security imperative was pragmatically cast in terms of US national interests rather than the abstract project of resisting communist incursions against the free world, of which Congress had become wary, and which had already raised enough consternation amongst the American people as well as traditional allies. Even established critics of the administration, including those who voiced objections to specific aspects of the CBI, agreed that the region was vital to US interests.

Senator Robert Dole, one of the co-sponsors of the CBI in the Senate, even went beyond the president in reaffirming the doctrinal basis of a security perspective on the Caribbean Basin:

> The message you [the president] bring today marks an important new chapter in US relations with our southern neighbors. It is perhaps in importance equal to another Presidential message pronounced on the subject long ago. . . . The core idea of the Monroe Doctrine that the new lands of this hemisphere must remain free from outside intervention in order to pursue their own destinies in peace today endures more vitally than ever. But the nature of the threats, enemies, and solutions have changed markedly in 160 years.[102]

Senator Daniel Inouye went beyond the Monroe Doctrine in articulating the scope of US interests:

> I am always convinced that if there is a riot in Bangladesh, it will affect us; if there is a civil war in El Salvador, it will affect us; if Nicaragua falls to an element that is not friendly to us, it will affect us. And if we are to maintain this democracy which we cherish so much, we cannot uphold ourselves as an island. It [the supplemental assistance] is a large sum, but when one considers the economic health and political stability of our country, I think it is a small investment to make.[103]

With respect to specific aspects of US interests, there was widespread support for the administration's position. Representative Gibbons, a leading sponsor of the CBI in the House, and now a co-sponsor of CBI II,[104] expanded on the strategic importance of the region in urging support for the passage of the CBI:

> A coherent approach to the security of the United States must include a strong Caribbean. Should a conflagration ever break out of any major size, the ports of the eastern parts of the United States would probably be inoperative, forcing most of the reinforcement of our Armed Forces, in fact, the deployment of our Armed Forces to go through the Caribbean.[105]

Similarly, the connection between the CBI, illegal immigration, and US security was also endorsed. Representative Shaw warned that illegal immigration threatened more than the jobs of US workers: it also posed problems of "political and military importance to the US."[106] Representative Lungren elaborated this concern with his observation that illegal immigration posed "the risk of losing one of the major evidences of sovereignty, that is, control of the borders and determination of what type of society one country or the other wishes to maintain."[107]

Finally, the administration's view of the relationship between the CBI and US economic and commercial interests was also endorsed. The House Committee on Foreign Affairs virtually repeated the administration's observations on the importance of maintaining the security of access to Caribbean sea lanes for US commerce and the region's markets for US goods and investments and concluded that "the economic and political stability of these countries affects our own economy."[108] The CBI as presented by the administration therefore had the effect of defusing, at least temporarily, apprehension in Congress over the militarist and confrontational posture of the Reagan administration's policy towards the Caribbean Basin, and especially towards Central America. The appeal of the CBI as an ostensibly trade-oriented, private sector-based, integrated, and multilaterally formulated economic strategy lay in the fact that it appeared to constitute a feasible and prudent alternative to the military approach to the region's instability.

4   The Political Realities of the CBI

To appreciate the politics of the CBI, it is useful to reflect briefly on its genesis. On the occasion of Jamaican Prime Minister Edward Seaga's visit to Washington in January 1981, barely two weeks after a change in US administration, President Reagan characterized Seaga's victory in the elections as "the turnover or turnaround of a nation that had gone, certainly, in the direction of the Communist movement: it was a protégé of Castro," and continued with a hint at a policy proposal: "I think this opens the door for us to have a policy in the Mediterranean [sic] of bringing them back in those countries that might have started in that direction or keeping them in the Western World, in the free world."[109] The administration then oversaw the formation of the US Business Committee on Jamaica, comprising 23 chief executives of large corporations and chaired by David Rockefeller at the request of Secretary of State Haig.[110] The purpose of the Committee was to advise private companies on Jamaican investment opportunities as well as to "bring to the attention of government, the need for changes in laws, or to suggest the need for technical assistance."[111]

The importance of this program to the Reagan administration is suggested by the fact that Venezuelan and Canadian counterparts were also urged to establish similar committees on Jamaica. A member of the Venezuelan committee, in endorsing the Reagan administration's position, remarked that the program represented "an extraordinary chance to build an alternative showplace to Castro in the Caribbean."[112]

The Reagan administration decided that this program on Jamaica could be usefully generalized to other countries in the region, and could prove "crucial to stability and democracy in the Caribbean." Jamaica was considered a symbolically appropriate place to start, since "it is the first country [which] by the decision of its own people, [has] thrown out a Marxist regime and turned back to private sector."[113] It is important to note, therefore, that the administration's view of an economic program for Jamaica and other countries in the region was, from the inception, motivated not only by the political objective of helping governments friendly to the US but, more importantly, to making them attractive alternatives to the "Cuban model."

It seemed that, concurrently, the administration was attempting to evolve an *official* multilateral economic program for the region.[114] During Mexican President Lopez Portillo's visit to Washington in June 1981, the possibility of a regional economic program for the region was discussed. A State Department spokesman reported that President Reagan introduced the issue of "the need to strengthen the economies of the less developed nations and to . . . bring about the social and economic development of the peoples of the region" and that "both Presidents agreed wholeheartedly that this is the way to assure future stability for the region and for individual countries."[115]

The Mexican position on recipients of the proposed program, according to an administration official, was that "it ought to be available to all nations in the hemisphere."[116] Asked about the US position, in view of the fact that the Mexican plan would include Cuba, the official responded that "we did not come to any hard and fast premise" and that "the question of eligibility was not addressed at the present" by the US, but would be raised later.[117]

A summit of foreign ministers of Mexico, Canada, Venezuela, and the US was held in Nassau, Bahamas, on July 11-12, 1981. The need for a regional economic program was reaffirmed, and the participants pledged to continue their consultations. According to the Joint Communiqué issued by the Conference of Ministers, no specific programs were agreed to, nor conditions for recipient countries discussed.[118]

In a press conference the next day Secretary of State Haig, responding to a question as to whether the Cuban government was being considered for assistance under the program, replied cryptically that "there are no automatic exclusions nor any obligations for inclusions."[119] Two weeks later, the truth was revealed: Assistant Secretary of State for Inter-American Affairs Thomas Enders declared that while "Mexico wanted Cuba automatically included . . . we can contemplate no aid to Cuba."[120]

These events suggest that the US probably hoped to garner multilateral support for an economic program that would bolster its allies in the region against radical opposition and, at the same time, render the "Cuban model" an unattractive alternative. It was obvious that the US would not include Cuba in a program that was meant to be anti-Cuban or "anti-Marxist" in the first place.

The Senate Committee on Foreign Affairs, which contributed to evolving the Senate's position on various provisions of the CBI, candidly noted that, amongst the donor countries, "there were sharp differences in interpretation as to the rationale for the program, the political conditions and appropriate policy regarding specific countries, as well as the appropriate level of contributions to the development effort by each donor."[121]

Representative Bonior was far more perceptive as early as February, 1982. He remarked:

> The President has not, unfortunately, . . . reached an accord with our neighbors to the South, the Mexicans and the Venezuelans, with respect to this program. I think that the administration has been offering a program in which we will help countries that are philosophically in line with us, and the Venezuelans and Mexicans will help countries that are philosophically in line with them. Basically, I think this translates into saying, "Therefore, we are not going to help Nicaraguans, we are not going to help countries that don't toe the philosophical line of this country that this administration would want them to adhere to." . . . I think this attitude risks, if you will, the demise of the whole economic program that the President is suggesting . . . [122]

Despite this obvious breakdown of multilateralism, the Reagan administration persisted in describing the proposal, and later, the US-formulated CBI, as "multilateral." Indeed, in the same testimony in which Enders confessed that differences existed amongst the donor countries, he continued to refer to the program as multilateral, though with a curious redefinition: "While the overall concept of action should be multilateral," he explained, "actual benefits should be given on a bilateral basis so that the conditions of each recipient and each donor can be satisfied."[123]

Why did the administration continue to refer to disparate bilateral programs as "multilateral"?[124] Apart from the fact that to do otherwise would have constituted a confession that the US could no longer impose its will even on traditional allies, it was apparently a useful tactic at a time when the administration was facing criticism for its ideologically based, "hard-line" policy in the region. We have already seen how Congress was lured by this and other "legitimacy" features of the CBI. The exclusionary eligibility criterion, based on an ideological litmus-test, was formalized as the first of seven mandatory criteria of eligibility for CBI participation: "The President shall not designate any country as a beneficiary ... if such a country is a Communist country" (Section 212 [b] [1]).[125]

Nicaragua was included in the CBI legislation as an eligible country but received beneficiary status only after the electoral defeat of the Sandinista government in early 1990. When asked to explain the effective exclusion of revolutionary Nicaragua, a State Department official in the Office of Regional Economic Policy explained that Nicaragua had simply not applied. When further asked whether revolutionary Nicaragua might have been favourably considered had it applied, he responded:

> There are a number of criteria a country has to satisfy to be designated, most of them relating directly to the economic policies that they have. I would think that Nicaragua, then, would have had difficulties with some of the economic policies. . . . I think that the CBI is mainly designed to promote economic development and to effectively do that, requires a certain range of economic policies that are conducive to growth.[126]

This consideration has been advanced since August 1982. At that time, when questioned about the eligibility prospects of Grenada and Nicaragua, Thomas Enders had replied:

> Let me say with regard to both of those countries, they would have to be examined not only under the Communist-country exclusion, but also to see whether they are running their economies in such a way so that they could in fact take advantage of free-enterprise type trade and investment opportunities of the kind proposed.[127]

However, technical economic arguments against Nicaragua's eligibility were unsustainable. It was estimated (by Abraham Brumberg, former editor-in-chief of the State Department journal, *Problems of Communism*) that under Sandinista rule about 60 per cent of the Nicaraguan economy remained in private hands.[128] In contrast, only about 20 per cent of Guyana's economy was in private hands, yet a State Department official expressed the conviction that "the prospects [were] quite good" for that country's admission to the CBI.[129] Further underlining the political-ideological character of the CBI is the fact that under the presidency of the late Forbes Burnham, who was known for his caustic forays against the US, the Export-Import Bank (EXIM-BANK), a US agency, had listed Guyana as a Marxist-Leninist state and therefore ineligible for further benefits.[130] Under new president Desmond Hoyte, however, a rapprochement with the US has occurred. Said the deputy assistant secretary of inter-American affairs, Caribbean Division: "The US government and the Hoyte government are breaking down a hostility and a distance that has been quite profound."[131] Indeed, in November 1988, Guyana was granted beneficiary status under the CBI.

To return to the case of revolutionary Nicaragua, when Enders was pressed further to reveal the State Department's position on this country, he reiterated that "it would be premature for us to determine that this country has in fact become a Marxist-Leninist country" and pointed out that "some private sector elements" and active opposition parties still existed. After more probing, he eventually declared:

> Well, I think it is a Marxist-oriented nation. I don't think there is any question about that at all. Whether it is in fact a Communist country in the same sense Cuba is, is a judgement we haven't yet reached but everything looks worrisome. There are some 2,000 Cuban military personnel in that country at the present time.[132]

Similarly, with regard to revolutionary Grenada, the assistant secretary noted:

> We are very worried . . . about the trends in Grenada. It is an oppressive one-party society. Whether it is in fact or should be so qualified at this moment as being a "Communist country" is uncertain to us, but we have to be very preoccupied about the direction of events there.[133]

Enders then proceeded to declare categorically that, with respect to the 1982 supplemental assistance designated under the CBI, "if this legislation were enacted there would be funds available . . . neither for Cuba nor Nicaragua, nor Grenada."[134] Indeed, the fact that the Reagan administration's proposal to Congress excluded these countries from the list of recipients indicated that a prior determination had already been made that they were to be excluded from the CBI.[135]

In his OAS address on the CBI, President Reagan had already implied that Nicaragua would be excluded: "We seek to exclude no one. Some, however, have turned from their American neighbors and their heritage. Let them return to the traditions and common values of this hemisphere, and we will all welcome them."[136] It was only in January 1984 that the State Department translated "the traditions and common values of this hemisphere" with which Nicaragua was expected to comply for access to the CBI. Langhorne Motley, assistant secretary for Inter-American Affairs, elaborating on "what the United States seeks from Nicaragua," presented a four-point demand: establishment of a genuinely democratic regime; a definitive end to Nicaragua's support for guerrilla insurgencies and terrorism; severance of "Nicaraguan military and security ties to Cuba and the Soviet Union"; and, "reductions in Nicaraguan military strength to levels that would restore the military balance between Nicaragua and its neighbors."[137] Motley then concluded:

> Nicaraguan implementation of these four points, whether unilater-
> ally, through negotiations, would remove the causes of the deterio-
> ration in Nicaragua's relationship with the United States. *A prompt
> return to a cooperative relationship, including economic assistance and
> the CBI (Caribbean Basin Initiative) beneficiary status would then be
> possible.*[138]

These demands would have been either impossible to accede to, as
they were based on fallacious premises, or would have meant political
suicide for the Sandinista government.[139]

What explains the initial attempt by the administration to stall on a
definition of Nicaragua's CBI eligibility through the use of technical
economic arguments? And why such obvious reluctance to confess that
political and ideological considerations were in fact paramount in a
determination of the country's status? The obvious answer is that the
Reagan administration was not prepared to disclose the politically
punitive nature of the CBI towards countries considered to be
unfriendly. In fact, administration officials consistently employed technical economic arguments to deny revolutionary Nicaragua loans from
international financial institutions in order to conceal its political
motivation.[140] This history of official rejection, combined with the
May 1, 1985, US economic embargo against Nicaragua (following
President Reagan's finding that Nicaragua constituted an "unusual and
extraordinary threat" to the US) could only have convinced the Sandinista government that applying for CBI beneficiary status would not
only be futile, but would afford the Reagan administration the pleasure
of *officially* labelling it "Communist."

In contrast to the exclusion of Nicaragua is the administration's and
Congress's extremely favourable treatment of "friendly" governments,
especially those at the centre of US efforts at "drawing the line" against
further challenges of the administration's proposed distribution of the
1982 supplemental assistance under the CBI.[141] The four Central
American countries identified for assistance (El Salvador, Costa Rica,
Honduras, and Belize) accounted for $243 million, or almost 70 per
cent of the $348 million in-country allocations (the other $2 million
were designated to the regional program of the American Institute for
Free Labor Development). Only $105 million, or about 30 per cent,
were designated for the insular Caribbean countries of Jamaica, the
Dominican Republic, Haiti, and the several countries of the Eastern
Caribbean. At first sight, it might be argued that the designation process was probably informed by the criterion of population distribution,
given that Central America accounts for 22 million of the region's 39
million people.[142] But the funds were not designated to every country
in each region, and if the population of only the designated countries is
considered, the disproportionate nature of the distribution becomes

evident. The population of the insular Caribbean recipients (10.09 million) is only slightly less than that of their Central American counterparts (10.59 million), yet the insular Caribbean was earmarked for only 30 per cent of the funds.[143]

An alternative argument, voiced by President Reagan himself, is that the funds were intended to "help make possible, financing of critical imports."[144] A country's balance of payments position relative to its Gross Domestic Product (GDP) may be considered a useful indicator of its ability to finance its imports. A comparison of the country allocations with balance of payments problems does not, however, support this rationale. From Table 2-1 it is clear that Costa Rica and the Dominican Republic were the most seriously affected. Yet, they were allocated far less than El Salvador.

Table 2-1
Balance of Payments Position (1983),
Major Recipients of CBI Assistance
($US millions)

Country	B.O.P.	as % of GDP	Proposed allocation
Costa Rica	−346.2	14.59	70.0
El Salvador	−74.4	2.07	128.0
Honduras	−52.2	1.87	35.0
Central America	−472.8		233.0
Dominican Republic	−410.8	5.14	40.0
Jamaica	−123.6	3.76	50.0
Haiti	−46.3	3.13	5.0
Insular Caribbean	−596.3		95.0

Source: Compiled from data presented in *International Financial Statistics: Supplement on Economic Indicators*, Supplement Series No. 10 (Washington, DC: IMF, 1985). Belize is excluded due to unavailability of data. The Eastern Caribbean is also excluded since figures for some islands such as Montserrat and the British Virgin Islands are not available.

Even if the general criterion of economic need is considered, the official argument remains equally questionable. Haiti, the poorest country in the hemisphere, and Honduras, the poorest in Central America (and one of the poorest in the hemisphere) should have been considered more deserving than their more affluent neighbours, yet they received the smallest allocations in their sub-region. Ironically, Haiti was the least favoured amongst all of the recipients of the region.

In contrasting the allocation to Haiti with that of Jamaica, Senator Proxmire appropriately asked: "Does that mean that Haiti is less needy, that Jamaica is 10 times as needy as Haiti? Is that the kind of division of aid that we ought to have a solid record on . . . ?"[145]

The allocation of assistance could only point to alternative, political considerations. That El Salvador should be earmarked for $128 million, or more than a third of the total funds, coincided with the Reagan administration's preoccupation with that country and has led to the conclusion that the CBI was merely a "channel for sending aid to such right-wing regimes as El Salvador."[146] Robert Pastor, hardly a critic of the paradigm of the primacy of US interests in the Caribbean Basin, observed that "the CBI may have been born of the struggle in Central America" and that "when [it] was announced, it rested squarely on a national security rationale."[147]

We have seen that the CBI was, instead, born in Jamaica, though it is certainly correct to say that it was nurtured in Central America, at a time when the administration's policy there had become a contentious issue. The emphasis on El Salvador in particular reflected an ongoing preoccupation of the Reagan administration. Indeed, in his message of transmittal of the CBI to Congress, perhaps his most ideologically muted statement on the Caribbean Basin, the president dwelt on El Salvador to the point where the rest of the region seemed to feature almost as an afterthought:

> El Salvador's economy is in desperate straits. The insurgents have used every tactic of terrorism to try to destroy it. El Salvador desperately needs as much assistance to stimulate production and employment as we can prudently provide *while also helping other countries of the region.*[148]

The position of the Congress on the allocation of the supplemental funds constitutes an interesting study in paradox. Congress, which was so volubly critical of the administration's political-ideological emphasis in its policy toward the region, not only sustained that emphasis in the CBI but even surpassed the administration. First it should be noted that Congress did reduce the administration's proposal for El Salvador from $128 million to $75 million, after the Senate conceded to the House position in conference negotiations "at the last minute, after every other item had been completed."[149]

Many members of Congress expressed concern over the administration's proposal of $128 million for El Salvador. Some, like Representative McHugh, objected to "the priorities" reflected in the proposal. In particular, it was argued that "although El Salvador has only one-eighth of the Caribbean Basin's people the President's proposal would have allocated more than one-third of the economic request to that nation," and McHugh expressed "serious reservations about the policy this administration is pursuing in El Salvador" as well as skepticism as to whether the Salvadoran government was committed to the reforms which the US administration had been commending it for.[150] The latter point was especially emphasized by Representative Harkin, who condemned the administration's certification of El Salvador (which was a prerequisite for granting US assistance), as "fraudulent" and as a signal to the Salvadoran government "that it had a blank check to continue its human rights violations," and suggested that "the $75 million to El Salvador is . . . too much by at least $50 million."[151]

Similarly, Senator Dodd, the most strident objector in the upper house, added: "Do you know why we are providing $128 million for El Salvador? Because the very rich are taking their money out and sending it to Miami and to Switzerland."[152] Dodd then pointed out the contradiction in giving assistance: "we are talking about $128 million going to a country in the middle of a civil war. Does anyone believe for one second that $128 million in economic assistance is actually going to provide economic help at this hour?"[153] On the program as a whole, the senator concluded:

> We are talking about $230-odd million to go to four countries, the balance of that money to go to the rest of the entire Caribbean. . . . The point is this: Call it what you will — call it a Caribbean Basin Initiative, call it economic assistance to the region. It is nothing of the kind. . . . This is just a bilateral aid program. That is all this is, $128 million for El Salvador. That is basically what it is.[154]

Despite the reduction, the allocation still represented a victory for the administration, which was successful in preventing Congress, especially the House, from going below the $75 million mark. In addition to this, the fact that after the congressional negotiation process El Salvador wound up with the largest allocation of any country represented a victory for the "spirit" of the administration's view of the CBI and its policy toward the region in general.

Another victory was scored with Jamaica, the administration's closest ally in the insular Caribbean. The $50 million allocated to Jamaica was unrevised by Congress, as there were few objections. Only Senator Dodd made reference to the political nature of the allocation:

> I have a great deal of respect for the prime minister there. . . . But let us be honest with ourselves. The economic problems of Jamaica are certainly not as serious as the economic problems of the Dominican Republic. Yet there is disparity there.[155]

In three other aspects of the allocation of the supplemental funds, the Congress went *beyond* the administration in the construction of political criteria for implementing the CBI. The decreased funding for El Salvador was compensated for by an addition of $20 million for financing land reform, whereas there had been no such provision in the administration's proposal. This addition was furnished notwithstanding the country-limitations imposed by Section 203 [c] of the Act and, more importantly, Section 620 [g] of the House Foreign Assistance Act of 1961 which "prohibits the use of US foreign assistance funds for the payment of compensation to owners of expropriated property."[156] In justifying this unusual suspension of its own stipulation in the CBI Act and of US law, the House Committee on Foreign Affairs emphasized the political urgency of committing these additional funds in terms of its conviction that "successful implementation of the land reform program is essential to returning that country to a state of economic and political stability."[157] In addition, the notion that the successful implementation of the land reform program was merely a function of financial assistance ran counter to the more informed assessment that the major obstacle to this program had always been the brutal military-oligarchy coalition. Further, the government lacked the power, autonomy, and popular support to resolve this problem (in which it was itself implicated).[158]

The administration originally refrained from proposing assistance to Guatemala under the CBI, probably out of an awareness that it might compound the credibility problems arising from an already fraudulent certification of El Salvador's human rights record. Congress, however, provided $10 million for Guatemala, in circumstances which demonstrated that it was even more willing than the administration to subordinate human rights considerations and standing US law to political imperatives. The House Committee on Foreign Relations noted, on the one hand, that it had received reports of widespread violence in the Guatemalan countryside, including "deliberate massacres and the burning of villages, attributable to extremists of both the left and the right, *but also to the forces of the Guatemalan government.*" It also expressed concern at the 30-day state of seige declared on July 1, 1982, by the Rios Montt government, "which effectively eliminate[d] all human rights and civil liberties."[159] The Committee confessed that "serious questions remain about whether the provision of economic support funds would be consistent with section 502 [b], the human rights provision of the Foreign Assistance Act." Nevertheless, it recommended the allocation of funds, on the grounds that the new Rios Montt government had "pledged respect for human rights and political and economic reform" and that:

encouraging reports have been received with respect to the declining level of violence in urban areas and gestures have been made to create a climate of more open political discussion within the country. In addition, the new government appears far more inclined to seek international respect for its policies than did its predecessors.[160]

This justification uncritically repeated the administration's consistent attempts to mis-characterize the Guatemalan conflict (as it did with the conflict in El Salvador) as one between extremists of the "left" and the "right," which the government wished to control. This act by the Congress may also be seen as consistent with the administration's resumption of military sales to Guatemala, which was described as a departure from the original human rights policy of "public threat" and "censure."[161] Those who criticized Guatemala on human rights grounds agreed, however, with the political rationale of strengthening "US-Guatemalan ties" introduced to justify aid to the government and expressed regret that a similar tactic was not seen fit for Nicaragua.[162]

Another allocation by Congress not initially proposed by the administration was a $7.5 million program for "scholarships and other training opportunities in the United States for citizens of the Caribbean and Central America."[163] The political rationale for the program was that it would "partially fill the gap created by curtailment in US scholarship programs while the Soviet Union and other Communist countries . . . dramatically increased educational and cultural exchanges for Latin American students."[164] Secretary of State Schultz later defended this program "for individuals in the Caribbean Basin with leadership potential" as important for "strengthening political ties between recipient countries and the United States."[165]

Finally, the political orientation of the CBI was summed up and formalized in a stipulation that spelled out the political conditions and political intent of the CBI. Public Law 97-255 of September 10, 1982, by which the CBI supplemental funds were authorized by Congress, concluded with an elaborate policy statement:

> Notwithstanding any other provision of this Act, none of the funds appropriated . . . may be obligated or expended in any manner inconsistent with the policy hereby reaffirmed, which is stated in SJ Res. (76 Stat. 697), to wit:
>
> "Whereas president James Monroe, announcing the Monroe Doctrine in 1823, declared that the United States would consider any attempt on the part of European powers 'To extend their system to any portion of this Hemisphere as dangerous to our peace and safety'; and
>
> "Whereas in the Rio Treaty of 1947 the parties agreed that 'an armed attack by any State against an American State shall be considered as an attack against all the American States, and, consequently,

each one of the said contracting parties undertakes to assist in meeting the attack in the exercise of the inherent right of individual or collective self-defense recognized by article 51 of the Charter of the United Nations'; and

"Whereas the Foreign Ministers of the Organization of American States at Punta del Este in January 1962 declared: 'The present Government of Cuba has identified itself with the principles of Marxist-Leninist ideology, has established a political, economic, and social system based on that doctrine, and accepts military assistance from extracontinental Communist powers, including even the threat of military intervention in America on the part of the Soviet Union'; and

"Whereas the international Communist movement has increasingly extended into Cuba, its political, economic, and military sphere of influence: Now, therefore, be it

"*Resolved by the Senate and House of Representatives of the United States of America in Congress assembled,* That the United States is determined —

(a) to prevent by whatever means may be necessary, including the use of arms, the Marxist-Leninist regime in Cuba from extending by force or the threat of force its aggressive or subversive activities to any part of this hemisphere;

(b) to prevent in Cuba the creation or use of an externally supported military capability endangering the security of the United States; and

(c) to work with the Organization of American States and with freedom-loving Cubans to support the aspirations of the Cuban people for self-determination."

Nothing in this Act shall be deemed to change or otherwise affect the standards and procedures provided in the National Security Act of 1947, as amended; the Foreign Assistance Act of 1961, as amended; and the War Powers Resolution of 1973. This act does not constitute the statutory authorization for introduction of United States Armed Forces contemplated by the War Powers Resolution.[166]

This amendment to the CBI, known as the "Cuba Amendment," was proposed by Senator Symms in early 1982, tabled by the Senate on April 14, 1982, and then forwarded to the Senate Foreign Relations Committee for hearings on it. The Senate had then declined to include the amendment in the CBI Act. On August 10, 1982, Senator Symms reintroduced the amendment with an extensive political-ideological rationale and, in an ingenious challenge to members to demonstrate their political and ideological credentials, persuaded the full Senate to pass his amendment.[167]

In addition to the three-part rationale reproduced above (a,b,c), Senator Symms noted that:

we do need to fully understand the Soviet threat from Cuba, both subversive and nuclear. The President has acknowledged that the Soviet threat from Cuba is as great or even greater than it was in 1962. . . . If we cannot muster the national will to oppose threats and dangers to our security, then we may never be able to safeguard our heritage. . . . I urge the Senate to approve the resolution as originally proposed. I fear that any action otherwise might be further misread as a sign that we do not have the will and determination to defend this nation and its neighbors — to stand up to nuclear blackmail by the Soviet Union.[168]

Senator Thurmond exhorted support for the amendment, citing a list of Cuban subversive activities in the region:

The Marxist Castro regime in Cuba has exported its subversion to Central America. Cuban activities have assisted in the overthrow of the government of Nicaragua, in the deterioration of the situation in Guatemala, and in the guerrilla violence that has resulted in bloody civil war in El Salvador. How long must we stand idly by as our neighbors to the South are engulfed by the Communist cancer?[169]

Senator Helms, a noted Republican "hard-liner," exulted that the amendment "has America acting like America again."[170]

The supporters of the Cuba amendment resorted to the familiar tactic of questioning the anti-communist resolve of others in Congress. In denouncing the Senate's earlier rejection of his amendment, Senator Symms noted: "I was . . . disturbed that the Senate did not see fit at that time to send a strong, clear message to the Soviet Union and Cuba that at least the Senate believes aggression and subversion in the Caribbean should be resisted."[171]

The senator also challenged his colleagues to state their position with regard to US policy toward Cuba.

Are we enforcing the Monroe Doctrine with regard to the Soviet Union and Cuba, or are we not? *Do we support the Soviet/Cuban-backed aggression in the Western Hemisphere,* or do we oppose it? . . . My amendment attempts to provide the Senate at least with an opportunity to answer in part these questions, *and express its will regarding American policy toward Cuba.*[172]

This tactic was even better displayed in an unattributed statement, "Points in Rebuttal to Critique of Symms Cuba Amendment," from which we quote at length:

[To] argue against the Cuba amendment is to argue for a foreign policy of accommodation of our friends and appeasement of our enemies. . . . By opposing the Symms amendment, Senators are sending a dangerous message to our friends and enemies alike. Senators would be telling the world that the United States refuses to even threaten force to defend our vital national security interest in our own front yard, the Caribbean. . . . Our enemies in the Kremlin and in Havana would be delighted to hear that America now declares itself defenseless, that the Senate refused to use force to defend our vital national interest even against Soviet-Cuban aggression. Even the third world could then feel free to attack US interests with impunity after such a dangerous signal was sent. . . . In summary, the arguments of the critics amount to nothing more than shameful appeasement. We remember the result of Neville Chamberlain's appeasement of Hitler. . . . Appeasement is not only dishonorable and un-American, it is also ultimately ineffective in preventing war. . . . *A vote against the Symms amendment is in fact a vote for Marxist-Leninist tyranny in our own front yard.*[173]

The administration's position is equally interesting. Perhaps for fear of *overtly* conveying the political nature of a program that was portrayed as economic, its initial response to the Symms amendment was that "while it was consistent with administration policy," its passage "at this time may not be necessary or helpful."[174] It seems that the statement, written in the White House, was cleared only by the National Security Council and took the State Department by surprise, apparently because it was perceived as a missed opportunity to lend support to an agreeable policy declaration without incurring the risk of appearing to take the lead in politicizing the CBI. The State Department, however, moved quickly to correct this "screwup," as it was characterized by the Deputy Assistant Secretary for Inter-American Affairs since, as the Assistant Secretary noted, "it does seem incredible that after a year of working to get a strong position on Cuba that something like this would have happened."[175]

On April 20, 1982, deputy assistant secretary Stephen Bosworth told the Senate Foreign Relations Committee that the Symms amendment "reaffirming the resolution adopted in 1962 on the US determination to oppose the efforts of Cuba to expand its sphere of influence . . . reflects the policy of six administrations, certainly this one" and indicated that this "finding was made at the highest level of the State Department by the Secretary of State himself."[176] Bosworth affirmed: "we will not accept that the future of the Caribbean Basin be manipulated from Havana" and noted that the US was enlisting regional co-operation in this regard, and that "*the Caribbean Basin program [the CBI] is in many ways a model of the type of regional cooperation we seek.*"[177] The Symms amendment also received endorsement from other high-level officials of the administration.[178]

In the context of wide official endorsement, and the "McCarthyist" inference that rejection of the amendment was tantamount to lack of patriotism or support for communism, it was passed by a vote of 65 to 30.[179]

5 Conclusions

From the Caribbean Basin point of view, the region's economies are so tied to the US market as to render the CBI important to any consideration of paths and prospects of development. Caribbean Basin development, insofar as it features in the deliberations of the US administration and Congress, became subordinated to, if not derailed by, imperatives originating from a larger conception of the political significance of the region to the US and, more precisely, to the desire to address the mounting challenges to US hegemony there. The CBI could not but reflect this preoccupation.

The benign presentation of the CBI as an economic program, multilaterally negotiated and formulated, was meant to assuage domestic and international apprehension at a time when the administration's militaristic and confrontational stance had called the legitimacy of policy towards the Caribbean region into question. The reality underlying this presentation was that, from the declaration of its *raison d'étre*, to its specific provisions, and finally to its underlying spirit as crystallized in the Symms amendment, the CBI stood true to the administration's overriding purpose of restoring and restructuring US hegemony in the region.

Intuitively, there is some appeal in the notion that Caribbean Basin countries should struggle to redefine the CBI as a developmental initiative. Indeed, a region unified in its conceptualization of the CBI could, in principle, bargain more effectively with US policy-makers. But the adage that "in unity there is strength" seems incapable of application for many reasons. From the US point of view the idea of a strong region is eclipsed by the more urgent question of whether or not its unifying political and ideological principles would accommodate US hegemonic concerns. If not, the US, as is historically indicated, seems more comfortable with a divided region and would even foster such division through bilateral policies like the CBI.

Caribbean Basin governments, sensitive to the importance of loyalty to the US, have also recognized that strength may not necessarily be predicated on regional unity. The experience of the CBI illustrates that those who are loyal to the US may receive lucrative rewards, while those who adopt an anti US stance can be punished through economic isolation. Moreover, Caribbean Basin governments, cognizant of the scarcity of market opportunities and foreign investment, are not above undercutting each other, even as they speak of unity.

Lastly, even if Caribbean Basin governments could articulate a concept of unity which would resolve the above problems, their credibility might still be questionable. There could be no real unity if the interests of the region's peoples were to be ignored. This would be a narrow unity of political elites, most likely in tandem with the region's private sector, sharing a concept of development which exploits and marginalizes the majority of the region's peoples.[180]

For this reason it is important to understand the political implication of the CBI as a model of development. For whether or not the CBI satisfies the general objective associated with it, it could substantially entrench a class-based form of development, allowing the political and business elites to use the agency of the state against the interests of popular groups and organizations. The regional struggle for the reconceptualization of the CBI is, therefore, ultimately a political struggle amongst the sectors of Caribbean Basin society which will be affected by it.

3

Britain, the Caribbean Basin, and the Caribbean Basin Initiative*

Colin Leys

It is not high on our agenda. Our files on it are pretty slim. We observe it hasn't been very successful and the countries concerned have said so. (A senior Foreign and Commonwealth Office official, on the USA's Caribbean Basin Economic Recovery Act — CBERA.)[1]

Grenada may be seen as a watershed, but I see no sign of a reassertion [of British interest in the Caribbean]. (Mr. George Gelber, Catholic Institute for International Relations.)[2]

1   Introduction

As Devanand Ramnarine and others have shown, the Caribbean Basin Initiative (CBI), while presented largely as an economic development initiative, was significant primarily as an aspect of a new assertion of US power in the region:[3] the very term "Caribbean Basin" is "a geopolitical concept defined by United States' security interests."[4] Britain's interest in the Central American part of the "Basin," never great, had become extremely modest since the expansion of US economic and political influence in the isthmus at the end of the nineteenth century. It would have been negligible by the 1980s but for the need to keep 1800 British troops stationed in Belize to protect it from Guatemala's territorial claims. The assertion of US power in Central America via the CBI, therefore, did not cause concern in the Foreign and Commonwealth Office (FCO). More significantly, while the FCO was internally divided over the assertion of US power in the insular Commonwealth Caribbean, those who felt concerned were keenly aware that such an assertion was consistent with the reality of a reduction of British inter-

---

Notes for Chapter 3 are on pp. 227-29.

45

est in the area, a reduction that had been in progress for two decades. As for the Caribbean Basin Economic Recovery Act (resembling in many ways the Lomé Convention, which gave Caribbean countries free access for manufactured exports to European Community markets), to the extent that it might prove valuable in attracting new investment to the Commonwealth Caribbean from firms seeking to supply US markets using cheap Caribbean labour, this could only reduce the need for British aid. Moreover, the firms could also be British; and, in general, the Thatcher government's commitment to market-based policies, and its support for the Reagan administration's anti-communist policies in the region led it to welcome the CBI. While the US-led invasion of a Commonwealth country, Grenada, conducted without consultation with Mrs. Thatcher, caused bitterness and some rethinking, it seems unlikely that it will lead to any significant renewal of an independent British commitment to the area.

2   Britain and the Caribbean Basin before the CBI

By 1980 Britain's exports to Central America were worth less than one-fifth of one per cent of its total exports; imports from Central America were worth little more than one-tenth of one per cent of its total imports. By 1986 even these shares had contracted significantly. As for investment, "we have no serious data on UK investment in the area," the Department of Trade and Industry official responsible for it stated.[5] Most British investment is of long standing, in the traditional products of the area. British aid, being concentrated on the poorest developing countries, is also modest: aid to the whole of Latin America in 1988 was about 12 m. per annum, including about 2 m. (non-military assistance) for Belize and 0.7 m. for Honduras (the poorest Central American country).[6] The net cost of Britain's military base in Belize was about 7 m. per annum (out of the total cost of 31 m. per annum, 24 m. would have been spent wherever the troops were based), but this was not seen as a permanent commitment.

Britain's involvement with the insular Commonwealth Caribbean was more substantial, but also diminishing. Jamaica, Trinidad and Tobago, Guyana, and Barbados had successively become independent in the 1960s; Grenada followed in 1974; five "associated states" opted for independence between 1978 and 1983 (Dominica, St. Lucia, St. Vincent, Antigua and Barbuda, St. Kitts-Nevis). Britain was left with only five Dependent Territories—Anguilla, British Virgin Islands, Cayman Islands, Montserrat, and Turks and Caicos Islands (with a combined population of 66 000 in 1986) plus Bermuda (population 57 200).

British interests in the Caribbean are less today than at any time during the last three centuries. From being one of the dominant imperial powers in the region, Britain has retreated to the point where it possesses very few remaining political commitments in the area. . . . The reality is that Britain's main interests in the region have now been effectively reduced to three considerations: trade, investment and aid.[7]

By 1980 even these interests had been in decline for some time. The ending of colonial political relations opened the way to trade, investment, and political relations between the Commonwealth Caribbean and other countries, especially (but not exclusively) the USA, and led to a relative decline in Britain's role, which still further reduced the significance of the area for Britain. Although Britain was still the Commonwealth Caribbean's main export market, "taking the bulk of the region's sugar exports, almost the entire banana crop and most of the citrus," Britain's imports from the Caribbean amounted in 1979 to only 0.3 per cent of its total imports, and exports to the Caribbean, to only 0.5 per cent of total exports.[8] British earnings from investments in the whole of Latin America and the Caribbean accounted for "just over 6 per cent of . . . total earnings from direct investment overseas," of which earnings from the Caribbean alone would have formed a small part.[9] Aid flows from Britain to the Caribbean, though the highest in per capita terms for any part of the world except the Pacific islands, remained static through the 1970s.[10]

At the end of the 1970s, British retreat finally became official policy. According to Tony Thorndike,

The Foreign and Commonwealth Office had decided in 1978 that the Caribbean was henceforth to be a low priority area now that virtually all the colonial territories in the region which had expressed a wish for independence had either proceeded to sovereign status or were well on the way to doing so. Britain's interests lay in Europe and, with the resounding victory of the Conservative party led by Mrs. Margaret Thatcher in the 1979 election, any lingering possibility of British withdrawal from the European Community had in its collective view thankfully vanished with the defeat of the Labour Party. In any case, the Caribbean Basin was widely acknowledged to lie within the sphere of interest of the United States, Britain's closest ally. Washington could be relied upon to respect the independence of the new and small full members of the Commonwealth and to assist in their development; after all, the U.S. had maintained a benign military presence in the English-speaking Eastern Caribbean since the 1940 Anglo-American destroyers-for-bases deal, while U.S. capital was increasingly dominant in the tourist industry. Furthermore, the responsibility for preferential trade agreements with Britain could be passed to Brussels with the signing of the Lomé Convention in 1975 while Canada, another traditional trading partner of the English-speaking Caribbean, was expected to expand its commercial and political interests. As time went on, there was also the imposition of increasingly severe public expenditure cuts which, in the context of Prime Ministerial scepticism about the overall effectiveness of Britain's diplomatic service, further rationalised the policy of effective withdrawal. After a review of resources, the policy was reconfirmed in 1981 (information from interview, FCO, October 1981).[11]

The Thatcher government's policy, in the words of another regional expert, Tony Payne, was

> founded upon the assumption that the best prospect for the economic development of the Commonwealth Caribbean [lay] in the region's wholehearted integration into the world economy as currently organised. It [sought] to encourage the flow of private investment, [saw] little need for extensive aid programs and believe[d] that traditional free enterprise policies pursued by Caribbean governments [could] still lead to the achievement of economic development.[12]

In these circumstances official British support for the Caribbean Basin Initiative was only to be expected.

3   Britain and the CBI – Economic Aspects

The official British response to the CBI was, however, essentially one of silent acceptance, rather than enthusiastic endorsement. The House of Commons Select Committee on Foreign Affairs, composed of six Conservative and five Labour MPs, and influenced by an accumulating body of opinion critical of the government's policies in Central America and the Caribbean, issued a report in 1982 which particularly attacked the US government's "paranoid antagonism towards any government in the area which may be remotely described as left wing, let alone Marxist," and criticized the CBI, saying it would "not remotely match up to the basic needs of the area."[13] In the government's formal reply, however, US policy, including the CBI, was not mentioned, while the Committee's recommendation that the UK should take an independent, not uncritical, but more sympathetic attitude towards the governments of Cuba, Nicaragua, and Grenada, and seek to influence the US to be less hostile to them, was ignored. It is a matter for speculation why the government chose this response, but by the end of the 1980s there could be no doubt of its implications. British economic interest in the area had continued to decline, and Britain continued to endorse the USA's hostility towards even social-democratic regimes (such as Michael Manley's PNP government in Jamaica from 1972 to 1980) and its uncritical support for repressive regimes of the right (e.g., in El Salvador, Haiti, Guatemala, Guyana, etc.).

Britain's trade with the Caribbean as a whole (i.e., including all the Caribbean islands plus Belize, Guyana, French Guiana, and Suriname) declined from 0.9 per cent to 0.4 per cent of total British exports, and from 0.7 per cent to 0.5 per cent of total British imports between 1983 and the third quarter of 1988 (see Table 3-1). For the four largest Commonwealth Caribbean economies, the figures fell from 0.52 per cent to 0.17 per cent of total British exports, and from 0.27 per cent to 0.15 per cent of total British imports over the same period. As Table 3-1 shows, the drastic drop in the relative share of British exports, as competition from other countries (especially the USA and Japan) intensified, led to the emergence for the first time of a substantial deficit in Britain's trade balance with the region. Britain was meantime purchasing virtually the whole of the Commonwealth Caribbean's banana crop at prices between 16 per cent and 51 per cent above the effective market price of "dollar" bananas (i.e., from US-owned suppliers in Central America and elsewhere). The additional burden of a trade deficit therefore threatened to weaken still further the government's economic enthusiasm for the area.[14]

With regard to investment, in 1984 the book value of British investment in the Commonwealth Caribbean islands was 413 m., a rise of 125 per cent since 1978, compared with an increase of almost 300 per cent in British foreign investments worldwide over the same period.[15] It is thought that total British investment in the Caribbean has not changed greatly since. In 1988, when overseas investment totalled about 100 billion, the Department of Trade and Industry estimated British assets in the Caribbean at about 2 billion, or 2 per cent of the overseas investment total. Most of this 2 billion was in the Commonwealth Caribbean.[16]

Neither the trade nor the investment figures indicate a significant response of any kind to the CBI (or indeed to the Lomé Convention). The Department of Trade and Industry, which is concerned mainly with export promotion, attributes the decline in Britain's share of Caribbean imports (from 50-60% to 10-15% since the 1960s) to intensified competition from other countries caused by decolonization and world trading conditions. The CBI was not seen as significant in this context, nor had it attracted much interest among British firms; only two British investments in the Caribbean Basin aimed at taking advantage of the access provided by the CBI to the US market, one of which had failed, were known to officials interviewed.[17]

As for British aid to the Commonwealth Caribbean, it had remained more or less static during the 1980s, averaging 31.6 m. per annum

Table 3-1
UK Trade with the Caribbean, 1983-88 (millions)

UK Imports

	1983	1984	1985	1986	1987	1988
Bahamas	24.0	38.5	70.8	10.3	15.9	22.9*
Barbados	11.9	22.5	13.6	11.7	23.3	19.1*
Jamaica	94.0	77.9	89.7	87.4	85.7	74.8*
Trinidad and Tobago	52.7	164.7	81.7	41.6	38.6	34.0*
Rest of Caribbean	290.0	531.0	475.0	380.8	295.6	308.2*
TOTAL	472.7	834.6	730.7	531.8	459.1	459.0*
Share of UK world imports	0.7%	1.1%	0.9%	0.6%	0.5%	0.47%

UK Exports

	1983	1984	1985	1986	1987	1988
Bahamas	17.8	220.3	74.1	95.8	27.1	18.6*
Barbados	31.9	30.7	36.9	38.3	33.1	28.3*
Jamaica	116.2	48.1	44.3	43.3	54.6	43.0*
Trinidad and Tobago	148.8	113.3	93.9	79.0	57.0	35.8*
Rest of Caribbean	213.9	211.8	271.3	220.2	199.3	178.5*
TOTAL	528.6	624.2	520.4	476.7	371.1	304.2*
Share of UK world exports	0.9%	0.9%	0.7%	0.7%	0.7%	0.41%

* January-October 1988.
Source: Department of Trade and Industry.

(plus an average additional 3.4 m. per annum directed through the European Community and other multilateral agencies). In 1986 and 1987 the value of bilateral aid was 28.1 m. and 29.1 m. respectively, indicating a significant decline in real terms.[18] These figures, however, do not include military assistance; in this area, a significant expansion of British expenditure occurred, especially in the Eastern Caribbean, following the Grenada crisis.

Before turning to Britain's response to the military security dimension of the CBI, however, brief mention should be made of the implications for the Caribbean of the formation of a single European market in 1992. Although in no way a response to the CBI, Britain's role in the preparatory process sheds some additional light on its attitude to the region.

4 1992 – The Single European Market

As the earlier quotation from Thorndike indicates, the British government had been glad to transfer to the European Community a large share of the burden of preferential trade agreements with Commonwealth Caribbean countries under the first Lomé Convention of 1975. The price advantage to Caribbean sugar producers, for example, of the guaranteed annual sugar purchases by the Community of 430 000 tons per annum, averaged 105 million ECU per annum over the period 1981 to 1986; for 1988 alone this figure increased "significantly."[19] For Barbados, Belize, Guyana, Jamaica, and Trinidad-Tobago, the EC has accounted for an average of between 45 per cent and 109 per cent of their net sugar exports, and allowed them to realize on these exports additional foreign exchange receipts of more than double what they would have obtained on the "world market." The cost to Britain, which consumed nearly all of this sugar, was no greater than before, or than it would have been had the sugar been purchased from protected British or other European beet sugar producers. The introduction of a single European market, so far, has implied no change in these arrangements.

Bananas, on the other hand, are not grown in Europe but are imported by each main European state under separate national arrangements which disappeared by 1992. Here the problem is that the cost of production of bananas in the Windward Islands, Jamaica, Belize, and Suriname is much higher than in "dollar" banana-exporting countries, such as those which supplied West Germany; under a single market, dollar bananas can be sold anywhere in the community, thus displacing the Caribbean producers. Since most of them have no alternative to banana production, and efforts made to improve productivity (via WINBAN, a British-aided regional agency) can have only limited results, given local conditions, there has been great anxiety.

In principle, the EC has an international obligation, under the Lomé protocol, to continue the necessary protection for bananas and some other "ACP" commodities, such as rum, whose access appears threatened by the 1992 changes, but as of 1988 the European Commission had given no indication as to how this might be done. Against the background of ruthless reduction of US quotas for Caribbean sugar since 1981, it is not surprising that the fate of these commodity preferences in Europe should have loomed much larger than the CBI in the thinking of both Caribbean governments and the British government at the end of the 1980s.

> In 1975-81, the Dominican Republic exported an average of 815,000 tons of sugar to America each year. Its initial quota in 1981 was 493,000 tons. This year [1988] it is only 123,000 tons. In 1982 for-

eign exchange earnings from its American sales earned the country $187 m., this year it will receive about $49 m. Only American congressmen will be surprised to hear that the country has signed long-term supply contracts with Russia. The effect on smaller economies is yet more drastic. St. Kitts and Nevis, for example, had an American quota of 16,000 tons in 1982 (itself 13% below its average yearly exports to America from 1975 to 1981). This year [1988] its quota is 5,770 tons. Over a third of the St. Kitts and Nevis workforce is employed in sugar; of these, half are now laid off.[20]

5   The Political and Military Aspects of the CBI

The broader significance of the CBI was forcibly impressed on British policy-makers, including the Prime Minister, by the Grenada crisis of 1983. The government had fully endorsed the hostility of the US towards the New Jewel Movement (NJM) regime, as it also had towards the Sandinista government in Nicaragua and the FMLN-FDR opposition in El Salvador. Nicholas Ridley, minister of state at the Foreign Office, was quoted as saying that "Grenada is in the process of establishing a kind of society of which the British government disapproves, irrespective of whether the people of Grenada want it or not"; the British government consistently refused all overtures from the NJM government that might have enabled it to secure, in return for friendly relations, the improvements in human rights and movement towards elections that ministers gave as their reasons for being hostile. When, therefore, the US invaded Grenada in October 1983 without even consulting the British government, it was a severe blow to the government's pride. It was a breach of international law from which Mrs. Thatcher subsequently dissociated herself, and it involved usurping the authority of the queen, as formal head of state of Grenada. It also humiliated Mrs. Thatcher personally: both because she was deceived and snubbed, after acting as a faithful supporter of the Reagan administration's policies, and because the Reagan administration proved to have had a better appreciation of the contradictions at work than her government did. As a Guyanese official of the Commonwealth Secretariat put it in an interview, "'we wish we could have done it' was the informal, *private* view, even if formally it [the invasion] was opposed." This view prevailed even among many Labour Party MPs.[21]

What the Grenadian revolution showed was that the contradictions in which the Caribbean countries were caught were creating a vacuum which would be filled by social forces uncongenial, or at least inconvenient, to the United States, if it did not establish its imperial control in place of Britain's. Male unemployment often exceeded 30 per cent (and was still rising with every reduction in the US sugar quotas); debt and balance of payments problems were accumulating that would soon lead to IMF-imposed "structural adjustment" cuts in already declining living standards; there were increasingly acute contrasts of wealth and poverty, exacerbated by the growing importance of tourism; in some islands there was increasing reliance on marijuana production for export (the US Drug Enforcement Agency estimated that Jamaica in 1985 received about $175 m. per annum from marijuana exports to the USA), while in others there was extensive official involvement in the hard drug traffic; Caribbean banks were increasingly being used by organized crime or tax-evaders to hold or launder funds; Caribbean company laws were used by the South African state to evade the arms boycott; there were a number of attempted coups of diverse provenance (two in Barbados, in 1976 and 1978, and three in Dominica, all in 1981); and various other illegal transactions or near-transactions. In general, the islands were too weak economically to solve their acute social problems, sometimes too weak politically to avoid falling prey to corrupt politicians, and mostly too weak militarily to defend themselves from coups d'état. The United States was increasingly concerned about the Caribbean drug trade, which was becoming a major domestic political issue in the USA, and about the laundering in Caribbean banks of profits from the trade; but even more about the possibility of left-wing governments coming to power, as had happened in both Nicaragua and Grenada in 1979.

> [The] awakening [of the Commonwealth Caribbean states to world realities] was due to the world depression from the mid-1970s which coincided with effective British withdrawal from the region. It led several of their leaders – Michael Manley in Jamaica and Forbes Burnham in Guyana in particular – and opposition groups and intellectuals both to examine the Cuban experiment and come to political terms with it, and to attempt to diversify trade towards socialist bloc markets, in spite of US preferences and disquiet. As the sub-region struggled to survive, familiar political patterns appeared undermined as hitherto alien racial and political ideologies surfaced. The Grenadian revolution was a clear indicator of disquiet with the old order, but it was countered by an insistence by the United States and much of the Commonwealth Caribbean elites that the new order that it purported to represent could not be tolerated.[22]

The self-destruction of the NJM regime in 1983, culminating in the murder of Maurice Bishop and other NJM leaders, provided the USA with an opportunity to intervene; but the groundwork had already been laid by the leaders of a majority of the Commonwealth Caribbean countries over the preceding three years. Prompted especially by the prime ministers of St. Lucia, Dominica, and Barbados, a "Memorandum of Understanding" was signed by these states, plus Antigua and St. Vincent, in 1982, and by St. Kitts-Nevis in 1983, which provided for security and military co-operation in the prevention of smuggling and other crimes and also "threats to national security." Although it was the Authority of the Organization of Eastern Caribbean States which resolved to remove by force the Revolutionary Military Council that had assumed control in Grenada in October 1983, and from which the USA secured the desired "invitation to invade," it was the Regional Security System established by the 1982 Memorandum of Understanding that formally authorized the "Caribbean Peacekeeping Force" introduced into Grenada following the US invasion. It was, moreover, the Regional Security System (RSS) which subsequently became the instrument for the consolidation of US military-political hegemony in the Eastern Caribbean and the emergence of a limited new British response.[23]

The development of the Regional Security System, as part of a wider Caribbean security system under US leadership, has been fully reviewed elsewhere.[24] Briefly,

> Military training, arms and equipment were allocated to Jamaica and Barbados, reinforced by joint manoeuvres of US and Jamaican troops in the United States. In the small Eastern Caribbean islands, however, [training and aid] took the form of police paramilitary training and the creation of paramilitary units within the National police forces dubbed Special Support Units (SSUs) . . . their size ranging from forty (St. Kitts-Nevis) to eighty (Grenada). . . . The finance for such work [mostly conducted in Puerto Rico] and equipment (including rocket launchers, machine guns, M-16 carbines, telecommunications and armoured vehicles) came from . . . the [US] Military Assistance Program and the International Military Education and Training budget . . . rising to an estimated $8.5 million in 1985.[25]

Muniz estimates that 400 SSU personnel were trained in this way down to 1986; in that year the US spent $31.75 m. on military assistance to the Caribbean (including the mainland states of Belize, Guyana, and Suriname, but excluding Puerto Rico), of which $10.4 m. went to the Eastern Caribbean.[26] Between 1980 and 1983, Muniz also notes, 286 Commonwealth Caribbean military personnel also received US military training. As the figures show, the program was still expanding rapidly so that the subsequent impact of US training is likely to have been much greater, especially with the inclusion of Trinidad and Tobago in the program since 1985.

US hegemony, based on these military outlays far beyond the budgetary capacities of the Caribbean states, was also entrenched by the decision to convert its military base in Antigua to serve as a training and communications centre for the Eastern Caribbean.

In appraising the significance of this program, the "national security" doctrine on which US "military assistance" to Latin America had long been based must be kept in mind. According to this, the US was engaged in a titanic struggle against a world communist conspiracy. The task of its military assistance program was to establish military and "paramilitary" forces imbued with this idea and to influence governments (by this means and through inculcating further dependence on US military support) to adopt domestic policies which were also imbued with the idea. This included giving priority to the suppression of socialist or "popular" political opinion and organizations over the maintenance of democratic processes and civil liberties.[27]

Table 3-2
Commonwealth Caribbean Military
Personnel Trained under
the US IMET Program

1980	1981	1982	1983
10	41	73	160

Source: Adapted from Muniz, *Boots*, Figure 4, p. 19.

These ideas were symbolized by the military exercises organized by the US in the Caribbean in 1985 and 1986, involving the SSUs alongside US and Caribbean forces in practice assaults against small islands whose governments were supposed to have been overthrown by insurgents (supported by "Carumba" and "Niggaro," according to the 1985 scenario; this exercise, the US commander in the Caribbean stated, would be "a graduation exercise . . . where we actually give the Special Service [*sic*] Units' people an opportunity to exercise the things they have learned during training").[28]

The "national security" ideology was also manifest, however, in the outlook and behaviour of the SSUs. Dressed in combat fatigues and travelling in jeeps, they were increasingly disinclined, it seems, to take orders from uniformed police officers; they showed themselves ready to be mobilized by unscrupulous governments against political opponents in St. Vincent in 1984 and Grenada in 1985. By 1985 a marked reaction was setting in, as Caribbean electoral opinion began to swing back to the centre. The new prime ministers of St. Vincent and Barbados expressed open opposition to the American-inspired Regional Security System as it had by then emerged; the latter especially rejected proposals for upgrading the 1982 Memorandum of Understanding to the status of a treaty, opposing "the use of our resources for militaristic purposes or for the unjustifiable usurpation of the sover-

eignty of our country by alien influences" (and calling instead for support for the idea of a "peace zone" in the Caribbean).[29]

6 The British Response after Grenada

The British response to the political dimension of the CBI was the
product of all these developments. Mrs. Thatcher's personal humilia-
tion over the invasion of Grenada and her consequent anger at the
hapless Foreign and Commonwealth Office was aggravated by the
knowledge that many of the same Caribbean leaders who had welcomed US intervention felt let down by Britain. Britain, however, had
not been called upon to intervene by the Grenadian governor-gen-
eral.[30] It was clear that Britain's relatively modest level of diplomatic
engagement in the area, and its record of withdrawal, had made her
appear ineffectual, whereas the US had been both eager and able to
act. There were also domestic critics, represented publicly by the
1981-82 Report of the Foreign Affairs Committee and privately by elements in the military as well as the Foreign and Commonwealth Office,
who entertained an "aristocratic" disdain for the American style of
imperialism. These would have liked to see Britain pursue a more dis-
creet style of domination, more sensitive to Commonwealth Caribbean
political culture (including its democratic traditions). There was,
finally, the "West Indian" factor in British politics to be considered. As
Payne noted, down to 1983 "nobody in Whitehall [had] dared to apply
their minds to an exploration of what might be the implications of Britain's increasingly politicized 'West Indian' minority."[31] But it constituted a potential problem for the future.[32]

In general, then, the Grenada crisis pointed to a rethinking of British policy, from which the following policy lines emerged. First, the
Foreign and Commonwealth Office ceased to put any pressure on the
remaining Caribbean dependencies to become independent, while
declaring that Britain remained ready to "respond positively when this
is the clearly and constitutionally expressed wish of the people."[33] Second, it was decided to improve the quality of diplomatic staff posted to
the area. After the invasion of Grenada "Prime Ministerial wrath was
directed at the Foreign and Commonwealth Office for neglecting the
area."[34] Third, "military assistance discreetly returned";[35] Britain and
Canada co-operated with the US and the Eastern Caribbean States to
fund the Regional Security Service, and in particular Britain and Canada shared in the improvement of coastguard facilities and equipment,
while Britain stepped up its contribution to "normal" police training (at
the Police Colleges in Jamaica, Barbados, Grenada, and also in the
UK), besides supplying military "advisers" to local military forces
(while the Belize base remained one of the largest foreign bases in
Central America). The stress on coastguard facilities (six stations were

built by Britain in the Eastern Caribbean for a total cost of over 6 million) and police training had an obvious symbolic role. Britain was training the "good cops" as opposed to the US-trained "bad cops" (the SSUs), and presumably getting credit for it with regional politicians. Fourth, Britain took a more serious interest in the US's anti-drug policies, passing the Drug Trafficking Offenders Act in 1986, under which agreements were then sought with other states, allowing the British police and customs authorities to examine their nationals' British bank accounts, with powers to freeze and, following convictions, confiscate funds found to be the proceeds of drug dealing. By 1988 the Bahamas had signed an agreement, and Jamaica and the Dependent Territories were expected to do so shortly; eventually the whole Caribbean should be covered. Fifth and last, Britain co-operated in the regional military exercises under US command referred to earlier.

7 Conclusion

Britain's response to the CBI went through two distinct stages, separated by the Grenada crisis. In the first, the CBI was seen primarily in terms of the CBERA and welcomed (though with understandable scepticism) as an additional lever for extending to the Commonwealth Caribbean more of the theoretical benefits of its proximity to the US market. In general, the Thatcher government looked to market forces to replace colonial subsidies and post-independence aid in the region's development, and looked to political accommodation between the Caribbean and the US to replace the colonial relation with Britain. The Grenada crisis showed that these expectations were naive. Britain's subsequent response was to seek to restore its standing in the region mainly by accepting an "orthodox" role in the Regional Security Service, and improving the quality of its diplomatic representation and intelligence. It did not, however, reverse in any significant way its more general policy of withdrawal. British exports to the region contracted, and no special effort was made by the Department of Trade and Industry to restore them; aid levels continued to be reduced in real terms; no new economic initiatives were contemplated.[36] US military, political, and economic supremacy was not contested. It is easier to understand the second phase of the response as an attempt to limit the political damage done to Britain by its progressive withdrawal than as a policy shift with significant new implications for the region. However, if the modification of British policies helped to reduce the threat to democracy, and hence to the possibility of social change posed by US-led militarization, this may be considered positive, even if the Thatcher government was no more sympathetic than the administration in Washington to the forces for social change that actually existed in the Caribbean at that time.

4

Caribcan: Canada's Response to the Caribbean Basin Initiative

Catherine Hyett

1 Introduction

In describing Canada's relations with the Caribbean region, a former vice-president of the Canadian International Development Agency (CIDA) observed: "After Columbus, we came."[1]

Indeed. In 1865, prior even to Confederation, the MacDonald/Cartier government dispatched the country's first commercial mission to the region. Canada's economic, political, and cultural ties with the English-speaking Caribbean, springing from the colonial history of the two areas, are particularly strong. Trade links were developed in the early eighteenth century when Atlantic Canada traded fish and timber for West Indian rum, sugar, and molasses.

Although financial links were not established until the late nineteenth century, Canadian banks and other financial institutions now have significant interests in the Caribbean. The Latin American Working Group estimates that by the early 1980s offshore financial investment accounted for approximately 65 per cent of total Canadian investment in the region.[2] Of the four major private banks currently operating in the Caribbean, three are Canadian. Together, Barclays, the Royal Bank of Canada, the Canadian Imperial Bank of Commerce, and the Bank of Nova Scotia dominate much of the region's financial activity and wield considerable influence in the areas of economic planning and development policy.[3]

In this century Canadian economic interests in the Caribbean have continued to expand and diversify into non-traditional sectors of the regional economy. Since World War II Canadian companies have invested heavily in utilities, transportation, mining, tourism, and the financial area. By the mid-1980s the total value of Canadian direct

---

Notes for Chapter 4 are on pp. 229-33.

investment in the Caribbean was substantial by any standard, exceed-ing $2 billion.[4]

While average annual merchandise trade flows between Canada and the English-speaking Caribbean barely exceed $0.6 billion — repre-senting a tiny fraction of Canada's international trade — trade with Canada comprises a significant proportion of total Commonwealth Caribbean business.[5] Growth in Canada's imports from the region was particularly marked in the early 1980s after the international economic recession ended. Between 1980 and 1985, Canada's imports from the Commonwealth Caribbean increased by over 70 per cent, at the same time as Canadian exports to the region were declining (see Table 4-1). Since then, however, the bilateral trade situation has undergone quite significant changes. These changes in the pattern of merchandise trade, and their implications for Commonwealth Caribbean economies, will be the primary focus of this chapter. Canadian trade data covering the English-speaking Caribbean[6] has been used for the purposes of this study.

2   Background to the Caribcan Program

Because of Canada's strong commercial links with English-speaking Caribbean nations and its shared heritage as a member of the British Commonwealth, Canada has enjoyed a more positive image and influ-ence in the Caribbean region than have many other developed nations. In large part Canada has been able to preserve its enviable interna-tional reputation as a benign donor nation because it has traditionally avoided any overt involvement in regional politics. Instead, it has depended on such major powers as Britain and the United States to create and maintain an operating environment in the Caribbean region which is conducive to the economic needs and interests of Canadian corporations.

With the erosion of British hegemony in the post-World War II period Canada relied more heavily on its superpower neighbour to ful-fil this policing role. One consequence of this alteration in the balance of international power has been that Canada's position as a hemis-pheric ally of the United States has emerged as a key conditioning fac-tor of its activities in both the Caribbean region and elsewhere in the Third World.[7]

Since the Progressive Conservative government assumed office in 1984, Canada's relationship with the US has been of even greater sig-nificance for foreign policy-making. As expressed by Prime Minister Brian Mulroney immediately following his victory at the polls in Sep-tember 1984: "Good relations, super relations with the United States will be the cornerstone of our foreign policy."[8] The desire for a more harmonious relationship with Washington has affected not only the

Table 4-1
Canada-Commonwealth Caribbean Trade, 1980-90

Imports to Canada ($000s)

Country	1980	1985	1986	1987	1988	1989	1990
Bahamas	38 537	38 876	29 808	42 178	20 882	32 636	59 042
Bermuda	1 180	1 654	27 091	5 454	967	3 091	2 031
Belize	1 752	4 958	1 211	5 849	13 166	8 861	10 606
Barbados	11 509	6 994	21 278	21 127	6 577	13 298	15 239
Jamaica	49 908	155 169	149 903	113 774	150 166	188 662	159 074
W & L*	2 340	2 446	5 386	5 525	6 818	2 862	10 361
T & T**	11 246	29 558	54 090	36 875	56 395	22 252	24 761
Guyana	35 720	23 323	26 917	33 777	15 267	19 999	24 577
Other***					120	35	4
Total:	152 192	262 978	315 684	264 559	270 360	291 696	303 695

Canadian Exports ($000s)

Country	1980	1985	1986	1987	1988	1989	1990
Bahamas	25 368	28 167	28 935	33 188	39 012	29 335	50 310
Bermuda	29 586	34 317	32 100	39 354	41 448	39 448	24 891
Belize	3 996	4 409	4 026	6 180	7 567	5 307	3 581
Barbados	34 778	34 295	43 771	44 454	43 404	47 893	34 647
Jamaica	65 179	54 775	73 347	99 338	130 968	131 660	108 759
W & L	29 130	43 148	81 015	48 990	48 844	40 743	30 827
T & T	123 673	100 537	91 041	75 280	58 144	58 864	61 788
Guyana	15 841	4 471	4 669	5 808	5 816	4 574	10 678
Other	4 939	6 068	3 370				
Total:	327 551	304 119	358 904	352 592	380 142	363 592	328 851

  * W & L = Windward and Leeward Islands.
 ** T & T = Trinidad and Tobago.
*** Cayman Islands and Turks and Caicos Islands (data presented separately from 1988).
Note: As of January 1990, trade data with the US includes those imports and exports associated with Puerto Rico and the US Virgin Islands.
Sources: Statistics Canada, *Trade of Canada, Imports by Commodity*, 1980-90, Table 1; Statistics Canada, *Trade of Canada, Exports by Commodity*, 1980-90, Table 1.

Canadian government's economic relations with Latin America and the Caribbean but also its military policy toward the region.

While the role of the Canadian government in the military and economic affairs of the Caribbean has become more evident since 1984, Canada had significant military involvement in the region prior to the Conservative Party coming to office. During the 1970s direct arms sales to Third World countries totalled approximately $50 million per annum. After 1978 exports of military goods rose substantially. During the 1980s direct sales of arms to countries of the Third World averaged $150 million per year. When indirect sales of military commodities are included (made largely via the United States, as a consequence of Canada's military production-sharing relationship with that country) some analysts estimate the real total to be in the region of $300 million. Canadian involvement in this sector grew in the 1980s, spurred by the aggressive marketing of the federal government. Canada's most important Third World market for military equipment is Latin America and the Caribbean. According to the Stockholm International Peace Research Institute (SIPRI), in the five years from 1983 to 1988, Canadian military exports to Latin America averaged $137 million.[9]

Insofar as the Caribbean is concerned, the increased economic and military role of Canada in the region during the 1980s proceeded with the active encouragement of the United States. In 1980, the Committee of Santa Fe provided a blueprint for presidential candidate Ronald Reagan that is by and large consistent with present policies in the hemisphere. The Committee urged that "Canada be induced to assume a greater responsibility in American defence and development by extending its influence into the former British West Indian colonies in the Caribbean."[10] Subsequent policy reviews by the US State Department continue to stress greater Canadian participation in hemispheric defence and economic development.

Increased Canadian involvement has gone largely unnoticed for a number of reasons. First, the massive and overt escalation of US military and economic activity in the region during the same period dwarfed the growing Canadian involvement. Second, such Canadian involvement has taken place under the umbrella afforded by participation in NATO and continental economic arrangements. For example, participation in the Canada-US Defence Production Sharing Arrangements (DPSA), which involves the use of Canadian-produced military components and sub-systems in equipment used by the United States for military operations in the region, has afforded a number of Canadian companies access to this lucrative market. These firms include Canadair, de Havilland, Fleet Aerospace, Marconi (Canada), Garret Manufacturing, Canadian Commercial Corporation (a crown corporation), Indal Technologies, and Bristol Aerospace. Canada reputedly has also issued permits for arms sales to four countries in the Commonwealth Caribbean: Bahamas, Barbados, Bermuda, and Jamaica.[11]

In the same fashion Canada has participated in joint naval manoeuvres in the Caribbean sponsored by the US and involving members of the NATO alliance. During the 1980s such military and naval activities were part of US strategy to increase psychological pressure on Nicaragua, as in the case of Operation Ocean Venture; and were part of the prelude to the invasion of Grenada in 1983. While Canada was not involved in the actual invasion of Grenada, it nonetheless participated in the post-invasion "stabilization" of that country, providing $800 000 in support for Grenada's police force in 1984. Another of the ways in which Canada has acted has been in the training of police and security forces in Grenada and other countries of the Commonwealth Caribbean. These forces are an important part of the Regional Security System established by the Reagan administration as a separate but related component of its Caribbean Basin strategy.[12]

The Conservative government's overriding desire to cement the US foreign policy "cornerstone," together with its strong commitment to the "Aid-Trade" approach to foreign development assistance, has seriously limited the country's development policy options for Caribbean and other Third World countries.[13] Nowhere has the attempt to harmonize Canada's foreign policy with US interests been so apparent as in the case of "Caribcan," the government's most recent economic policy initiative for the Caribbean. Although in his first Speech from the Throne in November 1984 Prime Minister Mulroney supported the development of strong multilateral institutions in foreign aid and in other major areas of Canadian foreign policy, barely one year later the government opted for a bilateralist regional policy for the Caribbean, one strikingly similar to that initiated by the Reagan administration in 1984.[14]

Caribcan was officially announced in February 1986 as a material expression of Canada's "special relationship" with the countries of the Commonwealth Caribbean. The legislation was passed into law in June 1986.[15] Aimed at strengthening the exporting capabilities of Commonwealth Caribbean nations and promoting Canadian investment and other forms of industrial co-operation with the region, Caribcan closely resembles the US program, the Caribbean Basin Initiative (CBI), launched two years earlier. While less elaborate in form than the CBI, Caribcan differs from it in few substantive respects.[16]

A Canadian economic and trade development assistance program for Anglophone nations had been proposed by Commonwealth Caribbean political leaders at a meeting of the Canada/Caribbean heads of government convened in Kingston, Jamaica, in February 1985. For the most part, the leaders sought to foster expanded trade with Canada through preferential commercial arrangements for non-traditional exports, particularly garments, cigars, and footwear.[17]

3 Principal Features

Caribcan offers to 18 English-speaking countries in the Caribbean a package of special trade and investment arrangements. In addition to the 13 Commonwealth nations, Caribcan covers imports from Anguilla, Bermuda, the British Virgin Islands, the Cayman Islands, and the Turks and Caicos Islands.[18] The program's single most important feature is that it confers on beneficiary countries preferential, duty-free entry to the Canadian market for almost all categories of exports.

As well, Caribcan provisions are intended to encourage Canadian private investment in beneficiary countries and promote other forms of industrial co-operation. These measures include a program to strengthen the export potential of Commonwealth Caribbean economies, particularly with regard to the Canadian market; seminars for the region's diplomats and business people focussing on strategies for developing markets for Caribbean products in Canada; and access to the regional offices of Canada's Department of Regional Industrial Expansion to assist Commonwealth Caribbean trade offices in promoting bilateral trade.

Market Access

Canada's Customs Tariff was amended to allow duty-free entry for imports from designated countries. This provision covers most Commonwealth Caribbean products already entering Canada, as well as goods that might be imported in the future. Although there is no time limitation to the Caribcan program, tariff concessions remain in effect for a period of only 12 years. This limitation applies because Canada was not able to waive the provisions of Article 1, paragraph 1, of the General Agreement of Tariffs and Trade (GATT) beyond 1998. At the end of this period the Canadian government must apply to GATT for an extension of the waiver to allow the tariff-free provisions of the legislation to continue.[19]

Before Caribcan was implemented 93 per cent of Caribbean exports entered Canada duty free. With the program in place, the Department of External Affairs estimates that less than one per cent of product categories are excluded from tariff-free treatment.[20] As with the CBI, however, the exclusion clause in the Caribcan legislation applied to textiles, clothing, footwear, and leather products, as well as to luggage, handbags, lubricating oils, and methanol. It so happens that these manufactured items are the ones which Caribbean governments had identified as offering the best opportunities for rapid economic diversification and export development.[21] All of these products remain subject to established duties under either Canada's Most Favoured Nation Tariff, the General Preferential Tariff or the British Preferential Tariff.

Like the Reagan administration before it, the Canadian government was prevented from extending comprehensive duty-free entry to Caribbean products by opposition from vulnerable domestic producers. Existing controls on textile and clothing imports, though extensive, were already viewed by many domestic manufacturers as inadequate protection from "low cost" producers in less developed countries (LDCs). Given the resistance to completely free trade, the Mulroney government chose to continue restricting imports affecting the handful of "sensitive economic sectors" referred to above.[22] Eligibility for non-dutiable access was further restricted by the "Rules of Origin Regulations" established by the Department of National Revenue (Customs and Excise).[23] Stringent rules of entry are imposed on goods grown, produced or manufactured in beneficiary countries which incorporate imported components or materials. In order for such products to remain eligible for Caribcan duty-free treatment, a minimum of 60 per cent of the value-added of the commodities must originate in the beneficiary countries or in Canada.[24]

Finally, all products must be imported directly into Canada from the region. Goods requiring transportation through, or storage in, an intermediate country must remain under customs control.

The program remains subject to limitation in two further ways. First, the "safeguard" provisions of the Canadian Customs Tariff may be invoked to protect the Canadian market from Caribbean competition. The Customs Tariff provides for the withdrawal or suspension of Caribcan duty-free treatment should Caribbean imports jeopardize the profitability of Canadian producers.[25]

Second, Agriculture Canada and Department of Fisheries and Oceans regulations continue to apply to Caribcan imports. These are intended to ensure quality grade standards for fruit, vegetables, fish, meat, poultry, dairy products, and other agricultural imports. In addition, Canada applies standards similar to those of the United States for pesticide residues, and regulates the packaging and marking of Caribbean imports.[26] All the above conditions must be met before the program's concessionary arrangements can apply.

Canadian Investment in the English-speaking Caribbean

The Canadian International Development Agency (CIDA) administers the bulk of Canada's Overseas Development Assistance (ODA) Programme. Within CIDA the Business Cooperation Branch has been central to the Canadian government's effort to consolidate its "special relationship" with the Commonwealth Caribbean by strengthening commercial links with the region. The Business Cooperation Branch advances this objective by assisting Canadian businesses to expand their interests in the region.

The Industrial Cooperation Program administered by the Business Cooperation Branch supports Canadian private sector investment initiatives by identifying possible joint venture opportunities in the Commonwealth Caribbean and assisting firms with feasibility and project definition studies. The Industrial Cooperation Division also helps Canadian companies develop contacts in the region and identify potential investment opportunities by organizing investment missions and seminars.[27] All English-speaking Caribbean countries, with the exception of the Bahamas and Bermuda, qualify for overseas development assistance.

4   Linked Programs

In addition to Caribcan itself, Canada's economic objectives in the region are being furthered by a variety of programs which seek to enhance the Act's effectiveness. One such service, provided by the Trade Facilitation Office (TFO) of the federal government, assists Commonwealth Caribbean countries in expanding exports to Canada. The TFO offers trade seminars; maintains a register of Caribbean exporters and funds their participation in trade fairs; organizes trade missions; and produces marketing information for the benefit of Caribbean exporters and Canadian importers.

As in the United States, private sector bodies with interests in the region have been incorporated into the Canadian initiative. The Canadian Council for the America's (CCA) and the Canadian-Latin America Trade Organisation (CLATO) fulfil roles similar to those provided by Caribbean/Central America Action in the United States. The main goal of both bodies is to strengthen private sector links between Canada, the Caribbean, and Central and South America. Both the CCA and CLATO publish information on trade issues, and provide a variety of other services to member companies. Chief of these is their function as channels of communication between private sector interests and the federal government.[28]

The Act provides for a review of Caribcan, two years into the program, to consider changes to its provisions. As a consequence of that review, in May 1990 the Government of Canada announced alterations to the program, to expand duty-free coverage. Such changes are, however, limited in scope and are unlikely to influence the pattern of bilateral trade.

5   Trends in Canadian Trade with the English-speaking Caribbean

While little official information on the impact of Caribcan on Caribbean economies has been made available by the Canadian government, it is possible to discern general trends in bilateral trade between Canada and the English-speaking Caribbean.

Aggregate Trade

Official data covering Canada's trade with the Caribbean in the 1980s indicate that changes have been occurring in the pattern of trade between the two areas. As Table 4-1 shows, trade flows between Canada and the English-speaking Caribbean totalled $479 million in 1980 (all figures rounded). This comprised $327 million in Canadian exports and $152 million in imports, representing a sizeable trade surplus in favour of Canada. By the end of 1985 bilateral trade amounted to $567 million, a rise of $88 million, or 18 per cent, over the 1980 figure. Notwithstanding the overall rise in bilateral trade in the period following the international economic recession, Canada's trade surplus with the English-speaking Caribbean declined significantly in the early 1980s, falling from $175 million in 1980 to $41 million for 1985. In 1985 the value of Canadian exports to these countries fell to well below the 1980 level.

In contrast to their Canadian counterparts, Caribbean exporters made gains during the early 1980s. While export sales remained erratic — reflecting continued reliance on a small number of primary goods exports — the general trend was upward. Imports to Canada from the English-speaking Caribbean grew by a hefty 73 per cent, from $152 million to $263 million, in the six years ending 1985.

Coincident with the launching of the Caribcan program, a trend began developing remarkably similar to that which pertained in United States-Caribbean trade relations after the Caribbean Basin Initiative was implemented. The year 1986 marked the beginning of a reversal in the bilateral trade situation. By the end of 1988 Canadian producers had regained their former dominance, increasing export sales by 25 per cent over the 1985 level, to $380 million. Caribbean industries, on the other hand, after achieving significant growth in exports to Canada in 1986 experienced a sharp fall thereafter. Despite the fact that international prices for a number of Caribbean commodities were rising in 1988, at $270 million, sales to Canada in that year were 14 per cent lower than for 1986, when Caribcan went into effect, and only 3 per cent higher than for 1985.[29] As a consequence of these changes, in 1988 Canada recorded a trade surplus of $110 million, its largest in five years.[30]

After 1988 a number of factors combined to affect the emerging pattern of bilateral trade between Canada and Caribcan beneficiary countries. This ensemble of factors included the signing of the Canada-US Free Trade Agreement, which intensified the process of integration of the US and Canadian economies and further eroded the

Canadian government's capacity for independent decision-making with respect to both domestic and foreign economic policy; the decision to maintain a high value for the Canadian dollar, which reduced demand for Canadian exports and attracted high levels of imported goods and services; and the general slowdown in the global economy, which affected both developed and less developed countries.

Developments within the Caribbean also influenced the pattern of trade with Canada in the late 1980s. Most notable were the impact of natural disasters (Hurricanes Gilbert and Hugo) in the last two years of the decade, the success of the CBI in facilitating US import penetration of the region, and the implementation of structural adjustment programs—as prescribed by the International Monetary Fund and the World Bank—by many of Canada's trading partners in the region. Structural adjustment programs—which involve trade liberalization, together with cuts in social services, policies to hold real wages down, the removal of subsidies and price controls on essential goods and services, and in some instances, massive currency devaluation—are intended to enhance the capacity of Caribbean countries to service foreign debts. By redirecting resources away from their populations and toward production for export, these austerity policies also depressed demand for imported goods. These developments have been particularly damaging for Canadian exporters to the region. Given the high value of its currency, Canadian products have become increasingly uncompetitive, particularly in comparison to US exports.

These changes are reflected in the bilateral trade figures for the period. Canadian sales of goods to beneficiary countries have been sluggish in recent years, falling by roughly 13 per cent between 1988 and 1990, to $328 million. During this same period Commonwealth Caribbean exports to Canada grew by 12 per cent, to exceed $300 million for the first year since 1986. One result of these changes was that the merchandise trade deficit with Canada was reduced to $25 million in 1990.[31]

As suggested above, the growth in value of Caribbean exports to Canada after 1988 was linked less to the generative effects of Caribcan than to more profound changes occurring in the Canadian, Caribbean, and international economies at the turn of the decade. Indeed, given its restrictive clauses, which exclude so many of the region's labour-intensive manufactured products such as garments and footwear from duty-free arrangements, little potential for expansion was possible under its terms. As was acknowledged by one senior economic officer in the Department of External Affairs in late 1988, the impact of Caribcan on the volume of goods entering Canada was "minimal."[32] A brief examination of trade data for Jamaica, Barbados, and the Windward and Leeward Islands attests to this.

Country Data

Figures for Jamaica, Barbados, and the Windward and Leeward Islands indicate bilateral trade patterns generally in line with the trends outlined in the previous section.[33] As Table 4-1 demonstrates, Jamaica's commodity trade with Canada suffered a setback in 1986 and 1987. Exports to Canada, which had grown in excess of 200 per cent in the five years 1980 to 1985, fell by 26 per cent or $41 million from the 1985 peak of $155 million, to $114 million by December 1987. Although exports recovered in the following year, by the end of 1988 they were still 3 per cent below the level recorded three years earlier. During the same period, imports from Canada, which had remained relatively stable in the early 1980s, jumped 139 per cent or $73 million, from $54 million to $131 million.

Barbadian exports to Canada fluctuated more than Jamaica's during the early years of the decade. As shown in Table 4-1, between 1980 and 1985 Barbados's merchandise sales to Canada fell by 39 per cent, from $11.5 million to around $7 million. During the first two years of the Caribcan program the island's export industries achieved a major improvement in sales to the Canadian market. By December 1987 Canada imported more than $21 million worth of goods from that country: three times the amount imported in 1985. In 1988, however, exports suffered a drastic reversal, falling beneath the level of 1985, when Caribcan began.

In comparison with Barbados's record, Canada's annual trade for the period appeared relatively healthy. For one thing, commodity exports to Barbados experienced only minor fluctuation. Moreover, although exports expanded only slowly in the early 1980s, from $35 million in 1980 to slightly over $34 million by the end of 1985, in the following year sales increased by more than one-quarter, to $44 million. While Canada's export sales did not expand further in the next three years, they suffered only slight variation, fluctuating between $44 million and $43 million in the period ending December 1988.

As in the cases of both Jamaica and Barbados, bilateral trade between Canada and the micro-economies of the Windwards and Leewards expanded during the 1980s, particularly in the middle of the decade. Between 1980 and the end of 1984 the annual trade flow grew by 9 per cent, compared to a 62 per cent increase over the following four years, from $34 million to more than $55 million. Once again, Canadian exporters were the main beneficiaries of the growth in trade. In 1988 annual sales of Canadian-produced goods were up by 68 per cent, or almost $20 million, over the 1980 figure, rising from $29 million to $49 million. Canadian imports from the Eastern Caribbean countries grew by 191 per cent between 1980 and 1986. This was, however, from a minuscule base of $2.3 million in 1980 to the still modest figure of slightly under $7 million in 1988. Moreover, Canadian imports remained low when compared with the country's exports to those islands.

Again, like Jamaica and Barbados, penetration of Eastern Caribbean markets by Canadian exporters was most pronounced from the mid-eighties. The year 1986 was especially lucrative for Canadian companies exporting to that region. In that year, commodity sales almost doubled, rising from $43 million in 1985 to $81 million. Subsequently, sales declined, reaching $49 million by the end of 1988.

The position of each of these Caribbean trading partners deteriorated relative to Canada in the 1985-1988 period. At the end of 1988 only one country, Jamaica, was enjoying a trade surplus with Canada. Even so, Jamaica's surplus had deteriorated to one-fifth of its 1985 value, from over $100 million then to less than $20 million in 1988.

The trade situations of Barbados and the Windward and Leeward Islands group were even more precarious. Both ran merchandise trade deficits with Canada throughout the 1980s. Despite the advent of Caribcan's one-way free trade arrangement in mid-1986, by December 1988 neither Barbados nor the Windward and Leeward Islands had shown any signs of rectifying these imbalances. Despite rallying in 1986 and 1987, Barbados's deficit was 58 per cent higher in 1988 than in 1980, increasing from $23 million to $37 million. Bilateral trade figures for the Windward and Leeward Islands indicate the development of similarly severe problems in the second half of the 1980s. The shortfall in trade with Canada rose from $27 million in 1980 to $76 million in 1986. Since then the annual deficit has fluctuated at around $30-$40 million.

It should be noted that the general deterioration in the trading position of Commonwealth Caribbean countries relative to Canada's during the 1986-88 period was not replicated throughout the region. One island which does not benefit from Caribcan, Cuba, achieved major reductions in its annual trade deficit with Canada after 1984. Between 1985 and 1988 Cuban exports to Canada almost doubled, rising from $44 million to $87 million. At the same time, imports were reduced from $330 million to $226 million, slashing the trade deficit by half, from $287 million to $139 million. This general pattern of falling sales of Canadian goods to Cuba combined with rising Cuban exports to Canada continued after 1988, resulting in a deficit of $43 million for 1990, the smallest of the decade.

As indicated by aggregate trade data for 1989 and 1990, the balance of trade between Canada and English-speaking Caribbean economies also shifted in favour of the latter at the end of the decade.

Movement was pronounced in each of the three cases examined in this section, involving in each instance a decline in the value of Canadian sales to the region as the country's exports became more uncompetitive in relation to US products. At the same time, the value of Canadian imports was rising. Jamaica, for instance, recorded trade surpluses of $57 million and $50 million for 1989 and 1990 respectively, while Barbados and the Windward and Leeward Islands substantially reduced their annual deficits with Canada (from $34 million to $19 million in the first case, and from $42 million to $20 million in the second).

As disaggregated Canadian import data covering these countries suggest, growth in Caribbean sales to Canada was largely unaffected by the Caribcan program. In the first place, little alteration in the composition of merchandise exports occurred during this period. Such changes as did occur reflected expanded sales of traditional (primary goods) exports rather than movement into new product lines. Moreover, even in those few instances where increased merchandise exports to Canada reflected sales of new product categories, the data do not support the view that such trade involved goods covered by the Canadian trade program.

As far as Jamaica is concerned, while post-1988 export sales were higher than for previous years, no significant changes occurred in the composition of sales to Canada; the dominant export item continued to be bauxite, followed by rum and other alcoholic beverages, and vegetables. Barbadian exports and those from the Windward and Leeward Islands were also far higher in 1990 than had been the case two years earlier. Once again, however, this change reflected large annual increases in sales of oil products by Barbados and St. Lucia as opposed to increased manufactured goods exports or sales of other items covered by Caribcan. In fact, when St. Lucia is excluded from the picture, Windward and Leeward Islands exports were significantly lower in 1990 than for 1988, falling from slightly over $6 million to less than $1 million.

6   Trends in Canadian International Trade

Before discussing responses to Caribcan by Caribbean political leaders and other interested observers, it is useful to assess the value of Caribcan to signatory nations in the context of changes in merchandise trade patterns between Canada and other nations and regions of the world. With regard to aggregate trade flows, it should be noted that in the four years 1985 to 1988 (during which time the Canadian import bill with the English-speaking Caribbean declined by 14 per cent and Canadian exports to these same countries increased by 6 per cent), Canadian commodity imports grew in value by 26 per cent, from $104 billion to $131 billion (see Table 4-2). Over the same period exports rose from \$116 billion to \$134 billion, representing a more modest 15 per cent increase.[34] The data therefore indicate that the bilateral pattern that was emerging between Canada and the Commonwealth Caribbean during that period ran counter to a deeper trend in Canada's international trade during the mid-late 1980s.

Table 4-2
Canadian Trade with Major Trading Partners and Country Groupings

Canadian Imports (billions of dollars)

Country/Region	1985	1986	1987	1988	1989	1990
USA	72.0	75.2	76.7	86.4	88.1	87.8
UK	3.0	3.6	4.3	4.6	4.6	4.8
Japan	6.7	8.4	8.3	9.2	9.6	9.5
LA & C*	5.1	4.6	4.8	4.5	5.2	4.6
EEC'86	10.7	12.9	13.8	16.0	14.9	15.6
OECD	92.7	100.0	102.7	116.1	118.3	119.8
All nations	104.3	112.5	116.2	131.5	135.1	136.2

Canadian Domestic Exports (billions of dollars)

Country/Region	1985	1986	1987	1988	1989	1990
USA	90.4	90.3	91.7	97.8	98.7	105.1
UK	2.4	2.6	2.8	3.4	3.4	3.4
Japan	5.7	5.9	7.0	8.6	8.8	8.2
LA & C*	2.8	3.0	3.2	2.9	2.4	2.5
EEC'86	6.7	7.8	9.1	10.7	11.5	11.5
OECD	105.0	106.1	110.1	120.1	122.3	128.7
All nations	116.1	116.7	121.5	134.0	134.8	141.0

Source: Compiled from Statistics Canada, *Trade of Canada, Imports by Country*, Table 2; and *Trade of Canada, Exports by Country*, Table 2.

In this period, imports from Canada's three main trading partners, the USA, Japan, and the UK, grew by 20 per cent, 37 per cent, and 53 per cent respectively, representing an average increase of 37 per cent. Increases were also recorded for imports from almost all other major regions. The single exception was the region including Central America, Latin America, and the Caribbean. On average, these countries suffered a 12 per cent drop in exports to Canada (and meanwhile a 3 per cent rise in imports of Canadian products) between 1985 and December 1988. As Tables 4-2 and 4-3 indicate, export growth generally lagged behind that for imports in this period. Overall, Canada's trade surplus with the rest of the world fell from slightly below $12 billion to $2.5 billion, reflecting a marked deterioration in the country's international trade position.

Subsequent data show fluctuation in the extant pattern of trade. By the end of 1990, while the country was recording larger annual deficits with most other countries and regions of the world, Canada increased its trade surplus with the US (see Table 4-3).[35] If US-Canada trade data are excluded, however, Canadian imports increased by 3 per cent in 1990, whereas no significant change occurred in the value of exports.

Table 4-3
Canadian Balance of Trade, 1985-90
(billions of dollars)

Country/Region	1985	1986	1987	1988	1989	1990
USA	+ 18.4	+ 15.1	+ 15.0	+ 11.4	+ 10.6	+ 17.3
UK	–0.6	–1.0	–1.5	–1.2	–1.2	–1.4
Japan	–1.0	–2.5	–1.3	–0.6	–0.8	–1.3
LA & C*	–2.3	–1.6	–1.6	–1.6	–2.8	–2.1
EEC'86	–4.1	–5.1	–4.7	–5.3	–3.4	–4.1
OECD	+ 12.3	+ 6.1	+ 7.4	+ 4.0	+ 4.0	+ 8.9
All nations	+ 11.8	+ 4.2	+ 5.3	+ 2.5	-0.3	+ 4.8

Source: Compiled from Statistics Canada, *Trade of Canada, Imports by Country*, Table 2, and *Trade of Canada, Exports by Country*, Table 2.

In this context, Canada can be judged to have fared well in respect to its merchandise trade with the region, including Latin America, Central America, and the Caribbean. The overall value of imports from these countries declined by 11 per cent between December 1989 and the end of 1990, at the same time as Canadian exports to them increased marginally.

7   Responses to Caribcan

Because Caribcan was implemented more than two years after the CBI and because its provisions bear such a striking resemblance to the earlier program, reactions to it have been influenced to a large extent by the sustained decline in Caribbean exports to the United States and the subsequent deterioration of the regional balance of merchandise trade with that country. The most substantive differences between the two programs relate less to content than to the criteria established for deciding beneficiary nation status. As one senior political officer of the Department of External Affairs put it: "The main contrast in how we approach the region on issues of economic development and assistance is that we don't attach a political price to our involvement."[36]

Hence, while the Reagan administration (which used the program as a means of channelling additional funds to the Salvadoran government for its civil war effort) included Central America in its definition of the "Caribbean Basin" and used the so-called "ideology" clause to discriminate in favour of its allies in the region and to exclude socialist countries like Nicaragua, Cuba, and revolutionary Grenada, the Canadian legislation contains no similar clause and confines the operation of Caribcan to the English-speaking Caribbean.[37]

Caribbean Political Leaders

Because it made no attempt to differentiate between countries on ideological grounds, Caribcan was initially greeted with genuine enthusiasm in the Caribbean. Objections were raised, however, to its limited character.[38] This is not surprising, given that disappointment over the CBI had been growing among Caribbean political leaders and business people. Even before the official announcement of the Canadian trade development program, Caribbean heads of government were expressing doubts about the value of the CBI to the regional economy. In a 1985 letter to the US President, Caribbean leaders focussed on the issue of product access, which was viewed as one of the program's most crucial flaws:

> It is . . . widely acknowledged that the CBI excludes products which are important to our industrial program. The most noted omissions viewed in terms of their exchange earnings and employment potential are textiles and garments, footwear and leather products. . . . In all our countries, this industry [sic] offers the best opportunities for quick development measures in terms of job creation with relatively low investment requirements.[39]

It was against this background that overtures were made to the Mulroney government for a Canadian development initiative for the region. Small wonder, then, that Caribbean politicians and leaders of the business community were generally dissatisfied with Ottawa's response when specific details of the trade components of the plan were released. Jamaican and Eastern Caribbean governments were particularly unhappy about the criteria of origin required to qualify for duty-free treatment (felt to be more onerous even than under the CBI), the "safeguard" provisions, and, in view of the marginal impact of Caribbean imports on Canadian domestic producers, the exclusion of garments, cigars, rum, and footwear from the duty-free arrangements.[40]

The viability of the domestic apparel industry in the Eastern Caribbean had already been undermined by the massive reduction in intra-regional trade (a problem exacerbated by such external stresses as the bilateralist emphasis of US economic policy in the region); the contraction of CARICOM sales had, in turn, forced local garment manufacturers into a desperate search for extra-regional markets.[41] In light of this, what many Commonwealth Caribbean governments sought from Canada was a trade deal which not only equalled, but significantly improved upon, product access provided under the Caribbean Basin Initiative.

That Ottawa has failed to address these basic concerns reflects the power of protectionist demands from those sectors of domestic industry likely to be most seriously affected by market liberalization. Despite completion of an official review of the program, the Mulroney government has to date given no indication that substantive revisions to the legislation are under consideration.

Objections to the program continue to be made by the very interests in the Caribbean which had initially sought greater Canadian economic involvement in the region. Only one year into the program, Douglas Vaz, then minister of industry and commerce in Jamaica, called for a review of the legislation, arguing that "Caribcan is not the answer, not in its present form."[42] The primary demand of such critics is that the duty-free program be extended to include all non-traditional products; above all, apparel, cigars, and footwear.

Canada has made little attempt to meet these types of objections. Moreover, given continued resistance to market liberalization on the part of domestic producers, there is no reason to believe that Canada will become more accessible to non-traditional manufactured products such as garments and footwear from the Commonwealth Caribbean in either the short or medium terms. Indeed, Caribcan's trade regime is less liberal than the Caribbean Basin Initiative in this respect, particularly since mid-1986, when the US program was amended to provide more generous "Guaranteed Access Levels" to the American market for Caribbean apparel items assembled from fabric manufactured and cut in the United States.[43] Imports in this category are now charged duty only on value added outside the US (in the case of the Caribbean Basin this amounts to roughly 30 per cent of total value).

With the signing of the Canada-US Free Trade Agreement in 1989, and with negotiations proceeding between the US, Canada, and Mexico to include the latter country in a North American Free Trade Agreement based on the Canada-US model, concern has been rising in the Caribbean, as in other areas of the world, about the potential of such arrangements to divert trade and investment away from third-party countries. As far as Canada's program for the English-speaking Caribbean is concerned, with duties on American products being removed over a 10-year period and the probability of duty reductions on Mexican imports, the benefits to be derived by Commonwealth economies from Caribcan's trade regime will be increasingly jeopardized as the trilateral negotiations proceed.[44]

Popular Responses

More fundamental criticisms, however, have been made of the approach to Third World economic development shared by Caribcan and the CBI. Objections have been raised by independent analysts, unions, non-governmental development agencies, and Caribbean "grass-roots" organizations, to the strategy of private sector-led, export-oriented development embodied in the CBI and Caribcan initiatives.[45] Such criticisms have gained ground with the failure of both the US and Canadian programs to ameliorate even the most glaring problems of development — debt crises, economic marginalization, growing dependency on food imports, grinding poverty, and rising unemployment — that continue to afflict Caribbean societies.

Economic restructuring occurring in the Caribbean and Central America as a result of the US program indicate that specific forms of industrial and agricultural development *might* be stimulated in Commonwealth Caribbean nations as a consequence of the Canadian initiative.[46] Given the limitations of the program, however, such developments are likely only to be weak.

Even so, any evidence of economic restructuring in these directions is viewed as problematic by many critics of the CBI and Caribcan. Much of the reorganization that has already occurred is the result of contraction in US markets for more traditional products (sugar, tobacco, petroleum, and petroleum by-products) which are excluded from free-trade provisions. By the same token, the products which received the greatest stimulus from the American program were either winter fruits and vegetables produced by large-scale, highly capitalized production units, or labour-intensive industrial products (chemicals, pharmaceuticals, electronic items, and since 1986, garments) which are produced in Export Processing Zones employing low-waged, non-unionized, unskilled or semi-skilled labour, and almost wholly on imports of US-made materials and components.[47]

For the most part, the types of changes engendered by the American program have resulted in a shift in export orientation away from traditional agricultural products towards non-traditional fruits and vegetables, industrial processing, and assembly operations. To date, the evidence of product or trade diversification is negligible. Nor have the changes already experienced made any real impact on unemployment levels or foreign exchange earnings. Instead, they have perpetuated and reinforced dependence on the US economy by integrating Caribbean countries more closely into the international production arrangements of American manufacturers. Needless to say, as many critics have pointed out, the chief beneficiaries of the proliferation of "re-export" industries in the region are not the people of designated countries themselves but the foreign companies who have turned the region's huge unemployment problem into its biggest "comparative advantage."

8   Concluding Remarks

As the data presented in this chapter indicate, new patterns have been emerging in commodity trading between Canada and the Commonwealth Caribbean since the early 1980s. From a Caribbean perspective, one of the most alarming developments during the mid-late-1980s was the deterioration of the balance of trade with Canada. This occurred due to a fairly sustained rise in the value of Canadian exports to the Caribbean, coincident with the decline and stagnation of regional imports into Canada. Whereas during the first half of the decade Commonwealth Caribbean economies significantly improved their trade situation relative to Canada, between 1985 and 1988 their position deteriorated quite markedly. There is no evidence to suggest that changes occurring in bilateral trade after 1988 were connected to the Caribcan program.

Furthermore, since Caribcan began in mid-1986, it has not advanced its stated objective, that being to "assist [beneficiary countries] in meeting their economic development goals." There has been no progress in this respect. As in the case of bilateral trade relations between the United States and the Caribbean region after the CBI was launched, for the bulk of the period the trend has been towards larger trade deficits with Canada.

As critics of both the CBI and Caribcan have pointed out, some of the most obvious deficiencies of these programs have developed in predictable fashion, given that there was little or no real consultation with, or input from, people in the region. In the United States pressure for fundamental changes to the CBI did have some effect. Largely as a result of the efforts of organizations like the Development Group for Alternative Policies, a number of US legislators were compelled to at least minimally address the realities of the Caribbean and the problems associated with past policies towards the region. They were, moreover, forced to acknowledge the need for more consultation not only at the government level but also with representatives of the people who stand to be most directly affected by changes to US regional policy: farmers, workers, women, small businesses, and non-governmental development organizations active in the Caribbean.[48]

Canadian legislators have lagged behind their US counterparts in exploring the issue of alternative development policies and options for the Caribbean region. With the failure of Caribcan thus far, however, this is clearly only the first in a long series of changes to the policy-making process that must be implemented if Canadian economic and trade development assistance programs are to be made responsive to the needs of Commonwealth Caribbean societies.

5

The Philosophy and Developmental Prospects of the CBI

Devanand J. Ramnarine

1   Introduction

This chapter focusses on the crisis which Caribbean Basin economies faced on the eve of the launching of the Caribbean Basin Initiative (CBI), the Reagan administration's interpretation of this crisis, its proposals for resolving it as embodied in the CBI, and the results and likely future effects of the implementation of the CBI. A brief overview of the main economic indicators of major Caribbean Basin economies is presented in section two. This is followed, in section three, by a summary of the Reagan administration's perspective on the economic crisis. The solutions offered for the region's economic woes constitute the underlying principles of the CBI and are the subject of section four. Section five addresses the performance of the CBI in the first three years (1984-86) of its implementation through a detailed statistical profile of its three prongs. The current assessment of the CBI by the US administration is presented in section six. This is followed in sections seven and eight by a critical evaluation of the performance and developmental prospects of the CBI. Section nine continues this evaluation by examining the development logic and likely future impact of the CBI. Finally, in section ten, we focuss on the inevitable question to be asked of any US foreign-policy initiative in the region: to what extent does US capital benefit from it (in this case, from the CBI)? Indications are that the CBI will deepen the process of partial relocation of US capital which had already begun in response to the need for the US to enhance its competitiveness in the face of declining relative productivity at home.

2   The Economic Crisis of the Caribbean Basin

The Caribbean Basin economies plunged into an economic decline after peak performances in 1978-79. By the end of 1983, the 12 major

---

Notes for Chapter 5 are on pp. 233-39.

economies showed an average negative 23.5 per cent change in real GDP at 1980 prices (see Table 5-1). This was particularly severe in the case of Costa Rica (–69.7%), El Salvador (–32.9%), Nicaragua (–33.2%), and Jamaica (–27.3%).

Table 5-1
Changes, Real GDP, and Real Per Capita Income, Selected Countries (percentages)

Country	Change real GDP 1980-83 (at 1980 prices)	Change real per cap. income 1980-83 (at 1980 prices)
Costa Rica	–69.7	–83.2
El Salvador	–32.9	–20.8
Guatemala	–17.7	–13.1
Honduras	–17.5	–10.8
Nicaragua	–33.2	–2.5
Panama	–10.4	+ 0.3
C.A. average	–30.2	–21.6
Barbados	na	na
Dom. Republic	–15.0	+ 0.3
Guyana	–14.3	–32.5
Haiti	–16.0	–8.3
Jamaica	–27.3	–45.0
Trinidad & Tobago	–12.3	–2.8
Insular Carib. average	–16.9	–17.6
Caribbean Basin average (12 countries)	–23.5	–19.66

Source: Calculated from figures presented in International Monetary Fund, *International Financial Statistics: Supplement on Economic Indicators*, Supplement Series No. 10 (Washington, DC: IMF, 1985).

Real per capita GDP showed an average decline of 19.6 per cent, with Costa Rica, Guyana, and Jamaica registering the most profound setbacks. Rapid population increases exacerbated this decline.[1]

The external sector of the region's economies experienced a similarly dismal performance. The combination of volatile export commodity prices and rises in import prices drastically affected the financing of imports.[2] Overall, therefore, the major Caribbean Basin economies were confronted with massive balance of payments deficits (see Table 5-2). At the end of 1983, the 12 major Caribbean Basin economies registered over $21 billion in long-term debt commitments alone (amounting to 61.6% of total GDP), the servicing of which required a huge portion of export earnings (see Table 5-3), to the detriment of expansionary economic activities.

Table 5-2
Balance of Payments Position of 12 Major
Caribbean Basin Economies
($ millions)

Country/Region	Of which total B.O.P	Of which current account =	Current trade balance =	Account as % of exports
Costa Rica	−352.8	−316.5	−45.3	−27.0
El Salvador	119.7	−65.0	−95.5	−7.2
Guatemala	−114.6	−223.9	35.7	−18.6
Honduras	−61.6	−225.2	−66.5	−27.8
Nicaragua	67.4	−443.2	−349.7	−94.4
Panama	−12.0	247.0	−648.0	
C.A. total	−353.9	1026.0	−1169.0	
C.A. average	−58.9	−171.1	−194.8	−28.6
Barbados	−7.6	−42.0	−292.6	−6.0
Dom. Republic	−481.2	−421.1	−497.0	−33.7
Guyana	−193.0	−157.5	−32.4	−69.9
Haiti	−33.1	−114.1	−139.3	−38.7
Jamaica	−355.9	−358.6	−438.5	−26.90
Trinidad & Tobago	−953.3	−883.4	−42.7	−29.9
Ins. Carib. total	−2008.4	−1976.7	−1,442.5	
Ins. Carib. average	−334.8	−329.4	−240.4	−34.1%
CB total	−2362.3	−3003.5	−2611.8	
CB average	−196.0	−250.1	−217.6	−31.3%

Source: Calculated from data presented in International Monetary Fund, *International Financial Statistics: Supplement on Economic Indicators*, Supplement Series No. 10 (Washington, DC: IMF, 1985).

The social dimension of the economic collapse has been devastating. The Kissinger Commission estimated that by 1980, 60 per cent of the Central American population was living in poverty, with 40 per cent in extreme poverty; about "half the urban population and three quarters of the rural population could not satisfy their basic needs in terms of nutrition, housing, health and education"; rural unemployment reached 50 per cent; and, "ten out of every one hundred babies died before the age of five . . . and 52 per cent of the children were malnourished."[3] This socioeconomic deterioration stimulated a significant increase in emigration to the US. Emigration has been a historical reality for the insular Caribbean but a relatively new phenomenon for Central America. The total number (age 14 and over only) of Salvadorans, Guatemalans, and Nicaraguans *legally* living in the US grew from 175 000 in 1980 to 270 000 by April 1983.[4]

Table 5-3
Long-term External Debt of Major Caribbean Basin Countries, 1983

Country	Total long-term external debt (private + public)	Debt as % of GDP	Debt service as % of export
Costa Rica	3 643.70	125.17	55.10
El Salvador	1 467.70	36.35	NA
Guatemala	1 555.00	17.18	17.20
Honduras	1 804.20	61.25	22.30
Nicaragua	3 413.60	95.87	NA
Panama	3 090.80	70.57	NA
C.A. subtotal	14 975.00		
C.A. average	2 495.83	67.73	–
Barbados	262.40	24.84	NA
Dom. Republic	2 394.40	27.92	27.90
Guyana	692.50	142.70	NA
Haiti	449.90	27.60	NA
Jamaica	2 076.60	98.69	15.80
Trinidad & Tobago	887.00	12.12	–
In. CB total	6 762.80		
In. CB average	1 127.12	55.64	
Total CB	21 737.80	61.68	

Source: Calculated from data presented in International Monetary Fund, *International Financial Statistics: Supplement on Economic Indicators*, Supplement Series, No. 10 (Washington, DC: IMF, 1985).

3 Official Explanation of the Caribbean Basin's Economic Crisis

US officials usually specify four determinants of the region's economic crisis. The first derives from what preceded it. The period from the 1950s to the late 1970s is deemed to have been one of unprecedented growth in the region and this, according to Deputy Secretary of State Kenneth Dam, created rising expectations for broad political participation, for which there were few democratic outlets.[5] The results were social conflicts and political uncertainty which prevented new investments and affected the process of development.

The second factor was a series of adverse developments in the world economy: slackening of demand and decline in the prices of export commodities and the second oil shock of 1978 and 1979, which sapped the buying power of export incomes.[6] The third cause of the crisis was the inappropriate response by governments of the region to these external developments. The resort to external financing of huge import bills, according to Secretary of State George Schultz, laid the basis for a debilitating debt problem and also reversed an earlier progressive tendency to rely on domestic savings for investment.[7] In addition, worsening balance of trade problems inspired a series of economic controls such as cutbacks on imports of raw materials, spare parts, and other capital goods, thus accelerating the economic slowdown. These were compounded by weak economic management, restrictions on the private sector, and increased public spending. Government intervention proved inefficient and prone to a concentration of power, which invited corruption.[8] Finally, intra-regional tensions and political unrest, beginning with the conflict between El Salvador and Honduras in 1969, initiated a breakdown of the Central American Common Market, a previous engine of regional growth. Isolationist measures were later adopted in the face of growing balance of payments and debt problems when Nicaragua, El Salvador, and Honduras suffered trade imbalances with Costa Rica and Guatemala. With "political turmoil" in Nicaragua and El Salvador, intra-regional co-operation reached its nadir; economic infrastructure was damaged; investment confidence waned amongst commercial banks, foreign investors, and the domestic private sector; and capital flight became substantial.[9] What was most heavily stresssed in all this was the allegation that Nicaragua, backed by Cuba and the Soviet Union, was supporting the guerrillas in El Salvador, who were damaging vital infrastructure and escalating tensions which resulted in people abandoning economic activities.[10] In addition, the Sandinista government in Nicaragua was deemed a "communist threat" to the whole of Central America, necessitating an economically debilitating regional arms race and a further loss of investor confidence and capital.

4 Solutions to the Caribbean Basin Economic Crisis: The Developmental Assumptions of the Caribbean Basin Initiative

In his 1982 OAS address in which the CBI was formally introduced, President Reagan made reference to "a fresh view of development" which "stressed more than aid and government intervention" in that it included trade and investment. The "fresh view" of development for which the administration claimed credit – a reaffirmation, in fact, of the staple developmentalist approach – derived its inspiration from two major speeches by President Reagan, the elements of which were subsequently elaborated upon by other members of the administration.[11] They are reflected in the CBI.

The economic component of the administration's multi-pronged Caribbean Basin strategy consisted of four policies which Caribbean Basin economies must pursue and two which the US would sustain. First, a commitment to an open international economy is required, and this is to be pursued through a vigorous export strategy. Trade is viewed as the "engine of development," since it enables the export and import sectors to furnish vital inputs to development, provides revenues to eliminate the debt problem, and ultimately promises a better standard of living for the peoples of the region. The alternative, "inward-looking" strategy of import substitution was considered to have failed badly, creating dual economies, crippling the agriculture sector, precipitating balance of payments deficits, and encouraging rapid urban growth with attendant political instability. Protectionism, in addition, was said to be "an administrative way of delaying adjustment and changes in technology and productivity."[12]

Through an export strategy, it was argued, Caribbean Basin economies could emulate "the economic success stories" of Taiwan, South Korea, and Singapore. First, the Caribbean Basin Initiative guaranteed access for a wide range of goods. Second, the region's economies enjoyed certain advantages over South East Asian countries. They had a comparable resource base, were in closer proximity to major markets,[13] and wages were generally low or competitive (see Table 5-4).

The second policy advocated was the expansion of private sector activities as a prerequisite for participation in the international economy, and a simultaneous miniaturization of the public sector, since it was said to have proven to be inefficient, inexperienced, corrupt, and unproductive. Middendorf, then US ambassador to the Organization of American States (OAS), argued that "[i]f government pursues policies that significantly distort private sector decision making, if it is inefficient and/or ineffective, then the overall prospects for economic development suffer, and international commerce with it."[14] In his testimony to Congress urging the passage of the CBI legislation, Peter Johnson of the influential Caribbean/Central American Action (C/CAA) noted that a private sector emphasis was already gaining wide currency:

> The electral [sic] shift in the region dovetails with current directions
> in US policy as well as a striking shift in the institutions like the World
> Bank and the CDB [Caribbean Development Bank]. This is occurring

not in response to political pressures among the various players, but [to] a discovery at various levels that alternative approaches have not worked, and this might be the missing ingredient.[15]

The provisions of the CBI were seen to provide "the clear runway from which the private sector can take off."[16]

Table 5-4
Country Comparisons of Wages in the Caribbean Basin

Country	Wages	Current major exports
Anguilla	NA	Lobster, salt, livestock
Antigua	Medium	Undergarments, cement
Bahamas	High	Petroleum products, shellfish
Barbados	Med.-high	Electrical parts
Belize	Medium	Sugar, undergarments
Br. Virgin Isl.	NA	Rum
Cayman Islands	NA	Fish, petroleum products
Costa Rica	Low-med.	Fruit, beef, coffee, sugar
Dominica	Medium	Undergarments, essential oils
Dom. Republic	Medium	Sugar, precious metals, coffee, cocoa
El Salvador	Medium	Coffee, electrical machinery, sugar, shellfish
Grenada	Medium	Nutmeg, bananas
Guatemala	Medium	Coffee, sugar, petroleum products, bananas, meat
Guyana	Medium	Shellfish, sugar, bauxite
Haiti	Low	Electrical mach., undergarments, sporting goods, coffee, leather
Honduras	Low	Bananas, shrimp, coffee, meat, sugar
Jamaica	Med.-high	Bauxite/alumina, sugar
Montserrat	Medium	Electrical machinery
Neth. Antilles	High	Petroleum products
Nicaragua	Medium	Beef, fruits, shellfish, sugar
Panama	Med.-high	Shellfish, fruits, sugar, petroleum products
St. Kitts	Medium	Sugar, undergarments
St. Lucia	Medium	Undergarments, electrical machinery
St. Vincent	Medium	Undergarments, games & sporting goods
Suriname	NA	Bauxite/alumina
T/dad & Tobago	High	Petroleum products, fertilizers, steel
Turks & Caicos	NA	Shellfish

Wages: Low = below $20/wk. Medium = between $20-$30/wk. High = above $30/wk. NA = not available.
Source: *Business America*, January 7, 1985.

While a strong private sector was essential for tapping the international economy, foreign investment — the third element of the Reagan administration prescription — was, in turn, "the key to a strong private sector, and thus to a healthy economy."[17] Foreign direct investment was preferable to other sources of capital inflow such as official aid and private loans, for various reasons. First, it "serves to transfer new technology and management skills in order to increase exports and reduce the burden on the existing export sector in achieving the dual goal of renewed domestic growth and servicing the national debt."[18] Second, official and private aid had dwindled due to fiscal problems in donor countries and apprehension amongst private banks over the ability of recipient countries to repay existing debts. In any case, these alternative sources could not be adequate, given the enormous capital inflows required.[19] Third, foreign investments contribute more per dollar than official and private aid, which can no longer compensate even for the capital outflows induced by political instability. Fourth, borrowing creates and sustains dependence through the imperative of debt-servicing, while "foreign investment, unlike foreign debt, is serviced by profits, not interest."[20] Foreign investment is not, however, automatically available, nor is it necessarily economically optimal. The important prerequisites are "open markets, an equitable and efficient tax system, sound monetary and exchange policies . . . a government commitment to encourage new enterprises . . . sound government policies and non-discriminatory legal procedures . . ."[21] — policies encouraged by the Caribbean Basin Initiative.

The fourth policy prescribed by Washington was the promotion of domestic private investment as a complement to foreign investment. Two measures were needed to dissuade capital exports and so retain domestic investments in the region. First, incentives must be made available. Schultz advised: "When people are rewarded for thrift, capital becomes available for investment. When they are rewarded for entrepreneurship, they respond with productivity and innovation."[22] Second, the state should acknowledge its practical inexperience, desist from economic intervention, and limit public sector spending to make more capital available for investment.

The final domestic policy change recommended by administration officials was to rectify the skewed distribution of investment between industry and agriculture so as to achieve balanced economic growth. In their view an excessive emphasis on industrial growth not only tends to obscure the successes of the agricultural sector but has created many social and economic problems.

Revitalizing the economies of the Caribbean Basin, so the argument went, necessitates continued economic-related assistance by the US, such as providing markets, economic aid, and investment promotion. The administration had, in addition, identified two other areas of assistance: promoting the process of democratization in the region and creating a "security shield" under which this and the process of economic development may be protected.

Secretary Schultz argued that democracy allows for the resolution of "complex issues" through a "public mandate"; but more importantly, from the perspective of development,

> [a] functioning democratic system provides the best chance for stability that investors need to plan ahead. Democracy provides the flexibility to accommodate change and relieve internal pressure, and the freedom that facilitates enterprise and promotes economic growth.[23]

Much was made of US contributions in this area: support for the transition to democracy in Honduras in 1981-82; co-operation with the Costa Rican government in its Supreme Electoral Tribunal, and with other countries of the region through the Regional Centre for Electoral Assistance; contribution to the "stunning success" of El Salvador's constituent Assembly elections in 1982 and assistance in rebuilding that country's "tragically inadequate justice system"; support for Costa Rica "and its associates" in the Central American Democratic Community; "restoration" of democracy in Grenada; relaying the "democratic message" to Cuba through Radio Marti; and providing miscellaneous assistance through the newly created National Endowment for Democracy (NED).[24]

The security shield was intended "not as a goal in itself, but to provide the necessary protection for . . . political, economic and diplomatic goals" by helping Caribbean Basin democracies to defend themselves, as well as to "underline [the US's] deterrent capability."[25]

The foregoing discussion of the internal and external conditions deemed necessary for the revitalization of the region's economies captures the essence of the US administration's perspective on economic development. These are all embodied in the CBI, rendering it, as Secretary Schultz observed, "a symbol as well as a program."[26]

5 Overview of the Performance of the CBI

This analysis of the impact of the CBI on Caribbean Basin exports to the US pertains primarily to the first three years of the program, i.e., 1984-86. The presentation of empirical data relies heavily on the second annual report of the International Trade Commission (USITC) which was mandated, under Section 215 of the CBI legislation, to compile annual reports on the impact of the CBI.[27] Wherever figures are presented for 1987, these are incomplete and tentative and are obtained from the US Department of State.[28]

5.1   The Free Trade Area (FTA) of the CBI

Over the three years for which complete data are available, total exports from the 27 eligible countries to the US registered a *significant decline* – from approximately $9 billion in 1983 to $6.2 billion in 1986, a drop of the order of 31 per cent.[29] The 1986 export figures were lower even than those of 1982, when the US economy was in a recession. The downward trend in exports continued in 1987. During the first half of the year, exports to the US were 6.2 per cent below those of the same period in 1986.[30] The overall effect was a drop in the Caribbean Basin share of US imports from 3.4 per cent in 1983 to 1.6 per cent in 1986. In 1986, the 22 beneficiaries accounted for 98 per cent of the region's exports to the US.

Of the designated beneficiaries, the oil-producing and oil-refining countries were principally responsible for the decline. The value of their exports fell by $3.58 billion between 1983 and 1986, or more than the decline ($2.7 billion) registered by all the 22 beneficiaries combined.

A comparison of major source groups categorized by the US International Trade Commission (USITC) shows that the non-oil-refining Central American and Central Caribbean regions increased their exports in absolute as well as relative terms. Their share of the region's exports to the US rose from 22 per cent and 16 per cent, to 41 per cent and 29 per cent respectively. In contrast, exports from the Eastern Caribbean declined drastically in absolute terms. The relative increase from 2.7 per cent of the region's exports in 1983 to 3 per cent in 1986 was due only to the decline of the region's total exports. The USITC attributed this decline to the closure of the INTEL plant in Barbados which had been established to produce semi-conductors.[31]

With regard to the performance of individual beneficiaries, the major quantitative increases in exports came from Costa Rica, Guatemala, and the Dominican Republic, which together accounted for 38 per cent of the exports of all beneficiaries to the US. In contrast, the major oil-producing and refining countries – Bahamas, the Netherlands Antilles, and Trinidad and Tobago – together experienced a massive decline from 60 per cent of all exports in 1983 to only 28 per cent in 1986. The region still relies on the export of relatively few products. Table 5-7 highlights the principal articles exported from the region from 1982 to 1986. In 1983, these items accounted for about 80 per cent of total exports, compared to 77 per cent in 1986. It is clear, therefore, that diversification of production for export has not been significant. While the export of traditional products – sugar and bauxite – registered declines, this was not compensated for by any significant introduction of new products, but rather by the expansion of other traditional products such as coffee, bananas, and shellfish. The Department of State reported, however, that coffee prices, which had been on a "rollercoaster" for several months in 1986, retreated "to below historical standards in early 1987."[32]

Exports under the CBI alone amounted to $578 million in 1984, declined to $498 million in 1985, and increased to $690 million in 1986. They represented 6.7 per cent of overall exports by beneficiaries to the US in 1984, 7.4 per cent of the total in 1985, and 11.4 per cent in 1986. This compared favourably with two other duty-free programs. Exports under the General System of Preferences (GSP) accounted for 7 per cent of the total in 1984, and 8 per cent each in 1985 and 1986. Exports under items 806.30 and 807 of the Tariff Schedules of the United States (TSUS) amounted to 6.8 per cent in 1984, rose to 8 per cent in 1985, and to 10 per cent in 1986. It must be remembered, however, that the figures for exports under the CBI do not necessarily represent new exports. When the CBI became operational, certain articles previously accounted for under TSUS 806.30/807 and GSP changed to duty-free treatment under the CBI. In the absence of quantitative estimates of the impact of the CBI alone on the region's export performance, it is not possible to know whether apparent increases in the export of CBI items are attributable to more than the mere change in accounting format. For duty-free imports under all existing programs, however, the US International Trade Commission estimated that "less than 3 per cent of 1983 imports from CBERA beneficiaries received new duty-free treatment and less than 6 per cent of 1986 imports benefited."[33]

The first report of the USITC, for the period 1984-85, provided a list of 25 major commodities eligible for CBI treatment, ranked by calculated duties in 1983. The USITC report for 1986 compared this list (see Table 5-5) with the list of the leading 20 products exported from the Caribbean Basin under the CBI in 1986 (see Table 5-6). Products which were eligible for duty-free treatment under the GSP and which, accordingly, did not enjoy new benefits under the CBI, are identified in the tables. It was pointed out earlier that their entry as CBI items represents only a change in bookkeeping, though baseballs and baseball equipment were an exception, since they became eligible for duty-free treatment for the first time in 1986 by virtue of increased value-added that conformed to CBI requirements. Sugar is featured at the top of the 1986 list of duty-free exports as well as the list of duties collected in 1983. The listing of coffee in the 1986 list was the result of a change in bookkeeping rather than any new benefit from the CBI, since this item has never been subject to duties. The other items which are only in the 1986 list but are not GSP or Most Favoured Nation (MFN) duty free are non-beverage ethanol, orange juice, and deformed concrete rein-

Table 5-5
Leading Exports of CBI Goods, Ranked
by Calculated Duties Collected in
1983 ($ 000s)

TSUS Item #	Description	Duties collected
155.20	Sugars, syrups, and molasses	32 560
170.80	Tobacco, n.s.p.f.	2 803
106.10	Beef and veal	2 105
687.74	Monolithic integrated circuits	2 006
169.14	Rum (large containers)	1 658
685.80	Electrical capacitors	757
437.56	Adrenocortical hormones	727
170.60	Scrap tobacco	718
685.90	Electrical switches, etc.	627
170.35	Cigarette leaf, stemmed	614
734.56	Baseballs, etc.	450
148.96	Pineapples	494
425.52	Other nitrogenous compounds	455
686.10	Resistors	423
138.35	Yucca	328
723.15	Film other than motion picture	316
688.43	Electrical articles and parts	305
607.17	Wire rods	300
676.52	Parts of office machines	300
136.00	Dasheens	261
146.30	Avocados	215
437.57	Other hormones	191
137.75	Chayote	187
170.45	Filler tobacco not stemmed	186
169.13	Rum (small containers)	169

Note: In several of the above items official calculated duties for 1983 have been adjusted for the amount of US products entered duty free under item 807.

Source: US International Trade Commission, *Annual Report on the Impact of the Caribbean Basin Economic Recovery Act on US Industries and Consumers*, Second Report, 1986, USITC Publication 2024 (Washington, DC: USITC, September 1987), p. 14.

forcing bars. Exports of non-beverage ethanol were high because firms were established "specifically to take advantage of the [CBI's] elimination of the additional 60 cents per gallon duty that other countries pay on fuel ethanol."[34] Exports of orange juice did not feature in the 1983 list owing to inclement weather, but the USITC report noted that they would have featured in a normal year. The report attributed the appearance of reinforcing bars in the 1986 list to "a possible diversion" from exports of wire rods, triggered by the anti-dumping and countervailing duties imposed on these products from Trinidad and Tobago.[35]

Table 5-6
Leading Duty-free CBI Exports to US, 1986 ($ 000s)

TSUS Item No.	Description	Calculated duties collected
155.20[a]	Sugars, syrups, and molasses	124 851
106.10	Beef and veal, fresh, chilled	121 184
412.22[b]	Analgesics, antipyretics	50 993
685.90[b]	Electrical switches, etc.	27 099
4 7.88	Ethyl alcohol for non-beverage use	25 092
170.70[b]	Cigars each valued 23 cents or over	18 820
734.56[b]	Baseball equipment and parts	17 114
148.96	Pineapples, fresh, in packages other than crates	13 446
606.79	Deformed concrete reinforcing bars	12 371
740.15[b]	Jewelry and parts	11 137
685.80	Electrical capacitors	10 244
170.35	Cigarette leaf, stemmed	9 284
607.17	Wire rods	7 908
110.35[b]	Fresh fish, whole	7 729
165.29	Fruit juices, not mixed, orange	7 498
686.10	Resistors	7 415
169.14	Rum (large containers)	7 172
136.00[b]	Dasheens	6 651
160.10[c]	Coffee, crude, roasted or ground	6 057
148.30[b]	Melons fresh, except cantaloupes	5 984

[a] Entries except those from the Dominican Republic eligible for duty-free entry under GSP.
[b] Eligible for duty-free entry under GSP.
[c] Column 1 duty rate is free.
Source: US International Trade Commission, *Annual Report on the Impact of the Caribbean Basin Economic Recovery Act on US Industries and Consumers, Second Report, 1986,* USITC Publication 2024 (Washington, DC: USITC, September 1987), p. 15.

With regard to the performance of specific products from 1983 to 1986, the second report of the USITC noted that "notable 1986 developments are generally absent."[36] The increased export of beef and veal in 1986, compared to 1985, was due largely to a dockworker strike in New Zealand which afforded the CBI countries a "temporary opportunity" to increase their exports of these products to the US. In addition, increased exports of fresh, chilled or frozen beef from Costa Rica, the Dominican Republic, and Honduras in 1986 resulted from good pasture conditions in Costa Rica, a new meat-packing plant in the Dominican Republic, and severe drought in Honduras which led to "distress cattle slaughter" and export of beef to the US. Exports of pineapple increased by 60 per cent between 1985 and 1986, due to both higher prices and larger volumes of exports. The USITC report attributed this surge to "heavy investments in pineapple since the beginning of the [CBI]." Decreased exports of sugar reflect the ongoing reductions in US import sugar quotas aimed at supporting domestic producers.

We now turn to the performance of non-traditional exports. Exports of monolithic integrated circuits from CBI beneficiaries decreased by 62 per cent, from $170.2 million in 1985 to $64 million in 1986, due largely to the closure of INTEL Corporation's semi-conductor assembly plant in Barbados. In any case, monolithic integrated circuits have been freed from duty since March 1, 1985. The CBI therefore offers no advantage to exporters. A decline also occurred in the export of electrical parts (ferrite core memories resistor/capacitor networks and other miscellaneous articles) from $7.3 million in 1985 to $2.5 million in 1986 (a 66 per cent decrease). The USITC report attributed this to a possible displacement of these products due to technology changes. Total exports of baseball equipment and parts remained stagnant in 1986 but the value entering under the CBI more than quadrupled compared with that of 1985. This resulted from the fact that more of the manufacturing operations have been moved from the US to Haiti and the additional value-added qualifies these products for more duty-free treatment.

Products not eligible for duty-free treatment under the CBI, as a category, declined by 58 per cent mainly owing to a 72 per cent decline in the value of petroleum exports. Petroleum apart, however, this category contains products which recorded the highest export increases. Apparel increased by 107 per cent between 1983 and 1986, followed by 81 per cent for textiles. This, no doubt, accounts for present efforts to include these products fully under the CBI.[37]

5.2 New Investments

At the time of writing, no comprehensive and credible record of new investments in the Caribbean Basin is available, though the Department of Commerce is reportedly in the process of completing one. The only survey of new investments attributed to the CBI was published in 1985 by the Department of Commerce but was found to be seriously flawed.[38] The Department published the results of a survey which indicated that 285 new export-oriented investments in CBI countries, valued at $208 million and creating approximately 35 891 jobs, could be "reasonably tied to the CBI" from the period of its inception to the spring of 1985.[39] Of these, 75 new investments were reported to have been made in Jamaica, making it the preferred location.

The General Accounting Office (GAO) conducted a study in June 1986 which refuted these claims. The GAO was able to contact and interview only 106 of the 285 businesses listed by the Department of Commerce, but the conclusions were significant. It was reported by 87 firms that they were exporting to the US and of these, 63 indicated that they were receiving duty-free or reduced-tariff concessions. However, only 23 of the firms were receiving duty-free treatment under the CBI.[40] On the basis of both these interviews and information on the 285 investments provided by the Department of Commerce, the GAO further claimed that 133 businesses were not related to the CBI provisions and that of the remaining 152 businesses, only 36, or 12.6 per cent of the total, exported, or were planning to export, under the CBI. The relationship of the other 108 businesses to the CBI could not be determined, owing to inadequate information, though available information suggested that at least 10 of them may have been entirely inactive.[41] The GAO report concluded that the erroneous reporting by the Department of Commerce on new business activity under the CBI was attributable to a flawed methodology. The Departments of State and Commerce had requested the information from US diplomatic posts in the region; these, in turn, relied on unverified data from in-country sources in the region; moreover, many of the "firms" listed had never opened, had closed, were double-counted, were exporting under provisions other than the CBI or were simply not exporting to the US.

An investment analysis contained in the first report (1984-85), of the USITC on the impact of the CBI relied on the figures furnished by the Department of Commerce survey and is therefore erroneous.[42]

The USITC second report on the impact of the CBI in 1986 made use of preliminary results of the investment survey currently being conducted by the Department of Commerce (DOC), and this allowed only for an appreciation of general investment trends.[43] According to the report, the DOC survey listed a total of 132 projects registered in 1986. The information thus far did not allow for a determination of the exact number of projects that were CBI-related. Broad product descriptions for 125 of these projects did, however, exist. Indications were that 68 of these could very likely be CBI-related. Most of these projects, the report indicated, were in the area of "winter fruits and vegetables, aquaculture products such as shrimp, and electrical and electronic assembly work."[44] So far, the report observed, 55 of the 132 projects identified seem to be ineligible for duty-free treatment.

The countries which enjoyed the greatest levels of investment in 1986 were the Dominican Republic and Costa Rica, with 20 and 17 respectively, followed by Jamaica and Belize, with 14 each, and St. Kitts with 10. Of the projects in these five leading countries, 34 were identified in categories that suggest duty-free treatment under the CBI.[45]

With regard to investment trends, the report noted that of seven product areas which have proved attractive over the past few years, investment in 1986 has remained mainly in five: apparel manufacturing, ethanol, agriculture, fish processing, and aquaculture. Two product areas experienced declines in investment in 1986: electrical and electronic components and cut flowers.

The manufacture of electrical and electronic components usually takes place in "twin-plant" operations. Inputs are imported from the US, assembled in free-trade zones, and re-exported to the US. These twin plants are usually "subsidiaries of US firms established to take advantage of lower labour costs for their labour-intensive operations."[46] The USITC report observed that firms which establish these operations are lured by the inexpensive labour rather than the tariff concessions under the CBI. Despite both these advantages, however, there was a negative net investment in some electronics categories for 1986. This was attributed to a slowdown of demand in the world market in general and particularly in the US, combined with increased competition from Far Eastern producers.

With regard to ethanol, the report noted that substantial investments have been made over the past several years. Three major plants, located in El Salvador, Costa Rica, and Jamaica, produced fuel-grade ethanol in 1985, and another five new plants were planned for 1986 in Costa Rica, Guatemala, Jamaica, and the Virgin Islands.[47] However, only three of these were being undertaken in that year, all in Jamaica. The reason for this retrenchment, the report observed, was the decline in the price of petroleum (from which substitutes for ethanol are produced) and recent US policy. From 1985 to 1986, US imports of this product from CBI countries increased by 37 per cent. Its future, however, remains uncertain following congressional legislation requiring that ethanol feedstocks be purchased locally by CBI countries.

Citrus is another product that faces uncertainty, owing to price fluctuations caused by periodic disruptions of US production. A major investment in Belize was initiated by Coca-Cola but has yet to become operational due to poor soil and lack of infrastructure.[48] In addition to these problems, the US citrus industry has launched opposition to tariff concessions for imports and also to US assistance to projects in CBI countries through the Overseas Private Investment Corporation (OPIC).[49]

Cut flowers were cited as a major investment area in the USITC report for 1984 and 1985. Nineteen major projects were reported for this period in Costa Rica, St. Kitts-Nevis, El Salvador, and Haiti, with many small projects also established. The USITC report for 1986 noted that "this trend changed drastically during 1986." The principal reason was that anti-dumping and countervailing duty cases were successfully brought against Costa Rica by US domestic producers. As a result, only three projects were initiated in 1986, two of which were located in Costa Rica, the other in Jamaica.

Pineapple production is seen as offering bright prospects. The USITC report did not specify the number of investments made recently but observed that land formerly used for sugar cane is increasingly being converted to pineapple production.

Finally, the report noted, without citing figures, that large numbers of investments have taken place in activities that do not fully qualify for CBI treatment (i.e., textiles and apparel, and tourism-related ventures).

5.3   US Bilateral Assistance

US bilateral aid to the Caribbean Basin more than quadrupled from a 1980 disbursement of $324 million to $1.5 billion in 1985. Economic aid alone also more than quadrupled, increasing from $238 million to $1.2 billion in this period. The acceleration point appears to be 1982 when, under the CBI bilateral assistance provision, an emergency supplemental appropriation of $350 million was allocated to the region.

The distinctive character of US assistance since 1982 has been an increased emphasis on Economic Support Funds (ESF) in relation to military aid. Whereas ESF constituted a mere 6 per cent of US assistance in 1980, it rose to 64 per cent by 1985.

In terms of sub-regional distribution, most of the $940 million increase in aid from 1980 to 1985 has gone to Central America (i.e., $770 million or 82 per cent of the increase). This trend has been more visible since 1982 when $620 million, or 96 per cent, of a total increase of $643 million went to Central America alone, with the insular Caribbean receiving a modest $23 million increase.

Differential allocations of aid are also striking within the sub-regions. Within Central America, the programs of El Salvador, Costa Rica, and Honduras were, in that order, accorded priority and in 1985 together accounted for $590 million or 83 per cent of a Central American country-allocation of $715 million. In the insular Caribbean, Jamaica and the Dominican Republic have attracted the lion's share of US aid.

Allocations to sub-regional programs follow the same trend. Insular Caribbean programs received only modest increases from 1980 to

1985, while those for Central America, modest up to 1984 ($71 million), rose sharply in 1985 (to $199 million). This reflected an increased support for the Central American Common Market (CACM) which in 1985 was allocated $95 million in ESF, $20 million to assist in financing new venture capital, and $45 million for the Central American Bank for Economic Integration.

5.4 Tax Incentives

This last component of the CBI extends to US citizens the principle of "North American Treatment," whereby they may claim deductions from taxable income for business convention expenses incurred in Caribbean Basin countries. This provision is intended to promote tourism in the region. So far, no data are available on the estimated economic impact of this tax provision and, indeed, any such data could only be highly impressionistic, given the obvious difficulty of measuring an impact that is so indirect, if not intangible. In any case recipient countries have been slow or reluctant to take the necessary measures — mainly the ratification of a Tax Information Exchange Treaty with the US — to satisfy condition for eligibility under the program.[50]

6   Official Evaluation of the Progress of the CBI

The tone of the official evaluation of the CBI has ranged from an early celebration of "positive" and "promising" indications of success, to a more qualified and cautious optimism in recent times. Officials admit their disappointment over the decline in total exports but point out that this resulted from the fall in commodity prices. Richard Holwill of the Department of State attributed the major part of this decline to "market-induced changes in the petroleum market."[51] Moreover, commodities such as petroleum fall outside of the scope of the CBI and, as Lawrence Theriot of the CBI Information Centre pointed out, "There's nothing the CBI could do to reverse trends worldwide in terms of commodity prices or even to influence it in any way."[52] With regard to declines in exports of sugar, officials have expressed disappointment at the cutbacks in quotas for Caribbean Basin exporters. Theriot captured the contradiction in US policy when he noted: "We're trying to help in so many ways and hurt them in sugar policy."[53]

Administration officials argue that the CBI can be properly assessed only by disaggregating Caribbean Basin exports into traditional and non-traditional goods. Richard Holwill explains:

> We believe the fairest way to evaluate the results of the CBI is to look at non-traditional trade to see if the program is meeting its goal of expanding and diversifying the region's productive and export base. Here, the picture is more promising . . . that is the success of the CBI: encouraging investments and exports in a diverse mix of

products and thereby helping Caribbean Basin economies move from an unhealthy dependence on a few traditional products vulnerable to external shocks.[54]

Accordingly, officials point enthusiastically to the increase in exports of certain non-traditional products.[55] In particular, they cite garment assembly, light manufacturing, and agro-business as the most promising activities.

Table 5-7
Exports from CB, 1983: Value of Products
Excluded from CBI ($000s)

Product	Value	Share of exports to US	Duty-free share of total	807 share of total
Petroleum products	5 005 617	55.6	1.8	—
Textiles	401 937	4.5	2.3	89.9
Certain leather products	20 443	0.2	0.9	57.9
Certain footwear products	14 591	0.2	0.1	11.0
Canned tuna	8	—	22.5	—
Total	5 442 596	60.4	1.8	6.9

Note: *Petroleum products* consist of schedule 4 of the Tariff Schedules of the US (TSUS). *Textiles* consist of schedule 3 of the TSUS. *Certain leather products* are certain leather, plastic and rubber gloves: TSUS items 705.35 and 705.85-86; luggage, handbags, flatgoods: TSUS items 706.05-16, 706.21-32, 706.34, 706.36, 706.38, 706.41, 706.43 706.55, and 706.62; certain leather wearing apparel: item 791.76; *Footwear products* are items 700.05-27, 700.29-53, 700.56-89, and 700.91-95. *Canned tuna* products are items 112.30, 112.34, and 112.90.

Source: Extracted from data presented by the International Trade Commission (Operation of Trade Agreements, 1983), 1984, p. 33.

The US government has generally argued that it has provided the best incentives it could to Caribbean Basin countries and that the rest is up to investors and governments in the region. Officials also point to recent enhancement measures — the "Super 807" for textiles, and availability of "section 926 funds" from Puerto Rico to Caribbean Basin investors — as proof of US commitment to the success of the CBI.[56]

In the view of these officials, however, Caribbean Basin governments are not uniformly fulfilling their obligations under the provisions of the CBI. A number of governments have responded by introducing measures to remove administrative bottlenecks to investment and to create a "hospitable environment" for foreign companies. These have included instituting special incentives such as "one-stop business development centers" to handle the needs of potential investors, and "long overdue macro-economic changes," particularly currency devaluations, to enhance the competitiveness of their exports.[57] Equally important, Caribbean Basin governments have generally come to accept the US administration's view of development. Theriot observes:

> the nature of the debate over economic development in the Caribbean has changed significantly. There is no longer a question in the CBI beneficiary countries of whether or not to encourage private sector-led development and foreign investment. Now the debate is over how to most effectively provide a business environment attractive to investors.[58]

Nevertheless, several governments, it is said, "have not sufficiently followed the Hippocratic Oath — do no harm," and have instead impeded private sector expansion by "adding risks of arbitrary government actions."[59] Alexander Good pointed to three impediments to CBI business expansion. The "single most important" is national customs services, which "impose unacceptable risks on doing business by their capricious application of complex and confusing regulations that are more appropriate to antiquated colonial trading systems."[60] He advised that "customs services must be made to realize that not all importers are smugglers and that exporters must efficiently import raw materials, equipment and spare parts."[61] The second impediment imposed on businesses is "the chore of negotiating a bureaucratic maze to obtain approval for proposed business ventures," and this must be eliminated by Caribbean Basin governments through "effective one-stop shops for approving business ventures."[62] The third impediment is fiscal policy. Richard Holwill argued that "the policy which is proving its worth in the real world is characterized by market-based exchange rates, interest rates reflecting the real costs of capital, a loosening of price controls [and] greater discipline over government spending."[63]

With regard to the private sector in the region, the appraisal is similarly mixed. Theriot noted, on the one hand, a major change in the philosophy of development:

> The private sector in the Caribbean generally has accepted that the wave of the future is export-oriented business. There is a generation of young business leaders, often educated in the United States, who have strong entrepreneurial spirit, and who are very eager to find US partners for export oriented business ventures in non-traditional industries. This new direction is fundamental to the long-term success of economic development in the region.[64]

Alexander Good argued that these business leaders could, however, change their traditional approach to business more profoundly. Many

Table 5-8
US Tariff Treatment of Leading CB Exports
to the US, 1982-83 ($000s)

Product	New Tariff concession under CBI	Mainly 806, 807 treatment[c]	1982	1983
Petroleum	No		3748	4053
Coffee	No		501	521
Naphthas	No		342	481
Sugars	Partial[a]		281	437
Motor fuel	No		476	401
Bananas	No		350	382
Shellfish	No		217	214
US goods returned	No		147	190
Integrated circuits	Yes	Yes	99	159
Aluminum hydroxide	No		77	147
Beef and veal	Yes		150	133
Gold or silver	No		64	125
Bauxite	No		228	114
Electrical switches	Yes	Yes	40	79
Lace or body garments	Partial[b]	Yes	57	69
Nitrogenous fertilizers	No		44	67
Cocoa beans	No		57	55
Analgesics	Yes	Yes	35	51
Asphaltum	No		23	51
Other wearing apparel	Partial[b]	Yes	24	39
Baseball equipment	Yes	Yes	42	39
Kerosene	No		3	36
Cigars	No		30	35
Capacitors	Yes	Yes	31	34
Body-supporting garments	Partial[b]	Yes	33	32
Beet or cane molasses	Yes		25	31
Tobacco	Yes		10	30
Ferronickel	No		0	30
Leather	No		13	27
Subtotal			7147	8062
Total			8008	9006

a Sugar products were exempted from "fees" collected at the border but remained under quota restrictions.

b Textiles from countries granted quotas are subject to tariffs.

c 806 and 807 products enjoyed some concessions prior to the CBI, as "intra-firm" sales.

Source: Newfarmer, 1985. Compiled from US Department of Commerce data as given in International Trade Commission (ITC) (1984).

of them continue to "hoard personal capital rather than invest it in new production facilities," are impatient with the fact that "it takes 3 to 5 years for domestic firms to become successful exporters," and have therefore "rationalized defeat before even trying."[65]

Finally, there is also a mixed assessment of the response of US investors to the Caribbean Basin Initiative. Alexander Good observed that an "impressive array of US firms, both large and small, are already in business in the CBI region" but expressed disappointment with "the pace of US business entry." He elaborated:

> Like their Basin counterparts, US business managers have also been somewhat paralysed by tradition, by a bias to sourcing products from the Far East. Most have not fully analysed the powerful combination of preferences: CBI, LOMÉ and CARIBCAN, which make building new sources in the Caribbean Basin highly attractive.[66]

The obstacles yet to be surmounted notwithstanding, officials are pleased with the performance of the CBI. Good captured the official optimism in the following way:

> In terms of the old adage, CBI business expansion is definitely a cup half full, not half empty. If all participants, governments and private sector leaders press ahead to fulfill their responsibilities, as each at the outset assumed they would, we will see the CBI cup overflowing soon.[67]

7   Critical Evaluation of the CBI

The following evaluation of the CBI will deal with three issues: the significance of the CBI provisions themselves, especially against the grandiose claims made for them; the CBI in relation to factors beyond its scope which are crucial to its success; and the plausibility and promise of the CBI as a strategy of development, in view of the Puerto Rican experience.

7.1   The Impact of the Free Trade Area (FTA)

The FTA has been repeatedly cited as the fulcrum of the CBI, and much scholarly attention has focussed on its projected impact on Caribbean Basin economies. In his testimony before the Senate, Dr. William Cline, a noted economist with considerable repute in the area of Central American development, presented the most optimistic appraisal. Extrapolating from the past impact of the Central American Common Market (CACM), he argued that the access to the US market afforded by the CBI could realize a comparable investment growth of 20 per cent (or raise investment from 22.4 to 26.9 per cent of GNP), which could stimulate growth by approximately $2 billion annually in the early years, and by larger amounts later. In addition, Cline forecast increased exports of about $1 billion by 1985, and $4 billion by 1990, which would in turn facilitate even faster growth.[68] This projection, he claimed, was a conservative one, given the greater size of the US market compared with the CACM. The expected expansion of trade did not materialize, however. On the contrary, exports fell below the 1983 level for every year of the FTA so far.

What went wrong? We wish to suggest that nothing did; the results of the CBI so far were predictable, and there will be no surprises in the future. The first reason is that the CBI offers little *additional* duty-free coverage compared with arrangements that had hitherto existed, and this, contrary to the assurances of officials of the administration, must be regarded as a significant defect of the CBI. Of the approximately $9 billion in exports in 1983, $5.5 billion, or 60 per cent, were accounted for by items excluded from the CBI. This means that only 40 per cent of 1983 exports would have been eligible for duty-free treatment in 1984 and subsequent years of the CBI's FTA lifetime. Further, most of these exports are already classified under items 806.30 and 807.00 of the TSUS, as well as the General System of Preferences (GSP). In effect, 2.7 billion or 75 per cent of an already small amount of duty-free products (40%), would have benefited from duty-free treatment anyway. Additional duty-free treatment provided by the CBI therefore amounts to only 25 per cent of all duty-free exports, or 10 per cent of all exports.[69]

Of course, the limited nature of additional concessions should not, alone, imply failure for the CBI, since the range of the exports affected, and the significance of the duties from which they are freed, may be compensating factors. However, even in these areas the CBI falls short. Of the 15 leading CBI exports to the US, accounting for over 70 per cent of all exports from the region in 1981-83, only four product categories were granted some new exemption from duties under the CBI; only one of these, beef, enjoyed such treatment for the first time.

With regard to tariffs, the average rate imposed on the region's products had always been small — 1.4 per cent, 1.7 per cent, and 1.8 per cent of total value in 1981, 1982, and 1983, respectively. For dutiable products alone, the rate had been 1.9 per cent, 2.4 per cent, and 2.6 per cent in those years.[70] Given the above considerations, other analyses have countered Cline's optimistic projections. Albert Fishlow foresaw trade increases of only one-half per cent over 1980s exports, and Richard Newfarmer, analyzing the export performance of the most valuable 15 products granted FTA concessions, predicted a similarly modest export increase of 0.2 per cent to 0.9 per cent in the first and future years of the CBI. Rousslang and Lindsey cite comparable figures and note that the benefits will be concentrated in the Dominican Republic, Costa Rica, Haiti, and Honduras, given their present ability to expand production in the products affected by the FTA (see Table 5-9).

Table 5-9
Estimated Effects of the CBI Tariff-eliminations
Beneficiaries ($000s)

Country	Gain in export earnings	
	Low	High
Guatemala	3 000	4 900
Belize	1 000	3 200
El Salvador	2 100	4 200
Honduras	2 500	6 800
Nicaragua	1 000	2 200
Costa Rica	2 900	8 500
Panama	3 400	5 000
Bahamas	1 900	6 000
Jamaica	1 200	3 800
Turks & Caicos Isles	—	—
Cayman Islands	—	—
Haiti	2 800	7 800
Dominican Republic	10 700	16 700
British Virgin Isles	100	300
St. Kitts-Nevis-Anguilla	—	—
Leeward & Windward Isles	100	300
Barbados	1 600	5 000
Trinidad & Tobago	500	1 500
Netherland Antilles	900	2 200
Guyana	700	1 800
Suriname	200	400
Total	36 600	80 800

Note: A dash (−) denotes less than $50 000.
Source: Rousslang and Lindsey, 1984. Cited in Newfarmer, 1985, p. 84

The second reason why the CBI's results have been, and may continue to be, modest is that the type of products excluded from the FTA are those which the Caribbean Basin countries are either historically equipped to produce, or have a comparative advantage producing and which, therefore, have reasonable export prospects. Petroleum products, though the largest exports, are not important in this respect, since they are produced only by Guatemala and Trinidad-Tobago (the other countries which export these products—the Bahamas and the Netherland Antilles—merely conduct refining operations).

The policy towards sugar and textiles is not, however, without significance. In 1983 and 1984 sugar ranked third, behind petroleum and coffee, as a regional export. It was subjected to a 185 per cent increase in effective tariffs over the pre-1981 level.[71] In addition, a quota system was re-introduced on May 5, 1981.[72] The Caribbean Basin was granted a 10 per cent increase in sugar quotas in 1984, but suffered a 16 per cent cut in 1985. A further cut of 46 per cent was implemented in 1987. Whereas in 1981, prior to the re-introduction of quotas, the Caribbean Basin exported 1480 thousand tons of sugar to the US (32 per cent of US worldwide imports of 4566 thousand tons), by 1987 this was reduced to a mere 351 thousand tons (though representing 35 per cent of reduced US worldwide imports of 1001 thousand tons). In terms of value, the region's sugar exporters experienced a revenue decrease from $501 million in 1981 to $153 million in 1987.[73] While the CBI provides for a remittance of import fees to producers, and the quota system guarantees a higher price than that which obtains on the world market (less than 5 cents per pound in 1984), protectionist measures will, in the long term, work to the disadvantage of Caribbean Basin producers. The estimated loss of revenue by the region between 1984 and 1985 alone was approximately $90 million (see Table 5-10).

Table 5-10
Value of Sugar Quota and Effects
of 1985 Cuts ($ millions)

Country	Value of sugar quota[a]	Change FY1984 to FY1985
Belize	9	-2
Costa Rica	17	-3
El Salvador	24	-5
Guatemala	39	-8
Honduras	16	-3
Panama	24	-5
Central America	129	-26
Dominican Republic	143	-63
Eastern Caribbean	15	-30
Grenada	0	-2
Guyana	10	NA
Haiti	4	6
Jamaica	9	25
Insular Caribbean	191	-64
Total Caribbean Basin	310	-90

[a] Value of sugar quota is equal to the total quota volume in pounds times the US price differential above the world market price.

Source: Newfarmer, 1985. Calculated from information provided by Bureau of Latin American Affairs, AID.

Protectionist measures have also affected textiles and apparel products subject to quotas under the global Multifibre Agreement (MFA), as these were excluded from the FTA. Tariffs averaged about 25 per cent, and the International Trade Commission estimated that these products alone accounted for 63 per cent of total duties collected from Caribbean Basin exports in 1983. Freedom from the high tariffs imposed on these products, together with the comparative advantage which the region's producers enjoy in labour-intensive operations, would have realized an estimated 295 per cent increase in the trade-related benefits of the CBI.[74] The introduction of the "Super 807" program for textiles in February 1986, which allows for guaranteed access to the US market of all eligible textile products from CBI beneficiaries, will definitely lead to increased exports from the region. But the stringent conditions—that these products be assembled from 100 per cent US cut and formed fabric, and that the same firm must act as importer and exporter—mainly ensures increased benefits for US producers and, at best, only some employment creation in the region.

7.2 US Bilateral Assistance

Much is made by US administration officials of the quantitative and qualitative changes in US bilateral assistance to the region. Not only has aid increased fourfold in absolute terms, but its economic component has dramatically eclipsed the traditional emphasis on military aid. While this, at first glance, seems to indicate a genuine commitment to revitalizing the Caribbean Basin economies, further inquiry uncovers little *economic* logic behind the change, at least from the perspective of the economic well-being of Caribbean Basin recipients.

First, almost all the increases since 1980 have been channelled to Central America. Within Central America itself, El Salvador, Honduras, and Costa Rica have been the main beneficiaries. This reflected more of a preoccupation with neighbouring Nicaragua than an interest in Central American development. In the insular Caribbean, Jamaica and the Dominican Republic have enjoyed the largest appropriations, and this, as Newfarmer correctly suggests, seems to conform to the US administration's view that these countries represent "models of democratic development."[75]

Second, the overwhelming portion of economic assistance has taken the form of Economic Support Funds (ESF), at the expense of development assistance programs to long-term projects.[76] ESF rose from 6.3 per cent of US assistance in 1980 to 64.8 per cent in 1985. "The consequence of such an emphasis," observes Albert Fishlow, "is to diminish attention to the poorest countries and to the fate of the lower income population in the richer."[77]

Third, the programming of ESF largely toward the improvement of balance of payments problems, and specifically toward the financing of imports by the private sector, does not reflect an overall appreciation of the factors involved over the long term. Fishlow notes:

> What one does *not* see is a longer term strategy that systemically takes into account present levels of indebtedness and hence future obligations, variability in the terms of trade, and import requirements imposed by higher rates of economic growth. The support funds are not a matter of one or two years alone. Seeking to deal with them as though they were, reduces their usefulness and provides an inaccurate picture of continuing financial requirements within the region. This is especially the case since limited trade benefits are likely to materialize even in the medium term.[78]

Lastly, the "dramatic" increases in assistance seem less dramatic when viewed in terms of the financial needs of the Caribbean Basin. For Central America alone, the Kissinger Commission estimated that $24 billion of capital inflows would be needed, as one element in an eight-point stabilization program, in order to restore the region's economies to their 1980 per capita levels.[79] Of this total, it was estimated that private banks and private investments would account for $6 billion, and official sources for the remaining $18 billion. The US alone would be expected to contribute $10 to $12 billion, while the remaining $6 to $8 billion would have to be met by other bilateral creditors and development banks. US assistance to Central America in 1984 ($1,001m) and 1985 ($914m) actually fell short of these goals by at least $600 million in each year. Moreover, Kissinger's was only a conservative estimate.[80]

Equally significant is that while the US administration has appealed to other agencies to supplement its contributions to the region, US policy has, in fact, been a major obstacle to this. A recent policy of tying the disbursement of Economic Support Funds (ESF) to the condition of participation in IMF stabilization programs has been backfiring. In 1983, the IMF program in Honduras was aborted and the same occurred in the Dominican Republic in 1984. The US reluctantly proceeded with disbursements of ESF, out of purely political considerations, according to Newfarmer.[81] Recently, there has also been evident hesitation to support IMF and World Bank policy changes. It was only with reluctance that the US withdrew its opposition to increased IMF quotas proposed by European members in mid-1982, and by 1983 it was advocating more stringent conditions of access to the IMF. Lastly, the US has adamantly insisted upon a limit to the scheduled increase of funds for the International Development Association (IDA), the agency of the World Bank which offers low-interest loans with lengthy maturities to low-income developing countries. All these policies have affected the Caribbean Basin, and surely contradict the professed aims of the CBI.[82]

7.3 Tourism Incentive

This last provision of the CBI requires little attention, due to the expectation that its impact will be very limited and elusive of examination. It is sufficient to note that the impact of deduction allowances for business conventions is likely to be restricted to the tourist industry rather than stimulate investment in industrial operations.

8 The Role of Factors Beyond the CBI

Apart from the scope of the provisions of the CBI, there is a wide range of factors crucial to its objectives which lie beyond its real and legislative control. These operate both within the US and in the world economy in general.

8.1 Factors within the United States

No amount of euphemistic recharacterization of the present trends of the US economy can conceal the reality of a crisis. Diminishing relative productivity has resulted in a loss in, and in many cases a reversal of, the competitive advantage which US producers have historically enjoyed in the world economy. There are, therefore, domestic pressures for protectionist measures, and so far, Congress has been obliging. The administration has attempted to resist these efforts, but it is likely that it will succumb more and more to protectionist pressures in order to avert loss of political support and injury to its relationship with Congress. This will continue to pose credibility problems for the CBI.

Though the FTA has an indefinite duration, the duty-free status of eligible exports from the Basin is subject to re-evaluation by the US Departments of Commerce and Agriculture and may be withdrawn if found injurious to US producers. The power of Congress and the president to ratify arbitrarily such revisions will lead to more circumspection by present and potential investors in the Caribbean Basin and has already aroused concern within certain regional governments whose co-operation has been viewed by the administration as crucial to the success of the CBI. In fact, the fear of protectionist measures has been justified in recent times, not only with respect to US sugar policy, but also to the new rules of origin policy toward ethanol and the successful anti-dumping and countervailing duty charges brought against Costa Rican exporters of cut flowers.

Another factor crucial to even a modest success for the CBI is the general state of the US economy and the consequent level of demand for Caribbean Basin products. In fact, it has been suggested that US demand is more significant than the provisions of the CBI for export growth in the region. Richard Newfarmer has estimated that a 1 per cent increase in the US growth rate may translate into as much as $2.9 billion in additional export earnings for the region in the short term. If this is multiplied through secondary effects in income and expenditure creation, over the long term, an increase in output of about $6 billion may be realized.[83]

8.2   Factors in the World Economy

Factors operating in the world economy are also crucial to the region. This is illustrated in the 1984 export performance of many Caribbean Basin countries. A fact not mentioned by US officials or in scholarly analyses is that while certain countries in the region dramatically increased their exports to the US in 1984, their total exports either declined (e.g., Trinidad and Tobago, Guatemala, El Salvador), remained unchanged (e.g., Jamaica), or grew considerably less than exports to the US (e.g., Dominican Republic, Costa Rica).[84] This suggests that increased exports to the US may have represented largely a *redirection of trade*, rather than a new stimulus to trade attributable to the CBI. The overall factors operating in the world economy may therefore have conditioned whatever impact the CBI may have had on the region's performance.

The concern by developed countries for export markets has led to increased protectionist sentiment throughout the industrialized world. In addition, domestic subsidies enable these countries to export on the world market at considerably reduced prices. Where Caribbean Basin countries compete with developed countries for the same space in the world market, they are therefore at a disadvantage. An economic recovery in the developed world is viewed as crucial to the dismantling of these policies, as well as to an increased demand for the region's exports. The InterAmerican Development Bank estimates that a one per cent increase in the real GDP of foreign markets will yield a short-term multiplier of 0.5 for the major commodity exports of the Caribbean Basin, and a multiplier of 1.5 in the long term if such growth is sustained (see Table 5-11).

If other factors are held constant, the rate of growth of the region's foreign markets is therefore of considerable importance. It was predicted that the real GDP growth rate of these foreign countries would decline by between 1.8 and 2.0 per cent in 1986 (well below the 1970s trend of 3.4 per cent). Some recovery was indicated for the following four years, but not enough to realize more than 2.7-3.1 per cent growth per annum for the second half of the decade (also well below the 3.3% growth rate during 1984-85).[85] The amount of imports was therefore expected to be sustained in the second half of the decade. But the expansion of Latin American exports in general was expected

Table 5-11
Response of Total Earnings to 1 Per Cent
Increase in GDP, Foreign Markets

Country	Implicit impact multiplier [a]	Implicit long-term multiplier [b]
Bahamas	0.5	2.5
Barbados	0.4	0.7
Costa Rica	0.4	1.2
Dominican Republic	0.7	1.9
El Salvador	0.4	1.7
Guatemala	1.0	0.7
Guyana	0.7	2.0
Haiti	0.6	2.4
Honduras	1.0	1.6
Jamaica	0.3	0.3
Panama	0.4	1.6
Suriname	0.9	1.8
Trinidad & Tobago	0.8	4.0
Total	0.5	1.5

[a] Measures the immediate, or same period, effect.
[b] Measures the total accumulated effect.
Source: Extracted from data presented in *External Debt and Economic Development in Latin America*, Inter-American Development Bank, 1984, p. 135.

to be smaller than foreign import demand due to the deterioration of the region's competitive position.[86] For Caribbean Basin countries in particular, this would have been even smaller, since their major exports are primary commodities, which face more sluggish demand than manufactured goods. In addition, a weakening of prices was anticipated over the 1986-90 period, except for the Dominican Republic which was expected to enjoy an increase.

Meanwhile, the unprecedented debt problem brings into sharper relief the inadequacy of expected export growth and export prices. Even if the latter factors improved, and a positive balance of trade position were achieved, the balance of payments would still be rendered negative by the burdens of debt servicing. The deterioration in the debt structure is regarded as more ominous than the magnitude of the debts. The operative factor in the world economy here is that the increasing unavailability of official, long-term credit has forced Caribbean Basin countries to resort to private sources with more stringent conditions for repayment schedules and interest payments.[87]

Table 5-12
Relative Export Prices of
Major Non-fuel Exports

Country	1983 price	Projected 1985-90
Barbados	100	100
Costa Rica	100	94
Dominican Republic	100	105
El Salvador	100	94
Guatemala	100	97
Guyana	100	100
Haiti	100	94
Honduras	100	97
Jamaica	100	99
Panama	100	97

Source: Extracted from data presented in *External Debt and Economic Development in Latin America*, InterAmerican Development Bank, 1984, p. 111.

In sum, factors operating in the world economy exert considerable influence on the economies of the Caribbean Basin which may negate even more generous CBI concessions or more vigorous trade with the US.

9   The CBI and US Economic Interests

The presentation of the CBI by the administration and the debates over the CBI in Congress reflected a significant preoccupation with US "national interests," of which economic interests have been seen as an important component. While the dominant theme throughout the debates over the CBI has been the relationship of the CBI to Caribbean Basin instability and, thus, to US security interests in the region, the economic aspect became steadily more prominent as the July 1983 vote on the CBI approached. This was occasioned by strenuous objections to the CBI by some members of Congress, who argued that it would cause injury to US domestic industries and thereby contribute to the unemployment of US workers. The response by other members of Congress, as well as by the administration, was to argue the opposite: that the CBI would bring benefits to US industries and the US economy as a whole. A brief summary of this debate will illustrate why the latter view is the more plausible.

At least three arguments were advanced in Congress in support of the view that the CBI would prove detrimental to US industries. First, it was thought that the CBI would lure US industries to the Caribbean Basin, thus exporting capital and jobs at a time of high unemployment in the US.[88] The second concern was that increased imports from the Caribbean Basin would further weaken domestic producers whose positions in the domestic market were already being undermined by foreign competition.[89] The third major concern, that the CBI would work to the disadvantage of US industries, came from those who thought that foreign, non-Caribbean Basin competitors would use the region as a duty-free conduit to the US market.[90]

Supporters of the CBI emphasized that Caribbean Basin exports were very small relative to total US imports and that the CBI, moreover, represented only a small addition to these exports. Representative Rostenkowski, a strong supporter of the CBI, presented this analysis:

> In order to demonstrate why we feel these concerns are unfounded let me describe the real economic impact of this bill in terms of total US trade. Caribbean imports accounted for only 3.3 percent of total US imports last year — $8.1 billion out of $244 billion. About 90 percent of these imports would not even be affected by this legislation, either because they are already duty free or because the bill exempts them from such treatment. This leaves less than $1 billion affected by the bill — about three-tenths of 1 percent of total US imports and only three-one-hundredths of 1 percent of our total GNP. This minuscule amount of trade cannot possibly cause harm.[91]

The administration led the defence of the CBI as a program that would prove economically beneficial to the US. On this basis it was supported by members of Congress as well as representatives of the US business community. The gist of the argument was that in both the near and distant future, the Caribbean Basin countries would become increasingly lucrative markets for US goods and attractive locations for investment in semi-processing operations that could enhance the global competitiveness of US industries. With regard to the first claim, Secretary of State Schultz assured the Senate Committee on Finance that:

> the long-term benefits of this initiative are far greater than the short-term costs. The region already buys nearly $7 billion of goods from the United States. A stable, democratic and prosperous Caribbean Basin means a much larger and growing market for our exports and consequently significantly greater job opportunities for our workers.[92]

In fact, Schultz pointed out that the CBI would be immediately beneficial to US businesses with the disbursement of the $350 million in Economic Support Funds, which will enable the beneficiaries to purchase raw materials and equipment from the US.[93] The House Committee on Foreign Affairs noted that establishing lines of credit between US businesses and the Caribbean Basin could create a wider relationship whereby "US firms will benefit from the numerous contracts that will be offered by the governments of the region to carry out development projects."[94]

It was repeatedly argued that US trade with the Caribbean Basin was already lucrative. Secretary Schultz noted that "It's worth remembering that if you exclude petroleum trade, we have a $2 billion trade surplus with the Caribbean Basin and are already the major trade partner of most countries there."[95]

The major argument made for the positive trade impact of the CBI on the US was that the region has historically been import-dependent on the US and that "the trade pattern of that part of the world has been to spend almost all of their import foreign-exchange on our goods."[96] Moreover, it was envisaged that as the CBI strengthened the economies of the region, the already high demand for US goods would also increase. Ambassador Brock, credited with formulating the administration's version of the CBI, noted:

> The first signs of revitalized economic activity in the region will be new orders for machinery and other producer goods, which must be imported into the region to put new and expanding enterprises into an internationally competitive position. Now . . . those goods are going to be by and large American produced goods. Annual US shipments of capital goods to the Caribbean region have run as high as $2.5 billion in recent years. On a per capita basis, the Caribbean Basin nations import more machinery and capital goods from the United States than does any other developing country region.[97]

Finally, the CBI was deemed beneficial to US economic interests on the grounds that the cheaper, unskilled labour of Caribbean Basin workers could supplement the skilled labour of US workers to produce goods that would be more competitive, without incurring the loss of US jobs. Sam Segnar of the Internorth corporation and trustee of the US private sector-based Caribbean/Central American Action argued that:

> To the extent that we can do subassembly work with low-cost labour, and ship the subassemblies back to this country to be assembled by more skilled labour, that makes us more competitive if we can get the job done for less. I do not think it's using the type of jobs that we are trying to protect in this country.[98]

Cameron Clark of the Committee for 806.30 and 807, a lobby group for the promotion of production-sharing, elaborated on these benefits on the basis of experience:

> [W]e find that production sharing arrangements reduce costs, increase sales and market share which in turn increase domestic production and employment, or at least, these arrangements minimize losses in sales and market share, and minimize domestic production declines and job losses.[99]

The sheer volume of the defence of the CBI as an economic asset to the US coincided with, and was perhaps designed to counter, the objections to the CBI summarized above. This is not to suggest, however, that the defence of the CBI in such terms was without foundation. On the contrary, given the nature of the crisis which confronted the US economy, US investors had already begun to regard the Caribbean Basin, and indeed, low-wage areas of the developing world in general, as attractive locations for investment. The CBI deepened this interest and provided, in important provisions of the Act, a number of significant guarantees for US investors.

In the 1970s US businesses and the US economy as a whole began to show signs of a decline in important economic indicators. The profit rate of non-financial corporations fell from 12.7 per cent in the late 1960s to 10 per cent by 1975.[100] Productivity growth declined from an average yearly increase of 3.2 per cent between 1948 and 1965 to 1.1 per cent between 1973 and 1978.[101] Between 1970 and 1980 basic US industries such as steel, textiles, automobiles, petrochemicals, rubber, and consumer electronics lost their previous competitiveness in international markets, and the share of US manufactured goods in total world sales declined by 23 per cent; over the same years, that of every other industrialized country, with the exception of Great Britain, maintained or expanded its share.[102] At the same time, US imports from developing countries increased from $3.6 billion to $30 billion.[103] It is therefore not surprising that even before the launching of the CBI, some US investors had come to regard the low-wage areas of the developing world as pivotal to regaining their competitiveness and market share. In this context, the role of the Overseas Private Investment Corporation (OPIC), a federal agency, deserves brief mention.

OPIC was created by the US Congress in 1969 and began operations in 1971, with a mandate to "mobilize and facilitate the participation of United States private capital and skills in the economic and social development of less developed, friendly countries and areas."[104] As a key federal agency OPIC has, however, provided significant assistance to US investors abroad, citing among other things, "the need to expand US export markets in developing countries . . . in light of a growing US merchandise trade deficit" as justification.[105] OPIC currently assists and promotes US businesses in 100 developing countries worldwide. In 1986 alone, 124 projects were supported, representing a total investment of $722 million and involving export of US machinery and supplies valued at $531 million. An additional $556 million were expected to be exported in the five subsequent years in connection with these investments.[106] With regard to the Caribbean Basin, OPIC insured or financed 63 projects (compared with only three for Latin

America) in 1981 and 1982 (i.e., before the advent of the CBI).[107] By 1984, with the introduction of the CBI, the number of projects had increased to 140. In 1986, of the 124 projects assisted by OPIC world-wide, 35 (or 28.2%) involved the Caribbean Basin, reflecting "OPIC's continuing commitment to the Caribbean Basin Initiative."[108] Nearly half of the 29 investment projects financed by OPIC in 1986 were in the Caribbean Basin, representing a commitment of $327 million.[109]

Also preceding the CBI were provisions 806.30 and 807 of the Tariff Schedules of the United States (TSUS), which enabled US investors to take advantage of the low-cost labour power in developing countries to enhance their competitiveness while ensuring demand for US exports in the form of input materials. These provisions allowed for duty-free treatment of US inputs, with duties allocated only on the value-added abroad. The success of this program is indicated by the fact that in 1980, 50 per cent of the value of imports from developing countries under these provisions of the TSUS were duty free or, in other words, entailed the use of US materials.[110] This compared to only 7 per cent of US materials used in goods imported from developed countries to the US under these provisions. For imports from the Caribbean Basin, the contrast is even greater—63 per cent of the value of imports under these provisions consisted of US materials. In 1983, 6 per cent of total US imports from the region were already duty free under this program, and this rose to 10 per cent by 1986.[111]

By the time the trade component (FTA) of the CBI became operational in January 1984, therefore, US investors had already enjoyed a certain measure of support from their government in investing in the region. US direct investments doubled in Central America, from $501 million in 1967 to over $1 billion in 1980.[112] In the insular Caribbean's larger economies, a similar influx of US capital was evident. Between 1971 and 1981, US investment increased from $450 million to $2987 million in the Bahamas, from $155 million to $373 million in the Dominican Republic, from $262 to $932 million in Trinidad and Tobago, and from $12 to $31 million in Barbados. The only significant declines took place in Jamaica and Guyana, where a policy of nationalization of foreign capital was being pursued.[113]

This investment was mainly in twin-plant, assembly-type, labour-intensive operations in certain countries of the region. The emphasis had been on manufactures in which US producers were being surpassed by producers in other areas of the world. In 1982, for example, electronic goods had already featured in half of the 10 most important manufactured products from the Caribbean Basin. Exports of electrical capacitors comprised over 56 per cent of total US imports of this item.[114] At that time, these and similar products registered some of the higher duties; their release from these under the CBI would certainly intensify production for the US market under the additionally favourable concessions granted by governments of the region. What seems significant, however, is that this export growth took place despite the fact that these goods benefited the *least* from duty-free treatment. This suggests that the push factor of declining relative productivity in the US is more crucial than the pull factor of the CBI in accounting for US investment in the region. The dramatic increases in exports of wearing apparel and leather goods further testifies to this.

How does the CBI fit into this picture? In the 1970s the nationalization of foreign investments in Guyana and Jamaica created political uncertainties for US investors. These increased with the rising instability in Central America and with the establishment in Grenada and Nicaragua of certain measures of state intervention in the economy. Representative Schulz expressed this concern when he observed:

> One of the major deterrents to investment in the area is fear of the political risks. Many businessmen have told me that were it not for fear of losing their investment through war, rebellion, expropriation, or the inconvertibility of profits or earnings into US dollars, they would consider investing in the basin.[115]

The CBI contains several important guarantees to US investors as well as guaranteed access to the US market. These have been formalized in Bilateral Investment Treaties (BITS) between the US and beneficiary countries and were mandated under Section 212 (b) of the Act. Briefly, the relevant provisions are:

> (1) Beneficiary countries are required to provide "prompt adequate and effective compensation," or to submit to international arbitration, if they nationalize or expropriate property owned by US citizens; if they repudiate existing contracts, agreements, patents or trademarks with US citizens or corporations; or if they enforce taxes or other exactions, restrictive maintenance and operational conditions on property so owned as to have the effect of seizing control of such property.
>
> (2) Beneficiary countries are required to recognize arbitral awards made in favour of US citizens and corporations.
>
> (3) Beneficiaries cannot give preferential treatment to products from a developed country other than the United States, which may adversely affect US commerce. *This is the only provision that the US President cannot waive, even in the interests of national security.* The House Committee on Ways and Means, which recommended this provision, explained that "while the United States would welcome other developed countries granting preferential treatment to Caribbean Basin countries, it would not want to see them seek 'reverse' preferences in the Caribbean markets in exchange."[116]

(4) a government-owned entity in a beneficiary country cannot broadcast copyrighted material without the consent of US copyright owners. The House Ways and Means Committee noted that "the increasingly frequent practice of foreign governments intercepting satellite transmissions or otherwise copyrighted materials . . . jeopardizes substantial foreign revenues received by copyright owners."[117]

Apart from guarantees to US investors and exporters, the CBI also provides for a Tax Information Exchange Agreement (TIEA) between the US and a beneficiary country wishing to be designated as a location for tax-deductible conventions. The treaty requires that beneficiaries extend a similar concession for conventions held by their nationals in the US. But more importantly, the treaty requires that beneficiaries be willing to disclose information which may be "subject to non-disclosure provisions of the local law," such as those relating to bank secrecy and bearer shares. This provision can be waived by the US president only in circumstances related to "the national security interests" of the US. As Representative Stark has suggested, this provision was intended to counteract "the abuses of tax haven countries" which are " delighted to harbour legal and illegal investments, with no questions – and no taxes – asked."[118]

While the CBI contains guarantees to promote US capital, beneficiary countries are also supplementing this effort in a bid to attract foreign investments. Free Trade Zones have been established in the Dominican Republic, Costa Rica, and Honduras and others will soon be introduced in Jamaica.[119] *Business America* reports that "The development and expansion of Free Trade Zones has accelerated the growth of assembling operations in the region, particularly in the areas of electronics and apparel."[120] It is not difficult to imagine why this would be so, if one considers the conditions offered by regional governments to investors in Free Trade Zones. Jamaica was typical:

- 100 per cent tax holiday on profits in perpetuity for industrial activities;
- total exemption from income tax on sales for commercial enterprises;
- exemption from import duty on raw materials, machinery, and equipment;
- exemption from any licensing or quantitative restrictions;
- exemption for foreign-based companies from exchange controls and work-permit fees for foreign personnel;
- factory space leased for approximately US$3.50 per square foot per year.[121]

To what extent US investors, exporters, and the economy have so far benefited from the CBI has not yet been documented. What is known, however, is that while Caribbean Basin exports to the US have been decreasing since the advent of the CBI, US exports to the region have been almost constant (see Table 5-13) and the US trade surplus with the region has grown.

Table 5-13
US Trade with CB Countries, 1982-86

Year	US Exports	Share of US exports to the world	US trade balance with the CB
1982	6338.6	3.1%	−1669.0
1983	5888.8	3.0	−3117.2
1984	6300.2	3.0	−2596.3
1985	5996.4	2.9	−853.6
1986	6292.2	3.0	+105.4

Source: *Annual Report on the Impact of the Caribbean Basin Economic Recovery Act on US Industries and Consumers*, Second Report, 1986 (Washington, DC: USITC, September 1987), p. 1.

6

The Impact of the CBI on Barbados, Jamaica, and Grenada: An Assessment

Catherine Hyett

1   Introduction

This chapter examines post-war economic development in three nations of the Caribbean: namely, Barbados, Jamaica, and Grenada. It is especially concerned with the social, political, and economic effects of the Caribbean Basin Initiative (CBI), the most extensive and coherent policy initiative of that period in the Caribbean.

The case studies are drawn from the countries of the Commonwealth Caribbean. Because they share language, geography, a common colonial history, and proximity to the largest economic market in the world, it might be reasonable to assume that the prescriptions of the CBI would have similar effects across the region. Certainly, this is the view of development presented in the CBI itself.

In fact, the three countries under examination represent the broad spectrum of development experiences existing within the English-speaking Caribbean, having unique political cultures, distinct histories of class development, and differing relations with regional neighbours and the United States. Barbados, for example, is one of the most politically stable and economically developed countries in the Commonwealth Caribbean, with the highest per capita income in the region for a non-oil producing nation, and with no history of an active socialist alternative in political parties or social movements.

Jamaica, by contrast, is commonly perceived as one of the more unstable—economically, politically, and socially. With some tradition of social democracy under the People's National Party, the country still experiences phases of intense instability, characterized by violence and significant swings between right and left. Although in comparison to many other economies in the region Jamaica's industrial infrastruc-

---

Notes for Chapter 6 are on pp. 239-51.

tural systems are highly developed, its record in the areas of social welfare and human rights has been greatly criticized.

Grenada is the least developed of the three, relying almost entirely on agriculture and tourism for its economic survival. It is also the only territory in the Commonwealth Caribbean to have experienced even a partially realized socialist experiment. As such, it has been affected in a much more immediate and explicit way by the economic, social, and political consequences of the Caribbean Basin Initiative.

This examination seeks to demonstrate that, even in the most similar of regions and under the most similar of conditions, the temptation to aggregate and homogenize the experiences of political, economic, and cultural development in different countries should be resisted. Beyond that it provides insights into the attitude of the US government towards bilateral trade and aid relationships with its neighbours, including those like Canada that are not members of the so-called Third World. In the Commonwealth Caribbean, as in other such relationships, the United States has proven to be the net winner throughout the 1980s.

2 Barbados

Barbados has a land area of 430 square kilometres and a population of about 260 000. Although the island had access to few natural resources apart from its workforce with which to support its development effort, in the period following World War II Barbados rapidly became established as one of the most developed economies in the Caribbean. Today the country boasts the third highest per capita income in the Commonwealth Caribbean, good infrastructural systems, and a well-educated and skilled industrial labour force. In addition, Barbados enjoys a higher level of political and social stability than many neighbouring countries due largely to the fact that income distribution is more equitable, and health and social welfare networks more comprehensive than have been developed elsewhere.[1]

2.1 Post-war Economic Development

The decade of the 1950s marked a turning point in the island's economic development. After 300 years of absolute dependence on sugar production for export, Barbados began a process of economic diversification and structural change.[2] Over the succeeding two decades the government established an Industrial Development Corporation (IDC) along the lines of Puerto Rico's Fomento and an export-oriented industrialization strategy based largely on Puerto Rico's post-war development model. Investors in light manufacturing (particularly export industries) were offered a variety of fiscal incentives by the IDC. These included tax holidays, exemptions from import duties, and accelerated depreciation allowances. Factory space was also put at the disposal of manufacturers at subsidized rents.[3]

Foreign companies were attracted, by fiscal and other incentives, to invest in sectors other than manufacturing which promised to maximize the country's foreign exchange earnings. A central part of this process of diversification was the expansion of Barbadian tourism, which became, by the 1960s, a leading economic sector catering to an affluent clientele from North America and Europe.

Following the revival of the international economy in the mid-1970s Barbados almost immediately returned to pre-oil crisis levels of economic activity. Between 1976 and 1989 annual rates of growth averaged 6 per cent.[4] Barbados also achieved some success in the commercial development of its oil and gas resources as a result of the oil crisis, joining the Bahamas and Trinidad and Tobago as one of a handful of oil-producing economies in the Caribbean. Rates of growth over these years in both tourism and manufacturing were impressive, averaging 13.7 per cent and 7.8 per cent, respectively.[5] Activity in the construction sector was strong, benefiting mainly from the expansion of tourist facilities and public works. Considerable gains were also recorded in poultry and milk production and in the fishing industry. In 1979 alone milk production rose by over 10 per cent, poultry by 26 per cent, and fish harvests by more than 30 per cent.[6]

By the end of the 1970s the most serious impediment to the continued growth of the construction sector was the shortage of skilled workers. Sugar was the only industry to remain in the doldrums long after the rest of the economy had recovered its earlier momentum, reflecting continued problems of labour shortage and wage militancy. Even here, however, prospects seemed to be improving by the end of the decade. In 1979 sugar production increased by 12.9 per cent, compared with negative growth the year before.[7]

During the late 1970s the country's balance of payments situation was strengthened as a result of demand management policies which maintained commodity imports at a level well below that of exports. At the same time the buoyancy of the economy overall contributed to a significant reduction in unemployment. In 1979 roughly 11 per cent of the labour force was out of work, compared with about 20 per cent four years earlier.[8]

2.2   Economic Activity in the Early 1980s

By 1980, as a direct consequence of the post-war economic diversification program, garments, electronic components, and tourism had become crucial as foreign exchange earners, although sugar remained the country's most important single export commodity.[9] The economy was also continuing to achieve healthy, if slower, rates of growth.

Earnings from sugar, rum, and molasses reached a record level in 1980. Construction was still experiencing a boom, growing 7 per cent in the same year. Value-added by manufacturing industry increased by 6 per cent, with manufactured goods accounting for 62.7 per cent of total commodity exports, compared with only 13.6 per cent in 1967.[10]

This situation of economic expansion and increasing prosperity was, however, short-lived. In common with many other Third World trading nations, Barbados suffered severe economic and social dislocation in the early 1980s as shock waves from the second post-war economic crisis took their toll on all the island's most important industries.[11]

The economy was also undermined by the collapse of the international oil market, which forced a cut in output of more than 50 per cent and reduced the price for Barbadian crude to one lower than that required to cover the operating costs of the producing company, the Barbados National Oil Company.[12] GDP contracted by 3.1 per cent in 1981, ending a period of five consecutive years of growth. Economic activity slowed significantly in all key sectors of the economy. Tourism receipts fell by 5 per cent, agricultural output by 30 per cent, and manufacturing by 5.5 per cent over the previous year. Only construction survived the recession to achieve positive rates of growth.[13]

In the two years prior to the commencement of the Caribbean Basin Initiative, the Barbadian economy bottomed out and began to stabilize. GDP, which had declined a further 4.6 per cent in 1982, grew 0.5 per cent the next year.[14] Among the leading sectors of the economy, only petroleum and non-sugar agriculture grew to any appreciable extent.

Other industries remained depressed. Among them were the country's most important earners of foreign exchange. Tourism receipts, accounting for more than half of foreign currency earnings, declined by 14 per cent and 8.5 per cent, respectively, in the two years starting 1982. Sugar production, which had stabilized in 1982, fell by 5 per cent the following year to reach the lowest point in a quarter of a century.[15]

Construction activity, which had increased by 4.6 per cent in 1981, dropped 11.9 per cent the following year. Although the manufacturing sector weathered the recession better than construction, output remained stagnant in 1982 and expanded by less than 2 per cent the year after.[16] According to the Inter-American Development Bank, the main factors contributing to the slow recovery of the manufacturing sector were the depressed state of the domestic market (resulting from an economic stabilization program implemented by the government in late 1981 which was designed to curb domestic demand) and economic problems within the CARICOM group (where import restrictions, devaluations, and payment delays reduced demand for manufactured exports).[17]

The residual effects of the international recession combined with deflationary government policies to depress living standards and contributed to a large increase in lay-offs. Latent race and class tensions were brought closer to the surface. The official unemployment rate, which had fallen to 11 per cent of the total workforce in 1979, edged upwards from 1981, exceeding 17 per cent by the beginning of 1984.[18]

2.3   Impact of the CBI

The Barbadian economy began to perform somewhat better than many other countries in the Commonwealth Caribbean by the mid to late 1980s.[19] During the period 1984-87 the country achieved an annual average rate of growth of 3 per cent.[20] The revival of the global economy after 1982 did restore a measure of prosperity to the island, but economic recovery was based largely on the expansion of markets for a very small number of manufactured products destined for a handful of countries outside the Caribbean.

Since World War II, trade between Barbados and Britain has become less important to the Barbadian economy as closer links with the United States have been forged. More recently, intra-regional trade — which typically accounted for between 20 and 25 per cent of Barbadian commodity exports — has been constrained by a variety of problems.[21] These difficulties have, in turn, contributed to the narrowing of export horizons, intensifying the country's dependence on the United States as a market for Barbadian products.

The USA is now the largest and most crucial market for goods and services provided by Barbados. By the early 1980s more than 35 per cent of the total value of exports was destined for that country. The United Kingdom and Canada, as the country's second and third largest individual trading partners, were far behind the USA in importance to the national economy, accounting for 8 to 10 per cent and 5 to 6 per cent of exports, respectively.[22]

Since the CBI went into operation Barbadian governments have redoubled their efforts to strengthen the island's economic links with the United States. Successive budgets have sought to expand the flow of foreign private capital to Barbados by enhancing tax and other concessions available to export-oriented industries locating in the country. The government also undertook a major investment drive in the United States and Canada in 1986 to promote investment in the tourism sector and to induce North American companies involved in "skill intensive" industries, particularly apparel, electronics, medical supplies, and data processing, to relocate offshore.[23]

In addition, Barbados is one of a few Caribbean nations to have signed and ratified a Tax Information Exchange Agreement with the United States. The agreement increased the island's capacity to lure American insurance companies away from the Bahamas (which had not at that point agreed to an exchange of tax information with the US) by exempting Barbados from a 4 per cent US excise tax on gross premiums paid to such companies.[24] Further clauses were intended to boost activity in both tourism and manufacturing industries. Under the first of these, US companies and individuals arranging business conventions in Barbados became able to deduct convention expenses from federal taxes. Under the second clause, signatories to the Tax Information Exchange Agreement became eligible to participate in the Twin Plant Programme initiated by Puerto Rico in 1986.

It is clear that the many concessions made to foreign capital by Barbados in order to promote export-oriented development did not pay the expected dividends. According to Inter-American Development Bank data, the amount of private direct foreign investment in Barbados declined each year from 1981-83. This situation deteriorated even more during the first two years of operation of the Caribbean Basin Initiative. During 1984 and 1985 there was a net outflow of almost $7 million in private direct foreign investment from the island. Although the situation improved in the following year, the flow of private foreign capital into Barbados was still well below the level achieved in 1981 when the economy was suffering the effects of the international crisis.[25]

During the initial period, however, the US program did assist in raising confidence in the Barbadian private sector.[26] With the recovery of the US economy and improved access for Caribbean imports under the CBI's Free Trade Area arrangements, commodity producers anticipated a rapid expansion of trade opportunities with the United States, and hoteliers a substantial rise in American visitors to the island. Many US industry observers at that time viewed the country's economic outlook in similarly optimistic terms. As expressed by Mary Raymond in an April 1984 *Business Week* report on the Barbadian economy: "With a revitalized US economy Barbados, too, is looking stronger."[27]

In the first year of the program's operation, it seemed that the CBI might also help alleviate the unemployment problem. A number of companies established new facilities in Barbados. Neal and Massy Holdings of Trinidad and Tobago opened a new automotive filter manufacturing plant; Geddes Grant, a major Caribbean trading house, moved operations to the island; and American Airlines relocated most of its data processing operation and well over 250 jobs to Barbados from Tulsa, Oklahoma, in order to take advantage of the combined benefits offered by the island's proximity, political stability, and lower wage costs.[28] Such assembly-type industries as electronic components manufacture also underwent significant expansion and product diversification. The American-owned Intel Corporation, which was by far the country's largest microprocessor and computer chip manufacturer, was at the leading edge of this development. In the spring of 1984 Intel invested heavily in its Barbadian assembly plant, adding new equipment, additional product lines, and enlarging its labour force.[29]

With the passage of time, however, popular perceptions of the country's economic and political relationship with the United States have been undergoing change. Overall, it has gradually been dawning on politicians, large sections of the business sector, and the community at large that greater concentration on the US at the expense of other markets may not be beneficial to Barbadian interests in either the short or long term.

2.3.1   Changes in the Volume of Trade with the US

This view has certainly gained greater prominence and support with the publication of several years' worth of US federal data covering post-CBI US/Barbados trade relations. As far as the country's commodity trade with the United States is concerned, the figures only confirm the negative assessment of the American development program made by then prime minister of Barbados, the late Errol Barrow, in the fall of 1986. After almost three years of operation of the CBI, Barrow concluded that the initiative had "brought no visible benefits" to the economy.[30]

During the early 1980s there was a massive expansion of commodity exports from Barbados to the United States. As shown in Table 6-1, in the years 1981 to 1983 goods exports rose by 150 per cent, from $82 million to $205 million. In the first year of operation of the CBI Free Trade Arrangement, US merchandise imports from Barbados expanded by a further 25 per cent, or $51 million, to total $256 million for 1984. After 1984, however, total sales to the US fell drastically. By the end of 1986, their value had plummeted to $110 million (just $1 million higher than recorded for 1982, during the depths of the recession) and in the following year experienced another large drop.[31] Export data for 1987 indicate the intractability of the problems plaguing the island's export industries despite the advent of the CBI. At $129 million, total commodity exports for 1987 amounted to half the value of sales to the United States only three years earlier, with the US market accounting for only $61 million, or 47 per cent of total sales.[32]

In view of the difficulties facing the island's economy, it is hardly surprising that American exporters began to experience problems selling US products in Barbados. During the early 1980s the country formed a growing market for American producers. As Table 6-1 illustrates, United States' commodity exports grew steadily from 1981 to the end of 1984, from $149 million to $241 million. After that, however, sales started to fall. During 1985 and 1986, imports of American products dropped to $173 million and again to $147 million. In 1987 US exporters suffered further market contraction, with sales falling 10 per cent below those made in the year previous.[33]

Table 6-1
United States Merchandise Trade with
Barbados, 1981-87 ($ millions)

Year	US imports from Barbados	Annual % change	US exports to Barbados	Annual % change	US trade balance
1981	82		149		+67
1982	109	+33%	155	+4%	+46
1983	205	+88%	195	+26%	−9
1984	256	+25%	241	+24%	−20
1985	205	−20%	173	−28%	−33
1986	110	−46%	147	−15%	+34
1987	61	−44%	132	−10%	+71

Sources: United States Commerce Department, Office of Trade and Investment Analysis, *US Foreign Trade Highlights* (Washington, DC: Office of Trade and Investment Analysis), 1986 and 1987 reports; and United States International Trade Commission, *Annual Report on the Impact of the Caribbean Basin Economic Recovery Act on US Industries and Consumers* (Washington, DC: USITC), First and Third Reports (1984-85 and 1987).

Although both the United States and Barbados experienced a major drop in exports after 1984, their economies have not suffered the effects equally. Balance of trade data show that by 1986 the United States had regained a positive (and growing) trade balance with Barbados that had been lost in 1983.[34] A more crucial point, however, is that regardless of the fact that Barbados now enjoys liberalized access to the American market, the US trade surplus is increasing and will probably continue to do so unless measures are introduced to restrict imports and to promote Barbadian exports to the United States in both traditional and non-traditional goods areas.

2.3.2   Sectoral Development

In the area of non-traditional (manufactured) commodities, which account for the bulk of Barbados's merchandise exports, and where the Caribbean Basin Initiative was intended to make the greatest impact, the overall effects of the program have been disappointing. From a value of $64 million in 1981, exports of manufactured items to the United States increased fourfold over the following three years to total $247 million in 1984. Thereafter, sales declined to only $107 million in 1986.[35] More recent assessments of the export trade in manufactured items by the Caribbean Development Bank (CDB), the Inter-American Development Bank (IDB), and the Central Bank of Barbados all indicate either marginal or no improvement in the situation in the period ending 1988.[36]

After the end of 1984 the United States also suffered a significant fall in the value of its manufactured exports to Barbados. Prior to that time Barbados had provided a growing market for American products. Between 1981 and 1984, the US almost doubled sales of manufactured goods, from $109 million to $204 million.[37] During the next three years, US-manufactured imports into the country fell by 28 per cent, from $140 million to $100 million.[38]

As in the case of total US exports, while the United States has been confronted with the problem of depressed Barbadian markets for manufactured items, the impact of this on the nation's economy has been minuscule. The precipitous decline in exports of manufactured goods to the United States dealt a crippling blow to the Barbadian economy.[39] Moreover, after reaching a low in 1985, the balance of trade in manufactured commodities began favouring the United States and appears likely to remain that way for the foreseeable future.

If one examines the experiences of the island's most important manufacturing subsectors, it is not difficult to see why exports of manufactured items declined so dramatically since 1985, despite the easing of US trade restrictions on non-traditional products from the Caribbean.

(a) Electronics Sector
Barbados has served as a base of operations for American electronics companies since the late 1960s. Hence, while electronic components manufacture is not in any sense "traditional" to Barbados, it was already a firmly established feature of the economy by the beginning of the 1980s. Furthermore, after a relatively slow start, electronic-components manufacturing rapidly became one of the most productive of the industries created as part of the country's post-war export-oriented development program. Winston Cox estimates that between 1968 and 1979 the average annual growth rate of electronic components exports was 36 per cent.[40] By the latter year electronic components had outstripped garments exports in value, accounting for nearly 12 per cent of total commodity exports.[41]

When the Caribbean Basin Economic Recovery Act (CBERA) went into effect, Barbados was already an important base of offshore assembly and sub-assembly operations for about a dozen US-owned electronics companies, including Intel, Corcom, Aerotron, Micro Data, and TRW. The largest company, Intel, had approximately $15 million invested in its assembly operation in Barbados and was providing employment for more than 1 000 workers assembling integrated circuits for re-export to the United States.[42] The CBI did little to improve access to the US market for electronic components and devices. Although sales of electronic components declined during the recession of the early 1980s, exports recovered rapidly with the subsequent upturn in the world economy. In 1984 exports to the United States grew by 30 per cent, a rate almost equal to that achieved throughout the 1968-79 period.[43]

The international decline in the electronic components industry beginning in 1984 proved crippling to the Barbadian economy. The effects of the recession were perhaps more devastating for Barbados because it coincided with the ending of the tax holiday enjoyed by the country's leading electronics firm, Intel. Manufacturing output declined by an estimated 11.1 per cent in the three years beginning 1985.[44] Divestment, such as the closure of the Intel plant in 1986, together with production cutbacks by other electronics firms, boosted unemployment, depressed foreign-exchange earnings, and further undermined the domestic economy. In 1986 and 1987 output in the electronics subsector fell by an estimated 10 per cent and 67 per cent, respectively. Total unemployment climbed to 19 per cent, and earnings from merchandise exports declined below levels achieved in 1983 when the economy was still recovering from the recession.[45]

(b) Textiles and Apparel

During recent years, the Barbadian garment industry has been experiencing similar difficulties in maintaining export sales. As with electronics, the apparel industry dates to the early 1960s. Information published by the US International Trade Commission indicates that Barbadian garment workers are well trained. Productivity, at 70 to 80 per cent of US standards, is significantly higher than the Caribbean average. At $2.00 an hour in 1985, the average pay of workers in the industry is also rather higher than that earned by counterparts in most neighbouring countries.[46]

The structure of the Barbadian apparel industry and the markets for its products have undergone considerable change during the last three decades. The first garment factory was opened in 1953. The main sources of domestic supply at that time were imports and local seamstresses. By 1966 more than half a dozen clothing factories were in operation, producing a wide variety of items for local, regional, and extra-regional markets.[47] Many more factories opened subsequently. Like other non-traditional industries, most are owned and controlled by American multinational companies initially attracted by generous fiscal concessions offered by both the federal and host governments, lower wage rates, and close proximity in terms of company control over quality and management.[48]

The proportion of output and the value of goods exported outside the region, and especially to the United States, has grown steadily in the post-war period. Despite the impact of the recession, exports of clothing and textiles grew by 38 per cent annually during the 1970s. At the beginning of the decade, the domestic market was still the most important single market for garments and textiles manufactured on the island, local sales accounting for 49 per cent of total production. Exports within CARICOM and to countries outside the Caribbean amounted to less than $10 million in total and accounted for 25 per cent and 27 per cent of output, respectively.[49]

By the end of the 1970s, the situation was radically different. Exports of clothing and textiles had grown fivefold, to $49 million. The proportion of total output sold outside the region had also changed significantly, almost doubling to 50 per cent, while the local economy and CARICOM diminished in importance as markets for the Barbadian apparel and textile industries. The combined share of total production destined for the domestic and regional markets fell by one-quarter, from 74 per cent to 49 per cent.[50]

For much of the 1980s Barbadian textile and apparel manufacturers faced increased difficulties in retaining export markets. Like other export-oriented industries, clothing and textile manufacturers were seriously affected by the global recession. In addition, the Barbadian garment industry was faced with growing protectionism in the United States and by increased competition from lower wage countries in the region, like Haiti, the Dominican Republic, and Jamaica. After peaking in 1983, overseas sales dropped off rapidly. In the first three years of operation of the Caribbean Basin Initiative, clothing exports fell by 50 per cent.[51]

As first implemented, the CBI did not improve conditions for entry into the US for garments manufactured or assembled anywhere in the Caribbean. Over 90 per cent of regional apparel exports to the United States were already covered by duty concessions available under Item 807.00 of the Trade Schedules of the United States (TSUS).[52]

The introduction of the Caribbean Basin Special Access Programme for Apparel under the CBI in 1986 (see Chapter 1) liberalized these concessions marginally. But welcome as this change was, it was not sufficient to turn the situation around for the Barbadian garment industry. The erosion of export markets for Barbadian clothing continued at a slightly slower pace in both 1987 and 1988. As in the electronics subsector, the results were layoffs and factory closures. Given the economic importance and the labour-intensive character of both the garment and electronics industries, it is not surprising that their decline raised unemployment levels and forced the country into an even heavier reliance on tourism, one of the few industries continuing to prosper.[53]

(c) Agriculture

Sugar has traditionally been the country's principal commodity export and foreign exchange earner. This once-thriving industry has undergone decline in recent times. During the early 1980s the difficulties facing the island's sugar producers were exacerbated by two external developments. The first of these, the international recession of 1981-82, hit Barbadian agriculture harder than any other economic sector. Production declined by almost one-quarter in the two years starting 1981.[54] Export earnings from sugar and sugar by-products (which comprised the bulk of agricultural exports) were cut to half of the 1980 level.[55] A further factor impeding economic recovery (which had begun in 1984) was the imposition by the United States government of a quota system intended to phase out sugar imports from all regions of the world. Non-sugar agriculture and fishing, on the other hand, which remained unaffected by the system, continued to expand, if only slowly.[56]

As with other sugar-producing economies in the region which had progressively reoriented their economies away from Europe and which, by the early 1980s, had become heavily reliant on the American market, the sharp contraction of imports into that country was devastating for Barbadian agriculture. IDB analysts suggest that reductions in American import quotas, combined with weak international prices, had by 1987 rendered the island's sugar industry unprofitable. Cutbacks were undertaken in geographical areas dedicated to cane, and workers made redundant. By the end of that year output had been so reduced that it was insufficient to satisfy both the domestic market and overseas preferential quotas.[57]

United States Commerce Department data show that throughout the period 1980-87 exports of US agricultural goods to Barbados remained relatively stable, fluctuating between $27 million and $30 million annually. Imports, on the other hand, fell from $40 million to $7 million and in 1986 amounted to only $2 million. As a result, by the end of 1987 the agricultural trade balance had reversed, showing a surplus of some $20 million in favour of the United States.[58]

The situation facing Barbados in the area of agricultural trade with the US contrasts sharply with that of many other countries and regions not benefiting from special trade arrangements with that country. In the main, during the 1980s, US overseas sales of agricultural products fell behind imports. Trade between the United States and less developed countries (LDCs), as a whole, strongly indicates such a trend. In 1981 the United States enjoyed an agricultural trade surplus with these countries which exceeded $4.6 billion. By the mid-1980s the United States' trade superiority had been seriously eroded. In 1985 the United States recorded its first deficit in this decade. During the three years beginning 1985 agricultural exports to LDCs fell by more than $3 billion, and the United States was showing deficits ranging from $114 million to $2.4 billion.[59]

2.4   Economic and Social Policy since the CBI

Since the Caribbean Basin Initiative went into effect, both of Barbados's leading political parties, the Barbados Labour Party (BLP) and the Democratic Labour Party (DLP), have held political office.[60] Although differences do exist between the economic policies of the two parties, both have affirmed their commitment to the private sector-led, export-oriented development strategy begun years earlier. In order to advance this objective both BLP and DLP governments have pursued fiscal policies designed to improve investment incentives and stimulate growth in export and tourism sectors.

Over the past few years a variety of other policies have been introduced which have sought to cut production costs, particularly in export industries, and to offset the loss of competitiveness in both tourism and export-manufacturing sectors. Land taxes payable by hotels as well as taxes on corporate income have been significantly reduced, excise duties on industrial inputs eliminated, and private sector credit facilities improved.[61]

In addition to implementing policies specifically oriented towards stimulating export manufacturing and tourism industries, both parties have pursued restrictive monetary and fiscal policies for much of their respective periods in office. Public revenues have been increased at the same time as expenditures have been reduced in a number of important social areas. One inevitable result of this is that a greater share of the burden of the development strategy has fallen onto the shoulders of working people. Savings have been achieved in a number of ways: through the imposition of levies for health and other public services; by raising consumer taxes; increasing stamp duties on imports of consumer durables; and/or shifting a larger proportion of direct taxation to individual wage earners.[62] US business analysts estimate that budgetary changes introduced in 1987 were responsible for slashing 4.2 per cent from workers' take-home pay, at the same time as they precipitated a rise in inflation of between 2.5 and 4 per cent.[63]

Because such policies discriminate against poorer social sectors, they also have the potential to undermine the social fabric of Barbados. Although they are affecting the vast majority of working people detrimentally, they have forced the poorest and most vulnerable people to bear the heaviest burden.[64] Allan Kirton, head of the Caribbean Conference of Churches, has argued that by 1986 accumulated pressures were now beginning to break the surface calm of Barbadian society. At the same time as people were struggling against rising inflation and a growing threat of unemployment they could hardly fail to see the many "signs of progress and superstructural development" proceeding all around them.[65] Clearly, the growing disparity between their own situations and those enjoyed by social classes benefiting from the development strategy has proven difficult for many to reconcile.

3   Jamaica

Covering an area of 10 962 square kilometres and with a population of almost 2.4 million, Jamaica is the largest and most populous of the Commonwealth Caribbean islands.[66] As such, changes in the political and economic orientation of the country have a significant influence on developments in both English-speaking and other nations in the region. Although agricultural goods, and particularly sugar, formed the mainstay of the country's export economy up until World War II, mineral products and manufactured items have now superseded agriculture in importance as export commodities.

Despite the country's advantages in terms of size and natural resources, Jamaica has not succeeded in bringing about the economic and social improvements that have been achieved in a number of other Caribbean countries which are not so well endowed. Education and health services have been accorded a lower priority, and the living standards of working people are generally lower than in Barbados, for instance.[67] In the mid-1980s nine of the 13 CARICOM territories, including a number of the Eastern Caribbean states, were showing per capita incomes higher than that of Jamaica. The literacy rate was 26 per cent below that of Barbados. Life expectancy, too, was slightly lower. Unemployment, infant mortality, and population growth rates, on the other hand, were significantly higher. Also, although industrial infrastructural systems were highly developed, large sectors of rural and urban populations had no direct access to such basic amenities as piped water.[68]

Nor has the political system served to erode historical divisions or promote democratic norms. Since their inception in the inter-war period, Jamaica's two main political parties — the People's National Party (PNP) and the Jamaica Labour Party (JLP) — have been linked closely to two competing trade unions which together represent about one-quarter of the labour force. The links between the parties and unions have tended to polarize the working class and have led to the emergence of a clientelist system based on the promise of a variety of political favours in return for electoral support. This system has led to a massive increase in the incidence of politically motivated crimes, including murder, that characterize Jamaican elections.[69]

3.1 Post-war Economic Development

Largely as a result of the discovery of huge, accessible deposits of bauxite, Jamaican economic policy after 1945 continued its pre-war emphasis on raw materials exports. Both major political parties, however, proved eager to move beyond the country's traditional role as a supplier of primary commodities by stimulating activity in new sectors of the manufacturing industry. A state agency, the Jamaica Industrial Development Corporation (JIDC), was established to oversee this process. Tax and other fiscal concessions were provided to approved investors. Incentive legislation was first passed in the late 1940s, prior even to the creation of the JIDC, with further enactments in later decades.[70]

Unlike the Puerto Rican approach, a key objective in the initial phase was to promote economic diversification by developing manufacturing industries supplying the domestic market. The strategy blended elements of an export-led development approach into what was fundamentally an "Import Substitution Industrialization" (ISI) model. By promoting the development of both capital and labour-intensive sectors of industry, planners sought to broaden and deepen the country's economic structure, reduce the cost of consumer imports, and generate new jobs. The earliest incentive program (the Pioneer Industries Encouragement Law) encouraged local businesses to manufacture consumer goods for local needs. At the same time, foreign firms were encouraged to form joint ventures with local enterprises and to become involved in export-oriented industries.[71]

During the 1950s the program did generate employment, particularly in the ISI sector. Increases in both gross investment (up from 11 per cent in 1950 to 21 per cent in 1965) and gross domestic product were also recorded. Owen Jefferson estimates that in the 15 years ending 1965, Jamaica's GDP grew at an annual rate slightly in excess of 7 per cent.[72] By the mid-1960s the bauxite-alumina industry accounted for 10 per cent of GDP, and the manufacturing industry had expanded sufficiently to emerge as the most important single sector. By that time, tourism and construction were also sectors of rapid economic growth.[73]

By the close of the 1960s the economic strategy was still achieving relatively high growth rates. In addition, the development process had brought about a major reorganization of the island's class structure. It was during this period that an indigenous class of capital emerged, based in the manufacturing sector.[74] Its impact on other social classes was, however, more problematic. Reduction of the land area devoted to agriculture (sold off chiefly for mining and tourism development) accelerated the process of peasant proletarianization and raised rural unemployment to alarmingly high levels. Massive out-migration followed, accompanied by a significant lowering of wage rates among unskilled industrial labour. The political and social upheavals which ensued were no less dramatic, culminating by the end of the 1960s in massive strikes and a wave of urban insurrection which shook Jamaican society.[75]

When the PNP gained office in 1972, the Manley regime sought to increase the level of state involvement in the economy to better control national economic development. Initially, policy was not intended as part of a "democratic socialist" development strategy.[76] Of equal importance in the government's view was the attempt to staunch the flow of private capital from the island by raising tax incentives and industrial subsidies. To attract foreign investment, an Export Processing Zone (EPZ) was established in Kingston (which offered export manufacturers a huge array of publicly subsidized services and operated with fewer import and exchange-control restrictions than elsewhere on the island). More generous tax concessions than had been offered under the previous (JLP) government were introduced.[77]

Beyond this, the PNP government implemented a policy of "redistribution by growth" designed to stimulate forms of economic development capable of producing widespread prosperity and political stability. Measures were introduced to assist and encourage small businesses and to promote domestic import substitution in food processing and other consumer goods industries. Importantly, the "redistribution by growth" policy co-existed with a rigorous system of quantitative restrictions and duties for non-capital goods imports which had been in force since the mid-1960s.[78]

Analyst Winston James argues that the strategy produced an "unparalleled improvement" in working-class living conditions during the PNP's first term. Free education was extended to secondary and university levels, work opportunities expanded through job-creation programs, and increases in real wages were achieved and generally maintained until austerity measures were introduced as part of the first International Monetary Fund (IMF) agreement, concluded in 1977.[79]

In contrast to ISI industries, many of which continued to thrive, Jamaica's export sector experienced crisis conditions during the early 1970s. It has been estimated that more than 60 per cent of the firms established under the 1950s Export Incentives Encouragement Law

(EIEL) were no longer functioning in 1973.[80] Mahmood Ali Ayub explains the problems faced by the Jamaican export-manufacturing sector with reference to the specific character and needs of the industry. Capital investment per employee was generally low in this sector, as were wage rates and benefit levels.[81] Ayub maintains that for most of the 1960s Jamaica was able to offer advantages as an export-production site. Its generous tax incentive system gave the country a comparative advantage in export activities over many of its strongest competitors in the region. In addition, as an English-speaking nation with an educated, inexpensive labour force, the country proved to be an even more attractive location than Puerto Rico to many companies involved in labour-intensive production operations. By the end of the decade, however, these advantages had been eroded by currency overvaluation and by mounting industrial unrest and social tensions. Many foreign companies were thus prompted to relocate production operations to more stable low-wage countries when their periods of approved status expired.[82]

Capital flight continued unabated during the 1970s, fuelled by organizing efforts to incorporate previously non-unionized sectors of the working class into the organized labour movement and by an upsurge of industrial militancy, which culminated in the enactment of minimum wage legislation in 1976. One consequence of these developments was that between 1968 and 1973 the percentage share in total manufactured exports of EIEL firms fell sharply, from 52 per cent to 27 per cent.[83] Regional trade, which had grown rapidly after Jamaica joined the Caribbean Free Trade Association (CARIFTA—later to become CARICOM) in 1968, thus became even more crucial to the economy than in earlier years.

Two of the most serious setbacks occurred in 1974. The first was the oil crisis, which dealt a major blow to the industrial strategy by reducing the country's capacity to purchase other imported inputs through the second half of the decade. The oil crisis in turn prompted the Manley government to expand its own revenue base by imposing a bauxite levy indexed to the price of aluminium on the American market.[84] Growth rates in all key sectors of the economy were affected by the massive flight of foreign private capital which followed. Bauxite exports plummetted, sugar output dropped, and tourism receipts fell sharply. Manufacturers fared no better: output declined in most industrial subsectors from the mid-1970s. Annual growth rates of between −15 and −35 per cent were not uncommon during the second half of the decade. Output declined by 5.1 per cent in 1976, and by a further 14.4 per cent during the next two years. Unemployment began to rise again, too, and real incomes to fall. By 1979 the official unemployment rate had reached 31.1 per cent; and by the following year incomes were below 1974 levels.[85]

Notwithstanding the massive contraction of export industries, Ayub maintains that a significant shift in official policy towards a more clearly export-oriented strategy was well underway by 1978. This shift might have been predicted, given the growing marginalization of progressive elements within the party leadership from the mid-1970s, and the escalation of external pressure — chiefly from the US government, the IMF, and multinational capital — to restructure the economy in ways acceptable to them.[86]

Arguably, the most crucial external actor was the IMF, which demanded massive exchange rate adjustments as a condition of balance of payments support. Currency devaluations, which began in 1977, were combined with a series of government measures provided for under the IMF arrangement to further depress domestic demand, revitalize private sector activity (particularly export-oriented activities), and reduce public spending.[87] Aggregate consumption fell by 7.3 per cent in the year following the IMF agreement, and gross fixed investment (mainly public sector) jumped by 9.1 per cent. Thus, well before the PNP left office, official policy had already raised incentives to produce for overseas markets.

3.2   Economic Activity in the Early 1980s

When Edward Seaga's Jamaica Labour Party was elected to office in October 1980, the party enjoyed widespread goodwill and support both from Jamaicans and from the Reagan administration, which supported the JLP's free market economic policies and the party's call for closer links with the United States.

Huge increases in the level of US bilateral aid to Jamaica during the initial phase of the Seaga government are indicative of both the "special relationship" that was forged between the two leaderships and the country's centrality to the United States' Caribbean Basin strategy. US assistance, which had amounted to only $56 million in the final three years of the PNP government, rose to $500 million for the first three years of the Seaga regime. With the increase, Jamaica became the second largest per capita recipient of American aid. Loans from USAID, the IDB, and the commercial banks also began flowing into the country. Multilateral aid poured in, too, during this period. In 1981 the Seaga government negotiated its first agreement with the IMF for over US$600 million, on terms more favourable to the country than had been previously allowed. The World Bank was equally supportive. In 1981-82 almost 70 per cent of the Bank's Caribbean loan allocation was channelled to Jamaica.[88]

Despite this infusion, the decline of the Jamaican economy was not reversed during the early 1980s. With the exception of mining and tourism, all other major economic sectors faced obstacles to growth in the first two years of the JLP's first term of office.[89] Gross domestic product continued the long-term decline which had begun in 1972. Total output fell by 5.4 per cent and 1.2 per cent, respectively, in 1980 and 1981 compared with a 2.5 per cent decline in 1979 and an annual average drop of 2.8 per cent in the three previous years.[90]

In the years between the JLP electoral victory and the implementation of the Caribbean Basin Initiative in January 1984, sectoral performance varied. Agriculture, which still provided employment for more than 25 per cent of the workforce, suffered from serious shortages of inputs as well as the ruinous effects of Hurricane Allen during the early period. The industry recovered strongly in 1983, registering an 8.2 per cent growth rate for that year. Growth was attributable largely to increased production of non-traditional crops. While output declined in the traditional export crop subsector due to weak sugar prices and a poor banana crop, non-traditional agriculture had expanded by around 7 per cent. This type of agricultural development, however, did little to reverse the decline in the production of domestic food crops. In the years between 1980 and 1982 domestic food production fell by 9 per cent, to reach a figure 30 per cent below 1978 levels.[91] Thus, in 1983 when the inflationary impact of currency devaluations really began to bite, food prices shot up, as did the incidence of malnutrition.

Mining, which had benefited from policy measures implemented by the Manley regime in 1979 to reduce the bauxite levy and increase investment in the industry, ended three years of decline. Growth rates of 6.8 per cent and 1.3 per cent, respectively, were achieved in the two years beginning 1980. Thereafter, recovery was inhibited by the onset of the international recession and other external developments. As a consequence of these difficulties, mining output suffered a massive 29 per cent fall in 1982, and achieved only marginal growth in 1983.[92]

Tourism performed consistently well during this period. In 1980 the political violence surrounding the election depressed demand for Jamaica as a holiday destination in the second half of the year. Tourism receipts for that year nonetheless remained slightly higher than the previous one. The industry fared even better in subsequent years. In the two years ending 1983, arrivals jumped by 38 per cent. In 1983 alone, arrivals jumped by 16 per cent, and revenues increased by more than 45 per cent.[93]

Aggressive advertising by the Jamaican Tourist Board was important in raising the profile of Jamaican holiday resorts, especially in the United States and Canada. Secondly, as a sign of American support for the Seaga regime and its economic development strategy, the US exempted conventions held in that country from corporate taxes.[94] Of equal importance was the positive impact of currency devaluations on the industry. By the end of the period increased tourism earnings had lowered the current account deficit by nearly 30 per cent.[95]

Industrial manufacturing, particularly export manufacturing, was at the very heart of the program of structural adjustment introduced by the Seaga regime. Even so, decline in that sector, which had begun in the second half of the 1970s, continued well into the next decade. Output was only slightly higher in 1980 than during the previous year, declining by 5.4 per cent as compared with 6.1 per cent in 1979.[96] However, as discussed previously in reference to PNP economic policy after 1977, the two main subsectors (import-substitution and export-manufacturing industries) were not operating under the same sorts of constraints and were therefore experiencing very different growth rates.

The first group, comprising industries supplying the internal market, were given few incentives to increase investment or expand output. In addition, they laboured under a variety of measures restricting imports of plant, raw materials, and spare parts which had been introduced by the PNP in response to the chronic shortage of foreign exchange. In 1980 alone, footwear, textiles, furniture, and other manufacturing and processing industries geared to the local market suffered an overall reduction of output of approximately 10 per cent.[97]

The situation of this sub-sector became even more precarious with the election of the Seaga government. The bulk of the increased flow of bilateral aid secured by the JLP regime in the first years of the decade was intended by donor countries to facilitate the opening of the Jamaican market to their own manufactured products. Moreover, much of the multilateral support received came with the more general intention of removing impediments to the free flow of goods, services, and investment capital into and out of the Jamaican economy.

Much of the money coming into the country during this period was not channelled into private sector investment or devoted to upgrading neglected economic and social infrastructures. Instead, it was used to finance the import of luxury items and other consumer goods into the country. One result was that the annual balance of trade deficit more than doubled during the JLP's first years in office, from $203 million in 1979 to $595 million in 1983, with consumer durables imports rising at a rate many times faster than that of total imports. In 1982 alone, in the midst of the international economic crisis, imports of consumer goods increased by 21 per cent.[98]

The influx of foreign consumer goods proved devastating for large sections of local industry. Output of locally produced manufactured goods and food-processing industries suffered a decline in the order of 10 per cent.[99] According to the Jamaica Manufacturers' Association, government policies had forced the closure of 33 locally owned factories in a six-month period during 1982, rendering hundreds of workers redundant. Plant utilization, moreover, fell to 39 per cent of capacity over the same period. Small businesses, and particularly garment and shoe manufacturers, appear to have been seriously affected by the flood of lower-priced imports. Michael Kaufman reports, for example, that during this same period three-quarters of a million pairs of shoes were imported into Jamaica, while six local factories closed down — with substantial loss of jobs — due to lack of business.[100]

Export-manufacturing industries, by contrast, were the beneficiaries of a broad range of programs offered through the Jamaica Export Credit Insurance Corporation and the Jamaica National Export Corporation. These bodies expedited the bureaucratic process for exporters, ensured them priority use of such public services as port and air transport facilities, provided them with training and travel grants, and with advisory, marketing, and promotional facilities.

The Certified Exporter Scheme (CES) was a key policy instrument aimed at export promotion. The CES accorded the highest priority in import licences to exporters and industries supplying inputs into the production process. The program was also linked to an Export Development Fund, established with World Bank funding in 1979, which provided a pre-shipment financing facility to eligible firms. Approved status was based on the strength of a company's past export record, or the ability of businesses to demonstrate a clear intention of achieving a major expansion ($200 000) in export sales in the immediate future.[101]

The various programs available to export industries were extended after the Seaga government took office. Particularly important was the removal of quantitative restrictions on imports of raw materials and intermediate inputs. Further measures, introduced in the spring of 1983, were designed to help the country's balance of payments situation by improving the terms of trade and profitability of the export manufacturing sector. These established a new import quota system which was to improve the allocation of foreign exchange to industry and gave official recognition to the parallel currency market.

In spite of the international recession, manufacturing output expanded slightly in 1981 by 1.3 per cent, and by a total of 8.3 per cent over the following two years. In the first half of 1983 currency devaluation, combined with the new policy measures and the recovery of international markets, helped export manufacturers to increase the value of sales by 23 per cent, most exports being destined for the United States and other extraregional markets.[102]

The restructuring required by the Seaga government's export-led development program, together with currency devaluation and austerity measures, levied heavy economic and social costs on huge sections of the Jamaican working class. Although the absolute decline in economic growth was reversed after 1980, the official unemployment rate hovered at around 26 per cent throughout this period, reflecting the contraction of key sectors of the Jamaican economy such as bauxite/alumina and sugar.[103]

Furthermore, while the series of currency devaluations demanded by the IMF from 1983 did help to boost the export performance of both manufacturing and food-processing industries, they also brought sharply mounting costs. At the same time as wage rates were declining, the price of imported consumer goods, utilities, transportation, gasoline, cooking fuel, medicines, school books, and staple foods were rising rapidly. The marginalization and growing impoverishment of vast sectors of the population intensified social conflicts and led to an alarming increase in crime rates and in political unrest. Mounting social turbulence was in turn countered by the creation of a "Special Operations Squad." Popularly referred to as the "Eradication Squad," it was responsible for much of the growing police brutality as well as for the rapid rise in police killings after its establishment in 1981.[104]

3.3 Impact of the CBI

With the implementation of the Caribbean Basin Initiative, Jamaica was allocated an extra $50 million in special economic assistance, bringing US bilateral aid for 1984 up to $200 million. In addition, Washington made two major purchases of bauxite to add to the US strategic stockpile. Part of this was paid in cash, the remainder in food commodities—chiefly wheat and dairy products.[105]

This increase in official US support did little to ameliorate the many economic, social, and political problems afflicting the country. The embrace of the Seaga regime as a regional ally of the United States did not translate into increased private sector activity in the Jamaican economy. On the contrary, in the first two years of the CBI's operation Jamaica suffered substantial loss of tax revenues, export earnings, and jobs due to the closure of US-owned plants. These included ALCOA and Reynolds Metals, which had both closed down bauxite operations and quit Jamaica by early 1985. Although a number of small investment projects were initiated in the wake of the CBI, there is no evidence of any major US private investments having materialized as a direct consequence of the program.

As the Private Sector Organization of Jamaica (PSOJ) noted in its economic review for that year, 1984 was "altogether, not a vintage year" for the Jamaican private sector.[106] The inability of the economy to recover from the international recession is reflected in Jamaica's annual economic growth rates. In the four years after the CBI went into operation, the country's economy did significantly less well in this respect than did Barbados, which received almost no additional US development aid. Gross domestic product in Jamaica rose by a total of only 1.6 per cent between 1984 and 1987 and, during the first two years of the program, output actually declined by 5.4 per cent. In fact, economic activity in 1984 and 1985 was far lower than it had been earlier in the decade at the height of the recession.[107]

The policy measures implemented by the Seaga government to fuel export-led economic development did not succeed in significantly boosting the level of foreign investment in the country. Although investment levels improved under the Seaga government after the massive decline experienced during the 1970s, Jamaica was not as successful as Barbados in securing or maintaining the level of private foreign investment over the course of the 1980s. Between 1981 and 1983 the amount of private direct foreign investment in Jamaica fell by more than $46 million. During the first year of operation of the CBI, net foreign private investment rose by $12.2 million, indicating a recovery of investor confidence in the Jamaican economy. The improvement of 1984, however, was only a temporary deviation from a more general trend downward. Figures for 1985-86 show a net fall of $13.6 million in private direct foreign investment, wiping out the gains of the previous year.[108]

Nor did the US development program assist in boosting earnings from commodity exports. Between 1980 and 1983, total overseas sales of Jamaican-produced goods declined by 22 per cent, from $886 million to $686 million. This trend was reversed in 1984, when merchandise exports expanded by slightly more than 2 per cent, to bring in $702 million. Although the increase is partly accounted for by US stockpile purchases of bauxite, a rise in extra-regional exports of non-traditional products of almost 50 per cent was also recorded.[109]

As in the case of private direct foreign investment, however, 1984 was only a respite from the longer-term decline in overseas commodity sales. Earnings for 1985 fell by 19 per cent, to the lowest point since the Seaga regime took office. In the following two years there were signs of only minor improvement. By the end of 1987 the value of commodity exports was still well below pre-1984 levels.[110] Part of the reason for this lies with the huge contraction of Caribbean Common Market (CARICOM) trade. In the first year that the CBI was in effect and extra-regional sales were growing, there was a sharp drop in CARICOM demand for Jamaican-manufactured products. Commodity exports plummetted, from $84 million to $52 million in 1984, a drop of 38 per cent. Nor was this trend arrested when extra-regional sales began to fall once again the following year. Exports to CARICOM continued to contract, declining by over $12 million, or 23 per cent, in 1985.[111]

Much of the popular support for the Caribbean Basin Initiative generated by the JLP prior to the program's commencement was based on a belief that it would generate jobs in new economic sectors. Reality, however, never matched this expectation, and there are few, if any, signs that unemployment will be relieved through the operation of the CBI. At 26 per cent of the labour force, the official unemployment rate for 1985 was little different from when the Seaga government took office. In the opinion of the Private Sector Organization of Jamaica, moreover, it is likely that the actual number of unemployed people had begun rising after 1983. Many of these remained unrecorded for a variety of reasons. These conclusions are not surprising, given that well over half this number were women, who were less likely to register as unemployed.[112]

3.3.1   Changes in the Volume of Trade with the US

The stagnation (and, at times, the absolute decline) of the Jamaican economy, as measured by output, investment levels, employment, and other economic indicators, is also evident in the data for bilateral trade with the United States. The United States has emerged as Jamaica's most important trading partner. Over the 1980s the proportion of commodity exports sold to that country rose rapidly. In 1982 the US market absorbed about 38 per cent of total merchandise exports; by 1986 the figure had jumped to half. During the first year of operation of the CBI, moreover, the United States accounted for 56 per cent of Jamaica's total merchandise exports.[113]

It is important to note, however, that Jamaica's total merchandise exports declined by about 18 per cent, from $723 million to $589 million, during this period. Thus the rising proportion of merchandise exports to the US did not necessarily imply increased earnings. As shown in Table 6-2, the value of exports to the United States in 1986 was barely higher than for 1982 ($278 million in 1982 compared with $298 million in 1986). Furthermore, excessive focus on the United States was accompanied by the contraction of other vital overseas markets especially, as was noted earlier, that of CARICOM countries. Jamaica's exports to nations other than the US fell by more than one-third, from $445 million to $292 million during this period.[114]

More recently, the pattern of bilateral trade between the United States and the Caribbean Basin has diverged radically from a deeper trend in US foreign trade. The US has run a constant and growing deficit during the 1980s. Trade with less developed countries as a group conformed with this overall global pattern. The situation of the Caribbean and Central America stands in marked contrast to this trend. In the period 1981-83, the US economy reduced its trade deficit with the Caribbean Basin by 8 per cent, from $3.4 billion to $3.1 billion. The improvement in the US trade position was even more pronounced after 1984. Within three years of the CBI going into effect, the deficit had not only been extinguished, but the United States had begun to show a surplus in commodity trading.[115]

Table 6-2
United States Merchandise Trade with
Jamaica, 1981-87 ($000s)

Year	US imports from Jamaica	Annual % change	US exports to Jamaica	Annual % change	US trade balance
1981	357		468		+111
1982	278	−22%	460	−2%	+182
1983	263	−6%	444	−3%	+181
1984	397	+51%	488	+10%	+91
1985	267	−33%	396	−19%	+129
1986	298	+12%	446	+13%	+148
1987	394	+32%	*		

* Data not published in either source.

Sources: United States Bureau of International Labor Affairs, *Trade and Employment Effects of the Caribbean Basin Economic Recovery Act* (Washington, DC: US Department of Commerce, National Technical Information Service), 1985 and 1987 Reports; and United States International Trade Commission, *Annual Report on the Impact of the Caribbean Basin Economic Recovery Act on US Industries and Consumers* (Washington, DC: USITC), First and Third Reports (1984-85 and 1987).

Trade patterns between Jamaica and the United States have conformed quite closely to the general (downward) trend for Central America and the Caribbean. Between 1980 and 1984 US merchandise exports to Jamaica increased by more than 60 per cent, from $302 million to $488 million. Sales suffered a setback in 1985, dropping by 19 per cent, but recovered rapidly thereafter, growing by 13 per cent in 1986 to reach $446 million (see Table 6-2).[116] According to Commerce Department data, US commodity sales continued to rise strongly in the following year. The recovery of exports to Jamaica is reflected in a rising US trade surplus. In the 1982-87 period Jamaica recorded an annual trade deficit with the United States. Although the deficit was reduced by half between 1983 and 1984, largely as a result of US government stockpiling of Jamaican bauxite, it grew steadily after that and by 1987 was larger than at any other point this decade.[117]

3.3.2   Sectoral Development

Although all sectors of the economy felt the effects of the Seaga government's restructuring policies, none were affected more profoundly than the manufacturing industry and agriculture. Both sectors underwent major qualitative changes in consequence of the government's aggressive pursuit of export-led growth. The magnitude of the transformation in both sectors can be gauged from changes in the composition and volume of manufactured and agricultural exports in the period ending 1987.

In 1987 the manufacturing sector contributed around 18 per cent of the country's GDP. Although aggregate output expanded more or less in line with GDP throughout the mid-late 1980s, firms involved in non-traditional export manufacturing tended to achieve much higher growth rates than other branches of industry. In the period 1981-83, total exports of manufactured goods to the United States fell by 19 per cent, from $36 million to $29 million, reflecting the huge contraction of demand resulting from the international recession.[118] In contrast to Barbados, however, which suffered a sharp fall in sales of industrial goods to the United States after 1984, Jamaican manufactured exports took off, expanding by almost 500 per cent in the four years ending 1987.[119]

According to the Private Sector Organization of Jamaica, the improved export performance of the manufacturing sector during this period was attributable to three factors. While acknowledging the importance of the CBI and "Super 807" programs in expanding US demand for Jamaican products, the PSOJ viewed the depreciation of the Jamaican dollar as the key factor: it made Jamaican manufactured exports competitive with Asian and Latin American goods marketed in the United States.[120]

Much of the rise in manufactured exports from the mid-1980s has been accomplished through a massive restructuring of the country's apparel industry. Developments in the garment industry therefore need to be examined closely, as they are suggestive of the types of changes likely to occur in other branches of industry if the current PNP government retains the economic-growth strategy inherited from Seaga.

(a)   Export-oriented Garment Manufacturing
At the beginning of the 1980s, the Jamaican garments sub-sector was based predominantly on small, locally owned businesses catering to

local and regional needs. In addition, a small group of largely foreign-owned, export-oriented producers existed, serving exclusively extra-regional markets. Since then, mainly as a result of efforts by the US and Jamaican governments to develop the country's potential as a "re-export" economy, the apparel industry has undergone fundamental transformation.

During its first years in office, the Seaga government took a series of steps to reorient the economy towards export manufacturing. The apparel industry was only one of seven manufacturing sub-sectors targetted for development under the Structural Adjustment Programme. Central to the restructuring strategy was the expansion of existing export-processing facilities in the Kingston port area. Thus, in 1980, the Kingston Export Free Zone Act was passed to regulate the Free Zone and to provide companies locating there with a wide variety of benefits, including "tax free and duty free concessions in perpetuity."[121]

Two years later, a government-funded project was initiated with the Singer Company and Kurt Salmon, an American management consulting firm, to begin a five-year construction and training program to develop the garment industry. A huge advertising campaign was launched by Jamaica National Investment Promotion Ltd. (JNIP) in North America, Asia, and Europe to attract companies engaged in export-processing activities to the country.[122]

Largely as a consequence of these initiatives, apparel manufacturing is now overwhelmingly in the hands of foreign companies producing for overseas markets. Although a small amount of production based on "Cut, Make and Trim" (CMT) has been maintained, a growing proportion of total output consists of apparel assembled from pre-cut imported fabric. The bulk of raw materials are imported from the United States and re-exported to the same market under the federal government's 807 and 807/A (Super 807) programs.[123] Companies involved in 807/A activities typically run high-intensity production operations employing unskilled and semi-skilled assembly workers. In the main, 807/A operatives are not represented by labour unions, and frequently unionization is actively discouraged by Free Zone employers. Moreover, because the set-up costs of 807/A facilities are modest, companies engaged in re-export activities tend to be "footloose" in character.[124]

In the period 1981-83, exports of garments from CBI-participating countries to the United States grew by upwards of 20 per cent. After that, the US market expanded even more rapidly, increasing at an average annual rate of 28 per cent between 1984 and 1986.[125] This expansion of regional exports to the United States, however, pales in comparison with the record of the Jamaican garment industry over the same period. As early as 1985 Jamaica had emerged as one of the four main Caribbean suppliers of 807 products to the United States. It is estimated that the average increase of apparel exports to the US market exceeded 580 per cent during the period 1984-87 and totalled $186 million in the latter year. Well over half of this amount ($101 million) was generated by 807/A operations, whose value increased by 92 per cent during 1986.[126]

As the Seaga government frequently pointed out, garment manufacturing became one of the most vibrant branches of the Jamaican economy. With somewhere in excess of 23 000 people working in it, the apparel industry also became the single largest employer in the manufacturing sector. As in other Third World countries, the vast majority of these (around 95 per cent) are female production workers. In the 1980s, and especially after 1983, the industry steadily increased its contribution to foreign-exchange earnings. According to the JNIP, income from apparel exports almost doubled, from $26 million to $50 million, between 1984 and 1985. Employment in the Kingston Export Free Zone, the largest of the country's Export Processing Zones, expanded from around 200 in 1981 to about 15 000 by late 1988, most of this dramatic rise being due to the proliferation of 807/A factories.[127]

The rise in non-unionized industrial employment in largely unregulated operating conditions has generated new types of problems for the Jamaican working class, and particularly for women workers. Although many Jamaicans face serious difficulty obtaining paid employment, the situation of women is especially critical. Young women are in the worst position, with 80 per cent unemployment in the 14-19 age group and 60 per cent in the 20-24 age group in 1987.[128] It is from these two groups that garment assembly operatives are overwhelmingly recruited.

Because they frequently head one-parent families and are the sole breadwinner in the household, desperation has driven many young women to accept work for low wages, in poor physical working conditions, and with a high level of job insecurity. According to one report published by the Joint Trade Unions Research Development Centre (JTURDC) and the Canadian University Service Overseas (CUSO), the average hourly rate of female garment workers was significantly lower in Jamaica in 1984 than in the East Asian economies of Singapore, Hong Kong, Taiwan, and the Philippines.[129] Given that the JLP development strategy involved stabilization policies and deregulation of basic commodity prices, it is not surprising that the study also found that three-quarters of all female workers were unable to meet their basic weekly expenses on the wages they received.[130]

The very buoyancy of the apparel industry in the midst of a sea of economic stagnation and decline intensified rather than alleviated problems faced by its growing workforce. Because 807/A operations were central to its economic-growth strategy the government was unwilling to act in ways that might reduce investor confidence. In the area of employment practices and conditions of work, this necessarily implied that the Seaga regime would, if at all possible, turn a blind eye to apparent abuses of worker rights. This attitude undoubtedly encouraged many Free Zone companies in their anti-union activities, impeding efforts to improve wages, work relations, and conditions of employment.

Other factors also intervened to make unionization of the Free Zone workforce more difficult. The extreme vulnerability of garment workers to redundancy was and still is a key factor. While many wish for workplace representation, they worry that foreign companies will quit the country if they appear too interested in pursuing this option. This view has been encouraged by the Jamaica Manufacturers Association (JMA), whose Economics and Business Development Division manager, Wes Vanriel, called for a sense of "pragmatism and national purpose" to prevail when considering the rights of workers in the context of Free Zone operations. Indeed, in the opinion of Vanriel, inasmuch as the Free Zone system functions "as a 'forcing house' for industrialization – where people are taught the discipline and the rhythm of modern production," the derogation of worker rights it involves cannot but benefit the industrial labour force over the long term. Only when workers accept this version of reality will "cost efficient and competitive production," and thus the industry's capacity to generate further investment and jobs, be assured. That such ideas exert a powerful influence on the attitudes of garment workers, deterring them from unionizing, can be gauged from the fact that by 1986 only 5 per cent of them had been incorporated into the organized labour movement.[131]

(b) Locally Owned Garment Manufacturing
There are approximately 150 garment factories operating in Jamaica. Between 60 and 80 of these are small, locally owned businesses which have traditionally catered to domestic and CARICOM markets. Businesses of this type were squeezed progressively by policies implemented by the Seaga government in the name of export promotion. Most local producers gained no benefit from government-subsidized infrastructure such as that made available to foreign garment manufacturers locating in the Free Zones. And while, in the mid-1980s, public monies and USAID funds were lavished on exporting firms to provide

fiscal incentives, training, technical assistance and a number of other crucial support services, manufacturers supplying local needs were explicitly excluded from the majority of programs.[132]

Because USAID consultants identified the "ideal" 807/A factory as one operating at least 75 machines, businesses employing fewer than 60 production workers benefited least from fiscal and other incentives. According to Hugh Shearer, then Deputy Prime Minister and Minister of Foreign Affairs and Foreign Trade, around half of all garment companies operating in 1986 fell into this category. As the bulk of these were also under Jamaican — as opposed to foreign — ownership, the USAID criteria tended to discriminate both against local entrepreneurs and the types of businesses which earlier had formed the backbone of the country's apparel industry.[133]

Other factors that have forced local garment manufacturers and related industries out of business have been the lack of low-interest, long-term, loan capital available to them and the flooding of local markets with cheap, imported garments and accessories. The shortage of loan capital meant that local manufacturers were unable to invest in plant and equipment to increase productivity and meet import competition. Moreover, because 807/A activities rely on imports of US-made components, accessories, and other inputs, the program has dealt a severe blow to local producers competing in this market. The JTURDC/CUSO study indicates that by 1987 several manufacturers of hangers, zips, boxes, and thread had closed or significantly reduced output, and only two of the seven textile mills previously operating in the country remained in business.[134]

Changes to Free Zone regulations in 1986 did alter the situation for local producers somewhat, expanding opportunities to move into export manufacturing through sub-contracting arrangements. In so doing, firms also became eligible for the various government incentive and support programs designed to promote non-traditional exports. Indications are that local firms have been attempting to reorient their businesses and now depend heavily on the 807/A programs. One such company, Crimson Dawn, included in the JTURDC/CUSO study because it typified locally owned small-garment manufacturing, reported that because of "severe financial restraints" the company had been forced to make this move. By 1987 Crimson Dawn was exporting 40 per cent of output, most of which was destined for the United States under 807/A arrangements, while only 12.5 per cent of total exports went to CARICOM.[135]

The restructuring of much of local industry towards export production has in turn further reduced markets for Jamaican-made fabric, components, and accessories, compounding the problems faced by indigenous manufacturers focussing on local and regional demand. Increasingly these businesses are falling victim to heightened competition from imports as the costs of locally produced inputs escalate. Taken much further, this process will mean the virtual disappearance of the Jamaican fashion industry, an increase in unemployment among skilled and semi-skilled operatives, and a substantial lowering of skill levels in the garments sub-sector.

Besides the loss of an indigenous fashion and apparel industry, the subsumption of domestic manufacturing under export production implies other costs for the Jamaican economy and society. First, the contraction of local garment and linked supplier industries reduces the country's capacity for self-reliance and increases the import bill. Second, because "re-export production" is premised on slack labour markets and the existence of unregulated, low-wage Export Free Zones, any shift in this direction inevitably poses serious problems for Jamaican workers and their class organizations. As research on Jamaica and the Eastern Caribbean has demonstrated, while wages and employment conditions in local industry leave room for much improvement, they nonetheless tend to be better than those offered by multinational companies involved in re-export production.[136] Moreover, because the organizational structure of Free Zone firms is designed to maximize the productivity of labour by minimizing barriers to its use, unionization is viewed as far more problematic than in local industry, as is group decision-making and other forms of worker participation. The shift of local producers towards export manufacturing already evident thus necessarily involves the extension of low wages and sweated labour conditions into the heartland of the local industrial economy.

Finally, while 807 production has been represented as the "star performer" in the Jamaican economy, the benefits of re-export activities to the national economy are far fewer than such an assessment would imply. As both 807/A and CMT operations rely entirely on imported raw materials and other inputs, the value-added locally is restricted to the labour costs involved at the Jamaican end of the production process. Thus 807/A local, value-added production averages 25 per cent, while CMT averages 30-35 per cent; and, in 1987, when 807/A exports totalled $186 million, foreign-exchange earnings were actually far more modest, amounting to less than $56 million.[137]

A progressive lowering of local content in Commonwealth Caribbean re-export production has become increasingly clear since the early 1980s. That this movement represents the dominant trend for internationalized production arrangements in the garment industry became evident in 1986 with the launching of the "Super 807" (807A) program by the Reagan administration. While the JLP government acknowledged a debt of gratitude to the federal government for expanding US access limits for 807/A products, it also conceded that, insofar as CMT production offered greater opportunity to generate employment, enhance local value-added levels, and transfer technology and skills, it was far more advantageous for the Jamaican economy than 807/A operations.[138]

(c) Agriculture

As in the case of the manufacturing industry, changes in national development strategy and in the international economic environment have profoundly influenced developments in the Jamaican agricultural sector. The Seaga government sought to reduce state economic involvement in order to give a wider role to private sector interests. In the agricultural sector this involved the discontinuation of the Land Lease program (instituted by the PNP to make more land accessible to small farmers and the landless), divestment of the government's share in Tate and Lyle Ltd., and a significant reduction of its banana holdings and shipping services, including the closure of the Banana Company of Jamaica (BANCO).[139]

"Agro 21" was regarded as a cornerstone of the JLP privatization strategy. Announced in 1983, the program sought to arrest the growing crisis of agriculture (itself intensified by the deregulation of food imports) by selling off government landholdings to private investors in parcels of 150 to 20 000 acres. Under Agro 21 the government undertook to provide infrastructure, assistance in pre-feasibility analysis, and research on the technologies necessary to develop non-traditional agricultural export crops.[140]

Policy-makers argued that by increasing local private ownership and raising the level of foreign investment in the country the program would not only earn $450 million in foreign exchange during its first four years of operation, but would also ease the problem of rural unemployment by generating almost 40 000 jobs over the same period. In 1983, the value of agricultural output grew by around 8 per cent, much of this attributable to the increase in acreage devoted to non-traditional export crops. Expansion continued in the following year. One agricultural analyst has estimated that domestic crop production rose by 23 per cent in 1984, and non-traditional exports by 38 per cent.[141]

The expansion of 1983-84, however, proved to be only a temporary deviation in the longer-term pattern of agricultural stagnation or decline. Negative growth rates of 3.4 per cent and 2.0 per cent were recorded for 1985 and 1986, and only marginal growth occurred the following year. IDB reports indicate that export crop performance was also mixed. Traditional crops like bananas and coffee registered pronounced production increases towards the end of the period at the same time that exports of sugar, coconuts, and cocoa were recording sharp declines. The performance of non-traditional export crops most favoured under CBI duty-free arrangements was fairly uneven, but generally weak.[142]

Developments in agriculture resulting from restructuring parallel in terms of their class impact experiences in the apparel industry. Measures designed to shift the agricultural economy away from sugar by encouraging crop diversification did not prove equally advantageous to large and small farmers. Government policy was geared overwhelmingly to the promotion of large estate production and did little to assist smaller, marginally efficient farmers to improve quality and yields.

Steven Driever estimates that by April 1986 about one-quarter of the 200 000 acres of land allocated for the program had been sold off, most of it to small producers rather than to large-scale investors as the Seaga regime had intended.[143] In the final instance, however, small farmers gained little from the divestment program. In its first three years of operation, the average land grant of just over 3 acres was not large enough to sustain viable production units over the long term.[144]

During the 1980s, small producers faced even stiffer competition in both domestic and overseas markets. The domestic food sector was affected first, by being undermined when food items flooded into the country in the early 1980s following the removal of import restrictions. Smaller growers producing export crops also found it progressively difficult to stay afloat, given the contraction of overseas markets for certain staple exports such as those resulting from cumulative reductions of US sugar quotas after 1984. Exports of sugar to the American market fell by three-quarters in the 1984-87 period, affecting smaller farmers in addition to the big producers.[145] Unlike the larger estates, which could be diversified with the help of Agro 21 resources, smaller growers were not only deprived of a market outlet, but were offered few opportunities or positive incentives to shift production into non-traditional crops.

One Agro 21 innovation, in particular, was represented by the JLP government as a program of support of the small farming sector. Under this program a small number of modern, highly capitalized "mother farms," owned and run by large local and foreign investors, were established. These were supposed to provide technical assistance, production inputs, and marketing services to many hundreds of smaller "satellite" producers contracted by them to grow winter fruits and vegetables for extra-regional markets. The "mother farm" program was a dismal failure. In the 1984-85 season only about 20 per cent of the produce grown by satellite farms was accepted as export quality. Predictably enough, it was the smaller farmers locked into contracts with the mother farms who sustained the largest losses, as they earned little or no income from their season's efforts.[146]

Developments in the banana industry also proved to be equally harmful to small producers. Restructuring in this subsector is of particular interest, as the types of changes that were implemented to boost banana exports are indicative of those that will likely follow in other branches of agriculture if the export-led growth strategy is maintained. While the reorganization of the industry halted the spectacular decline of the late 1970s and early 1980s, it did so at enormous human cost. As Driever notes, prior to 1980 small farmers accounted for the bulk of Jamaica's banana exports. Since then, services crucial to small farmers were reduced or curtailed, and access to incentive programs, credit facilities, and technical and other support programs were limited mainly to larger investors. As a result, several thousand small local producers have been displaced by large-scale, capital-intensive production units. Today, a handful of growers established largely due to this restructuring process dominate the industry, accounting for most banana exports, while small farmers who have survived have done so by focussing primarily on the local market.[147]

As the export figures attest, although large agricultural units displaced small producers over the 1980s, their contribution to the national export drive has not been impressive.[148] As evidence from the "mother farm" project indicates, the difficulties faced by export-oriented farmers were not simply the result of adverse weather conditions, although this was undoubtedly a factor. Even high-profile projects with official backing collapsed. One of these, a high-technology experimental vegetable farm established in 1982 by the Jamaican government and an Israeli investor, at a cost of $30 million, folded four years later with heavy financial losses. That venture, which was intended to spearhead the country's entry into North American and European winter vegetable markets, foundered when the soil was found to be unsuited to vegetable cultivation.[149]

Even after restructuring, Jamaica is no nearer to dealing with some of the country's most pressing problems. In the area of agricultural policy the priorities for the Jamaican government should be to lower rural unemployment, reduce dependency on food imports, and reverse the massive imbalance in agricultural trade with its primary trading partner, the United States. IDB data indicate a particularly serious situation with regard to food self-sufficiency. Food imports grew much more rapidly in the 1980s than at any time in the previous two decades. Imports of cereals increased most, followed by fruits and vegetables, oil products, and many other major food groups, including sugar and honey. Whereas in the 1961-70 period Jamaica was a net food exporter, by 1986 food imports had shot up to almost double the value of commodity exports.[150]

The situation in terms of the overall balance of agricultural trade with the United States is equally alarming. Despite the reduction of sugar quotas, the Caribbean Basin as a whole ran a surplus in agricultural commodities with the US throughout the 1980s. Jamaica, on the other hand, maintained a substantial annual deficit with that country.[151] Although some headway has been made since 1984, there is little sign that non-traditional export crops have the potential to compensate for the loss of the US sugar cane market, let alone reduce significantly the overall agricultural trade deficit which had existed before sugar quotas were reduced.

Nor, finally, have the agricultural reforms contributed to economic and social development by creating expanded rural employment opportunities. The government's agricultural policies did not attempt to assist small farmers to adapt to heightened market competition, but tried to compensate for the collapse of the sugar industry by encouraging the development of large-scale, capital-intensive production units. The effect of this policy was to hasten the decline of rural communities. While demand for wage labour did increase, this was achieved at the cost of displacing large numbers of marginally efficient farmers. This added to already serious problems of rural unemployment and out-migration.

3.4 Social and Political Effects of Economic Restructuring

Throughout the 1980s Jamaicans experienced the harsh realities of Reaganomics, Caribbean-style. Between Seaga's election victory and March 1986, consumer prices rose by almost 120 per cent. Unemployment also increased sharply, while wages generally stagnated. The rise in living costs affected not only the poorest sections of society, but increasingly, the middle class. It is in the period since 1983, when the effects of the US/IMF stabilization strategy began to bite, that the deterioration in living standards became most dramatic.

After failing the IMF "economic performance" test in March of that year, the Seaga administration instituted a severe economic program of budget cutbacks, government layoffs, tax increases, a rolling currency devaluation, and the elimination of price supports on food and fuel. These undermined educational, health, and other social programs and sent prices spiralling for basic goods and services. In 1984, following a major jump in food prices, the National Consumers' League began expressing its "very grave concern" about the relentless rise in living costs. "The latest increase relating to rice, saltfish and chicken necks and backs," the League argued, "have made rather fragile the already threadbare existence of the poor and needy, the unemployed and the sick, the aged and the forlorn."[152]

Nor did the situation improve in the second half of the 1980s. Despite some growth in the economy after 1986, few benefits trickled down to the impoverished majority. The cuts in government expenditures not only reduced employment opportunities that existed previously in such areas as teaching and nursing; they also further undermined the nation's already hard-pressed educational and health services.[153]

Inevitably, while the middle class also suffered, the cuts hit the most vulnerable sectors of society the hardest. Infant mortality, maternal mortality, and malnutrition are all increasing and, according to one physician working in the nation's capital: "Health services have never been worse in the twentieth century."[154]

The pain caused by the Seaga government's free-market policies and austerity programs was reflected in political developments in Jamaica. Popular resistance to the continual price hikes erupted into violent protests and blockades in the mid-1980s, and a general strike was called by all five major public sector unions. While, in the short term, these expressions of disaffection brought little immediate relief, they did invigorate the PNP, which began to push for the return of a two-party system of government. With the massive defeat of the Seaga regime in the 1989 general election, the Jamaican people rendered their verdict on the JLP's US-inspired economic strategy. That the People's National Party government now in office has not yet heeded the verdict of the electorate is, of course, another matter.

4 Grenada

Grenada is the most southerly of the Windward Islands. Smaller than either Jamaica or Barbados both in size and population, the main island covers 344 square kilometres and has a population of approximately 110 000.[155] The state of Grenada also encompasses the tiny Grenadine Islands extending from Grenada northward to Carriacou and Petit Martinique.

Like many of its Eastern Caribbean neighbours, Grenada is not especially well endowed with natural resources. Its economy is based primarily on export agriculture, with tourism becoming an increasingly significant source of foreign exchange over the last two decades. Within agriculture, cocoa, bananas, and nutmeg are the largest export earners, followed by fresh fruit and vegetables. Industry exists, but despite ongoing efforts by the successive governments and the United States Agency for International Development (USAID) to promote investment in export-oriented manufacturing, this sector accounts for less than 5 per cent of GDP.[156]

In the period since 1979, Grenada has been the proving ground for two alternative and, in some respects, diametrically opposed strategies for development. Under the leadership of the New Jewel Movement (1979-83), an attempt was made to develop a mixed economy based loosely on principles of socialism but receptive to the presence of private capital in all sectors of the economy.[157]

The United States' invasion of Grenada in 1983, ostensibly on a mission to rescue American nationals studying on the island, was the catalyst for a process of systematic dismantling of the political and economic structures put in place by the New Jewel Movement (NJM) in the preceding years. In place of these a model for national development was installed which more closely reflected the regional interests of the United States.

A comparison of the results of these two approaches to development is instructive, particularly in light of the comprehensive way in which the United States has attempted to define the development agenda in countries of the Caribbean under the auspices of the Caribbean Basin Initiative.

In order to make sense of such a comparison and to arrive at some conclusions with respect to the economic, political, and social implications for the future, it is necessary to examine briefly the development of Grenada between 1945 and the overthrow of the Gairy government in 1979.

4.1 Post-war Economic Development

Grenada remained a British colony until 1974, when it was granted full independence. The period between 1945 and independence was characterized by an essentially stagnant economy. Based on plantation and peasant agriculture for centuries, first in sugar cane then in cocoa, nutmeg, and mace, the economy remained virtually unchanged in this respect until the late 1970s. The only major economic developments throughout this period were the introduction of bananas in the 1950s and the emergence of a tourism industry in the following decade.

The installation of Eric Gairy as the head of the newly independent Grenada by no means indicated the likelihood of progress in the future. The chief elected official of Grenada for a total of 13 years prior to 1974, Gairy had risen to prominence as leader of the Grenada Manual and Metal Workers Union (GMMWU) and had been at the forefront of an islandwide rebellion of agricultural workers in 1951. Once in office Gairy repudiated his allegiance to workers and peasants, shifting his political allegiance to a minority fraction of black capitalists within the dominant class.[158]

By the time the island became independent, much of the popular support Gairy had enjoyed in the early post-war period had long since disappeared; and he had developed a reputation for financial misman-agement, corruption, and repression noteworthy even in a regional context which included the Duvalier regime.[159]

Although a number of estates and hotels were taken over by Gairy, this move was in no way intended to contribute to a process of prop-erty socialization. Some confiscated land was subdivided and parcelled out to private individuals as payment for political support. The remain-der was retained, but much was left to fall into a state of neglect.[160] No action was taken to remove structural obstacles to economic develop-ment or to encourage productive activity. Rather, by reducing the amount of land under cultivation, starving small producers of loan cap-ital, allowing infrastructure to fall into disrepair, obstructing the emer-gence of an independent labour movement, and pursuing a generally corrupt form of economic management, Gairy strengthened barriers to progress. Real GDP fell significantly during the 1970s. Agricultural exports declined, while other sectors, such as industry and construc-tion, experienced stagnation. By 1979 tourism and government serv-ices were the only growth areas, and the country's economy and infra-structural systems were on the verge of collapse.[161]

The agricultural sector was particularly incapable of expanding out-put. According to one report, before the revolution 49 per cent of all arable land was owned by 93 farms, much of this prime arable land which was left uncultivated. Of the remainder, 23 per cent (mainly poorer land on mountainous terrain) had been divided and subdivided into tiny lots worked by 14 000 subsistence and semi-subsistence producers.[162]

Given the difficulties under which they laboured, peasant farmers still managed a significant contribution to export production. Amburs-ley estimates that proprietors with holdings of less than five acres pro-duced 93 per cent of sugar cane, 63 per cent of nutmeg, 50 per cent of cocoa, and 30 per cent of bananas exported by the country. In addi-tion, they produced all but 15 per cent of locally produced food sold on the island.[163] Even so, the shortfall in the country's food requirements was both massive and rising. To maintain domestic supplies Grenada had to import three-quarters of the island's food needs — a shocking statistic for an economy based largely on peasant and estate agricul-ture, particularly when it is considered that more than half of the avail-able arable land lay idle.[164]

The manufacturing sector grew slightly during the 1960s, but out-put remained stagnant at below 4 per cent of GDP throughout the next decade. What little dynamism there was in this and related sectors, such as construction, can be attributed to the development of tourism and the service sector generally. By the end of the 1970s tourism and service activities were the only bright spots on the economic map.

Together they contributed about 20 per cent of GDP on average during the 1970s.[165]

In view of the political and economic context, it is not surprising that the living and working conditions of the majority of the Grenadian population deteriorated in the 1960s and 1970s. Unemployment increased throughout the period, particularly among youth and women; by 1979 it had reached almost 50 per cent.[166] Those with work, however, fared little better than the unemployed. In the 10 years ending 1975 the cost of food increased by an estimated 200 per cent, housing by 135 per cent, and clothing by 164 per cent. Agricultural wages on the other hand rose much more slowly, increasing by only 100 per cent in the 20 years ending 1975.[167]

What medical and educational services were available had also been starved of funds and were breaking down. Health care suffered from a major shortage of medical staff, and the few clinics that existed were poorly equipped and in a state of general disrepair. As a consequence of these difficulties medical services were not only scarce and costly but also of inferior quality. Education, too, deteriorated under Gairy. Teachers were largely untrained, and secondary education became the domain of children of the economic elite. Access to subsidized higher education was also curtailed because the government discontinued payments to the regional university system, the University of the West Indies.[168]

In the face of a collapsing economy and growing social unrest the regime maintained its ascendancy by increasingly resorting to bribery and ballot-rigging. It also unleashed the army and the Mongoose Gang, a paramilitary force which operated in much the same fashion as the Tonton Macoute in Haiti.[169] Gairy meantime focussed less on the economic crisis and more on his obsessions with the occult, mysticism, and UFOs.

Maurice Bishop was at the forefront of political opposition to the ruling regime from 1970, when he returned to Grenada from abroad, until the coup of March 1979. Progressives focussed much of their organizational efforts on that constituency which formed Gairy's base of political support: agricultural workers, peasants, and the small, urban working class. The year 1970 marked another milestone in the political disintegration of the Gairy regime. With the passing of the Emergency Powers Act in that year, rights of movement and assembly were restricted, police powers expanded, and a new era of heightened repression begun that continued throughout the remainder of Gairy's period in government.[170]

The New Jewel Movement became a key actor in the struggle against Gairyism. The NJM was formed in early 1973 by the merging of the Movement for the Assemblies of the People (MAP), co-founded by Bishop and Kenrick Radix, and the Joint Endeavour for Welfare, Education and Liberation (JEWEL) which had been started by Unison Whitemen. As state violence mounted against members of the NJM in late 1973 and early 1974, the party began to occupy the political terrain which Gairy himself had monopolized two decades earlier.[171]

Two factors influenced the development of the NJM after 1973: political repression at home and revolutionary struggles abroad. The NJM leadership, during this period, transformed the party's organizational structure and *modus operandi*. Political activities shifted beyond the electoral sphere, and the party developed a Leninist cell structure and an overtly Marxist orientation.[172]

4.2 Economic and Social Policies in Revolutionary Grenada

The overthrow of the Gairy regime did not occur until some five years later. Throughout the intervening period, however, organizers widened substantially the NJM's base of support in both urban and rural areas and made inroads into the state's security forces.[173] In the countryside, the GMMWU's popular base was undermined, while NJM members gained policy positions in several urban trade unions. By the time the New Jewel Movement gained power, although it had less than 50 full members, the party had sympathizers within the security forces and had won overwhelming popular support.[174]

Notwithstanding the persistence of formidable obstacles to economic development and social prosperity, the progress of the People's Revolutionary Government (PRG) towards these goals was impressive by any standard. In the period between March 1979 and the US intervention in October 1983, the economy registered considerable economic growth. This stood as an achievement in marked contrast to the records of Jamaica and Barbados (and most other economies in the region) which, in the same period, were following the private sector-led, export-oriented development prescriptions offered by the US government and multilateral financial institutions like the International Monetary Fund (IMF) and the World Bank.[175]

Grenada's economic performance was all the more remarkable in that it took place amidst an international economic recession and in the face of concerted efforts by the Reagan administration to destabilize the Grenadian economy and derail the People's Revolutionary Government.[176]

4.2.1 Economic Strategy

Grenada, in this four-year period, struggled to integrate not only public and private enterprise, but also domestic and external economic policy in a sympathetic and mutually reinforcing fashion. The PRG's development strategy sought to create a mixed economy in which the public sector took a leading role.[177] The economic program was intended to increase foreign-exchange earnings by diversifying the country's commodity exports and markets and developing its tourism industry. Of equal or greater significance, however, were the imposition of punitive duties on many extra-regional imports, the establishment of a state trading corporation which challenged the monopoly of existing import-export houses, and state-sponsored agro-industrial projects designed to promote self-sufficiency in food production by developing processing, preserving, and canning facilities for fruit, vegetables, and fish.[178]

The PRG inherited from the Gairy government a national debt of $57 million and a deficit of $1.3 million.[179] Eighteen months after the installation of the revolutionary government observers were reporting significant progress towards the regime's economic and social objectives. More than 1 000 jobs had been created, roads, sanitation, and water supplies had been improved, and construction had begun on a new international airport at Point Salines to facilitate the development of the tourism industry.[180]

Through its "Idle Lands for Idle Hands" program the PRG simultaneously expanded the amount of land under cultivation and attacked the country's massive unemployment problem. Several plantations were added to the 25 state farms inherited from the previous regime, and legislation enacted to allow for compulsory leasing of idle lands. As well as improving the sector's productivity, land reform had the added benefit of furthering another key revolutionary objective — the erosion of the economic ascendance of the planter class.[181]

As well as expanding the area of cultivated land, the government's program sought to attract people to agriculture by developing and expanding the co-operative sub-sector. To implement this policy the government founded a National Co-operative Development Agency (NACDA) to undertake feasibility studies, negotiate land purchases, train co-operators, and to provide loan capital, technical and marketing assistance.[182]

Another aspect of PRG agricultural policy focussed on barriers to increased production in the private, small- and medium-farm sector. Credit facilities were provided by the Grenada Development Bank (GDB) to enable small producers to buy basic inputs and tools and improve access roads. A farm school was opened offering training in modern farming techniques, and a Marketing and National Importing Board (MNIB) created with responsibility for expanding agricultural exports. By providing farmers with an alternative outlet for their crops, the MNIB also made it possible for them to bypass private trading houses which had previously monopolized the export trade.[183]

These programs were not entirely successful in meeting PRG objectives. At the time of the invasion, although a few state farms were showing profits, the sector was still losing money overall. Co-operative enterprises were also still encountering difficulties. A major constraint was the social stigma attached to agricultural labour which deterred many young people from choosing farming as an occupation. The inability of newly formed co-operatives to pay high wages did not improve the situation. Similarly, in the private sector small farmers continued to confront serious problems. Peasant incomes were stagnating and in some cases even falling due to praedial larceny and declining international prices for traditional agro-exports.[184]

Despite these setbacks the PRG's structural reforms, infrastructural programs, and support networks were promoting agricultural efficiency and national self-reliance. Training programs were improving husbandry methods; projects to diversify livestock production and develop domestic sources of animal feeds were lessening the island's dependence on food imports; road construction projects were expanding marketing opportunities by opening up previously inaccessible areas of the countryside; and, while still fairly primitive, the quality of state farm management was improving so that only two years into the revolutionary period, several were able to implement profit-sharing schemes for workers.[185]

International trade data make it clear that Grenada also made significant progress in expanding agricultural exports. The single exception to this was bananas, which registered a decline in the volume of exports in each year 1980-83. Exports of cocoa, nutmeg, and mace all rose dramatically between 1980 and 1983.[186]

However, these gains were not reflected in higher foreign-exchange earnings. Prices for Grenada's traditional agricultural exports fell sharply throughout the NJM's period in office. Between 1979 and 1980 the PRG estimated that the decline was 22 per cent. By 1983, despite the fact that cocoa exports had grown by almost 50 per cent, they were worth less than half the amount earned in 1980 (falling from $8.6 million to $4.1 million). Nutmeg growers increased output by a similarly impressive amount, only to find their earnings falling even more steeply.[187]

While such developments depressed farm incomes and the economy, they also spurred efforts to improve the country's trade balance by diversifying markets for traditional and non-traditional products and by developing domestic agricultural production and local value-adding industries. Major strides were made in all these areas. New trade relations were established with both socialist and non-socialist economies. And, whereas in 1979 between 94 and 97 per cent of commodity exports comprised traditional products, by 1983 the figure was nearer to 70 per cent.[188]

Grenada's progress in the area of export diversification was based largely on fresh fruits and vegetables and to a lesser extent on higher value-added products such as processed foods, flour, and garments. Exports of fresh fruit and vegetables rose by 40 per cent between 1980-81 and by a further 220 per cent in the following year. Agro-industrial products also appear to have found ready markets. According to the Caribbean Development Bank, the True Blue agro-industrial plant (which manufactured jams, jellies, nectars, and preserves for both domestic and overseas markets) had begun to make a contribution to export earnings in 1981, its first year of full operation, enabling the factory to generate a small profit in that year.[189]

Market diversification was another area in which the regime was moving ahead. One notable development was a five-year trade deal with the Soviet Union which guaranteed producers relatively stable prices for part of their nutmeg and cocoa crops.[190] Progress was also made in promoting intra-regional exports. Grenada increased its sales of garments, agricultural products, and fish to CARICOM countries. Before the revolution there was no fishing industry on the island, and most of its salt fish imports were supplied by Canada. Three years into it, Grenada had not only begun to develop a deep sea fleet to supply its own needs but was also exporting fish to neighbouring islands.[191]

Policies were also implemented that were intended gradually to disengage the Grenadian economy from "the world system of imperialism" and to promote national self-reliance.[192] Duties were imposed on imported fruit, jams, soft drinks, and clothing of non-CARICOM origin in order to protect the national and regional economies from import competition. Consumers were, however, protected from rising living costs by government-imposed price controls on many items.[193] Private companies were also given incentives to shift activities into priority areas of the economy. The government enacted an investment code offering attractive tax concessions to foreign investors establishing manufacturing facilities in Grenada, and existing businesses engaged in productive areas of the economy were rewarded by a 15 per cent tax reduction.[194]

Viewed as a whole, government policy was largely successful in stimulating productive activity in both public and private sectors of the Grenadian economy. Notwithstanding the deleterious impact of international recession, the economy experienced several years of sustained expansion, recording one of the highest national growth rates in the region in the early 1980s. The average annual rates of expansion in GDP during the 1980-83 period was 3.7 per cent—much better than either Jamaica or Barbados, at 1.5 per cent and –1.2 per cent, respectively.[195] Double-digit inflation was also reduced to manageable proportions, and unemployment had been lowered to 14 per cent from a pre-revolutionary level of almost 50 per cent.[196]

4.2.2 Social Policy

The success of the NJM in so quickly effecting a turnaround in the Grenadian economy was based to a large extent on the popularity of its social and political agendas. Indeed, if political and social programs facilitating the establishment of, say, co-operative ventures and small-scale agriculture, had not been implemented, there is little doubt that many of the economic reforms would have been stillborn.

This is based in part on the material effect of PRG social programs on the daily lives of Grenadians. Under the Gairy regime education and health care had been perhaps the lowest of government priorities. In 1978, the year before the revolution, there were only 23 doctors in the country. After 1980 public expenditures on health care were second only to those on education. The arrival of Cuban volunteers at the time of the revolution doubled the numbers of doctors in Grenada. A system of regional medical facilities was created, with medical clinics in every parish and smaller medical stations dispersed throughout less accessible areas of the island. Most importantly, public medical and dental care was available free of charge. At the clinics and stations, a systematic program of health education was put in place with the objective of making preventive medicine part of the daily lives of Grenadians.[197]

Under Gairy, students entering the education system had an 86 per cent chance of dropping out before they reached the secondary level.[198] A curriculum based on the British colonial model of education — itself a bastardized version of the British educational system — had little to say to young Grenadians and unemployed or underemployed agricultural labourers.

The PRG made education its highest priority in social spending. A Centre of Popular Education was created to address the problem of adult illiteracy. Primary and secondary curricula were revamped. Education was made available for a nominal fee on a universal basis at the primary school level, and free for secondary students. The development of an "in-service" teacher program combining formal and on-the-job training was begun in 1981. Within 18 months this program was employed as a model for educational outreach programs in other countries of the region.[199] In addition to making training available to over 600 teachers in an effort to enhance skill levels, the government made good on national payments to the regional university system, thus making education accessible from elementary to post-secondary levels.[200]

In addition to health and educational reforms, a number of other social programs were put into effect. These included free milk and lunches for school children, a national public transportation system, cheap loans for home improvements, rent review procedures to control rent increases, compulsory recognition of trade unions, paid maternity leave for women workers, and the exemption of significant sections of the population from income tax.[201] In line with revolutionary objectives, the reforms benefited the poorer sectors of society most directly, demonstrating in material ways the government's commitment to combine economic development with progressive social change.

4.2.3   Politics

The leitmotif of much of the period of economic and social progress was a system of political organization which was at best contradictory and at worst proved to be the Achilles heel of the revolution. Throughout the country mass organizations of workers, farmers, women, and youth had begun to participate in the shaping of government priorities and policies. A number of writers observing the revolution at first hand have remarked on the dignity and confidence instilled in Grenadians as a result of these progressive initiatives.[202]

At the same time, the participatory nature of the relationship established between the party and mass organizations, co-ops, trade unions, and parish and zonal councils has been seriously questioned.[203] Colin Henfrey points out that the tendency to vanguardism, along with what often appeared to be a deliberate baiting of the Reagan administration on issues which were of little immediate importance to the PRG (combined, in turn, with US efforts to destabilize the country), corroded the government's commitment to participatory democracy, strengthened authoritarian tendencies, and left the party centralized and insulated from the mass movements.[204]

In general, these observations appear to be true. In a sense, the participatory democracy experienced at the grass-roots level developed in such a way and at such a rate that, given the charged political atmosphere created by US destabilization activities, the party could not effectively accommodate itself to these changes. Instead of attempting to work through the problems of incorporating mass organizations more fully into the political process, the party Central Committee attempted to control and direct the democratic impulses rather than to be guided by them.[205]

4.3   Economic Development in Post-revolutionary Grenada

American troops landed on Grenada on October 25, 1983, only days after the *putsch* led by Deputy Prime Minister Bernard Coard had provided an opening for US aggression. More than 6 000 military personnel were involved in the logistics and actual invasion of a country roughly the size of the Islands of St. Pierre and Miquelon. The US invasion and occupation of Grenada lasted seven months, during which time a paramilitary Special Service Unit was created to maintain social order and political stability after the last of the occupation forces had left.[206] The defeat and incarceration of the surviving PRG leadership was the prelude to the installation of a non-elected government, the composition of which had been decided upon prior to the US intervention. The interim government administered the island until elections were held in December 1984, at which time political control passed to a coalition government headed by Herbert Blaize.

In the period immediately following the invasion, US officials sought to minimize the impressive economic and social advances achieved during the revolutionary period and to cast Grenada as a showcase for the private sector-led, export-oriented development model supported by the Reagan administration. After four years of tightening the screws, US aid began to flow into the country, and positive predictions were made by Washington about its economic future. Arriving on the island as head of the newly installed USAID mission, Edward Morse fuelled popular expectations by describing US policy on Grenada in particularly extravagant terms:

> The United States has made a major political investment. If the government of Grenada can stand up to totalitarianism and say, "So far, no farther," then that gives great confidence. Investors want elections, security, infrastructure. We will give all three.[207]

The post-revolutionary era thus began optimistically, with the resumption of official American assistance to the country and its elevation to the status of a CBI beneficiary. Between October 1983 and January 1986 the United States committed $73 million in economic aid to the island, channelled through USAID. By 1988 that figure was around $100 million.[208] In return for continued US financial support, the interim government agreed to restructure the economy along lines "recommended" by USAID.[209]

The American plan proposed sweeping changes to national development policy, changes that reflected the Reagan administration's desire for a more market-oriented economy based on export promotion. Its key proposals emphasized:

1. Privatization of state-owned enterprises (including marketing services provided by the Marketing and National Importing Board).
2. Promotion of private investment, locally and from abroad.
3. Return to a free market economy (through a gradual reduction of import duties and price controls).
4. Direct financial support for infrastructural development and for export-oriented private enterprise.

5. Development of a union movement based on the American Institute for Free Labor Development (AIFLD) model.
6. Fiscal (budgetary and tax) reform, intended to reduce government expenditure and improve the environment for private sector initiatives by shifting the burden of taxation to consumers through a Value Added Tax system.[210]

Whatever reservations the interim government might have harboured regarding the likely economic and social impact of the US development strategy, it immediately proceeded to restructure the economy precisely on the lines indicated by USAID advisors.

In some respects the initiation of the US-sponsored restructuring program served to buoy the economy and maintain popular optimism about the country's longer-term development prospects. US-funded construction (and reconstruction) projects and infrastructural programs such as the rebuilding of the psychiatric hospital destroyed during the invasion and the completion of the international airport at Point Salines eased the problem of rising unemployment, if only temporarily. A series of high-profile investment missions, co-sponsored by the US government and the newly formed Grenadian Industrial Development Corporation (IDC), brought droves of US business executives to the island to assess investment opportunities in the tourism, industrial, and agricultural sectors.[211] By mid-1985 the IDC had already processed 33 applications for investment incentives from both foreign and local companies, and two small manufacturing plants had been established, employing a total of 112 people.[212]

By late 1985, however, the problems and limitations inherent in the US development strategy were already becoming obvious. Disenchantment was widespread and was not confined to those sectors of society which had derived the greatest benefit from PRG structural reforms, but included members of the ruling coalition and the island's business community.[213]

Protests erupted early the next year with the announcement of the February 1986 budget (itself a further outcome of the "policy dialogue" associated with USAID Economic Support Fund grants). The budget abolished taxes on personal income (which had previously applied only to high-income earners) and replaced them with a tax on unused land and a Value Added Tax (VAT) system, which imposed a 20 per cent purchase tax on consumption goods.[214] Since taxes on personal income had applied previously only to the rich, the poor were the worst affected by the budgetary reforms, while the wealthy were its primary beneficiaries. After the budget, people had to pay VAT every time they purchased all but a few unprocessed foods.

The money saved by wealthy families, however, appears not to have been channelled into productive investment as US advisors had argued would occur. According to one observer, the most noticeable result of the tax reforms was the rash of new imported cars (most of them Japanese) which appeared on the streets in the months after the budget.[215] In addition to the poorer consumers, manufacturers supplying the domestic market were affected adversely by the changes. Mainly in response to protests by this group, the government reduced the VAT charged on certain locally produced items.[216]

The government, too, found itself increasingly beset by acute financial and political difficulties as a consequence of its tax reforms. Loss of revenue — resulting from income tax reductions in the February budget, together with the VAT changes demanded by the local business lobby — was substantial. The government's financial problems were, moreover, compounded by its inability to collect a number of the taxes imposed in the budget. These problems resulted in a rising fiscal deficit and, by the following year, in a political crisis involving resignations by prominent members of the ruling coalition.[217]

Joblessness had been rising steadily since the time of the invasion. Much of that increase was also attributable to the structural reforms implemented by the Blaize regime as part of the *quid pro quo* for continued US economic assistance. The shedding of labour from the state sector, which began in earnest in 1987 with the disappearance of approximately one-quarter of the island's 7 000 public service jobs, caused major social dislocation. The adverse economic and social effects of the redundancies were exacerbated by the inability of the private sector to absorb even a fraction of those put out of work.[218] Although official figures suggest an unemployment rate of between 30 and 35 per cent from mid-1984, unofficial estimates put the real figure at nearer 60 per cent. More recent data do not suggest that the private sector is proving any more capable of generating employment than it was in the early post-invasion period.[219] The reasons for this become clear when developments in international trade and sectoral development are examined.

4.3.1 Trade with the United States

From the outset, and with US troops still present on the island, Grenada's economic future was bound to a new trade relationship with the United States economy. According to USAID advisers, stronger bilateral ties would lead to a secure and prosperous future for the Grenadian economy.

If in fact this really was the intention, one can only say that US foreign policy in this respect was a failure from the perspective of the majority of Grenadians. American policy-makers made maximum mileage from the fact that Grenada's exports to the United States more than tripled in the year after the invasion, rising from $211 000 to $766 000.[220] While this leap was substantial, it might well have been predicted, given Washington's desire to demonstrate the superiority of its own free market approach to national economic development in comparison to the "statist" strategy adopted by the PRG.[221]

When total earnings from exports are considered, however, the picture is far more gloomy than the US Commerce Department data would suggest. Overall, foreign-exchange earnings from commodity exports declined by nearly 10 per cent in the year following the US intervention. In spite of the damaging effects of the international recession, Grenada's export earnings had risen by 8.7 per cent between 1980 and 1983, from EC$47 million to EC$51.1 million. In 1984 earnings dropped to EC$46.2 million – almost EC$1 million below the 1980 figure. Even more ominous, both traditional and non-traditional merchandise exports suffered declines of similar magnitudes.[222]

If anything, non-traditional products (which had been identified by US economic planners as the main springboards for export-led growth) fared slightly worse than traditional goods, falling by 14 per cent and 13 per cent, respectively. Moreover, within the non-traditional goods area, only fresh fruit indicated any real potential. Even so, at 7 per cent the growth of fresh fruit exports was hardly impressive compared with the massive gains made in earlier years. All other major categories of non-traditional goods exports (clothing, flour, furniture, and wheat bran) had a disastrous year. Declines of between 42 per cent and 99 per cent were recorded, due principally to the disintegration of regional trade relationships during this period.[223]

Even when the island's trade situation is placed in the context of long-term bilateral relations between the United States and a number of other countries in the region, it must be concluded that the gains made by Grenada by the end of the CBI's first year of operation in that country were modest. Despite receiving by far the highest per capita US aid allocation of all CBI-eligible countries, the increase in commodity exports to the United States in the four years ending December 1984 was still impressive when viewed in the context of such neighbouring islands as Barbados and Montserrat. By December 1984, the value of Grenada's commodity exports to the US had risen 110 per cent above that achieved during the revolutionary period four years earlier, compared with increases of 213 per cent and 284 per cent accomplished by Barbados and Montserrat, respectively.[224]

Trade data for the period ending in 1987 show a gradual increase in the country's export earnings, particularly those accruing from traditional agricultural crops. While improvements in agronomic practices may have accounted for some of this increase, much of it was attributable to the fact that international prices for nutmeg, mace, bananas, and other primary commodities were higher than in previous years.[225] This improvement in the country's export position was not, however, reflected in healthier annual trade balances. The cost of food, construction, and raw material imports was also rising rapidly throughout the post-invasion period, resulting in growing annual trade deficits.[226]

4.3.2   Sectoral Development

(a) Manufacturing

It was the manufacturing sector that was intended to be the keystone in the process of economic restructuring in Grenada in the post-invasion period. To this extent its success or failure in securing an economy based on export growth is a measure of the success or failure of the overall US economic agenda for the island.[227]

As indicated above, under the People's Revolutionary Government, manufacturing industries had been established with a certain degree of success. By increasing Grenada's involvement in value-adding activities (such as garment and furniture manufacturing, flour milling, and food processing) the government sought to build upon the economy's existing strengths. During this period these industries flourished by expanding both domestic and regional sales.[228] So it is not as though healthy manufacturing industries did not exist in Grenada prior to 1983. Rather, it was the *kind* of activity that was questioned by the United States, and the social basis which underlay it.

The post-revolutionary era in Grenada is also the CBI era. Throughout the Caribbean, US economic policy was hastening the disintegration of long-standing regional trade relationships and establishing in their place bilateral arrangements between the United States and countries in the region. In Grenada, the breakdown of regional trade alliances spelled the quick and untimely end of both the garment and furniture industries. Prior to that point, these industries had been expanding rapidly on the basis of local sales and exports to neighbouring countries.[229] Instead, the face of the Grenadian economy was to be turned outside the region. The creation of low value-adding re-export industries, based primarily on foreign capital and with products targetted to US and European markets, was the model envisaged by American planners.[230]

Experts in export promotion were hired to market the island as an investment site. The US consulting firm Coopers and Lybrand opened an office in the Grenadian capital and began developing an international publicity campaign to entice labour-intensive industries, and segments of industries, out of the United States and the Far East and into Grenada. Understandably, the company highlighted the availability of cheap ($4.50 per day), literate, female labour in its advertising.[231]

Given the objectives of US industrial policy for Grenada, obstructing the re-emergence of strong, independent trade unions was clearly an issue of vital importance. To reduce this danger US occupation forces harassed and jailed labour leaders, and the AIFLD was mobilized to restructure the Grenadian labour movement and "reorient and train" its leadership along appropriate lines.[232]

Efforts to attract foreign export industries met with some initial success. The Ingle Toy Company of New Jersey, persuaded by a $450 000 Overseas Private Investment Corporation (OPIC) loan, set up shop in Grenada in 1984. A few more US companies followed, producing a variety of export goods from pharmaceutical and surgical supplies to prefabricated housing panels and packaged spices. Some, like Smith Beckman Inc., involved production-sharing operations linking Grenada with plants in Puerto Rico.[233] Other potential investors included MacGregor Sporting Goods, Control Data, and Agro-Tech International.[234] Finally, a handful of US garment manufacturers indicated interest in the island, which was known to possess excess capacity due to the collapse of the regional apparel market. One US investor entered into a sub-contracting arrangement with a local manufacturer which had previously been supplying local and regional markets. The local firm switched to lower value-added activities assembling garments from imported fabric. The clothing was then re-exported to the United States under TSUS 807.[235]

Perhaps spurred on by the initial show of enthusiasm, new incentives to foreign and local investors were announced in late 1984. These included significant improvements to the existing investment incentives program and streamlining of the approval system, USAID-subsidized financing for "enclave" industries, reduced stamp duties on imports, upgrading of access roads and industrial infrastructure, the construction of factory space, and planning for the development of an industrial park.[236]

After the first blush of success in 1984, events quickly began to turn sour for the US-inspired industrial development plan. The little investment that actually materialized in the early post-invasion period was not sufficient to absorb an unemployed workforce that by 1985 exceeded 35 per cent of the adult population. Even with an amount of United States aid in the hemisphere second only to El Salvador, the manufacturing sector was sliding into a recession, while the Grenadian economy as a whole was stagnant.[237]

Notwithstanding the lacklustre effects of CBI policies in stimulating productive investment and extra-regional trade, and the emergence of acute fiscal and political difficulties associated with the US-sponsored development program, the New National Party government continued to rely on both the CBI and US financial assistance to revitalize the nation's flagging economy.[238] This was to little or no avail. By 1985, not only were new investors not coming, the original ones were not staying. Ingle Toys, post-revolutionary Grenada's first, and much-lauded, overseas investor, shut down within a year of opening and was later to be prosecuted for defrauding the US government of $350 000. Of the garment firms that were part of the initial wave of investment, five had closed by the end of the year.[239]

Manufacturing output and employment both declined throughout this period. According to *Caribbean Contact*, industrial employment had dropped by 900 people at the end of 1985. And despite the Reagan administration's attempt in early 1986 to bolster interest in garment and twin-plant manufacturing, indications are that export processing industries still did not locate in Grenada in sufficient numbers to reduce unemployment.[240] The Caribbean Development Bank reports that while output rose subsequently, the performances of individual manufacturing sub-sectors were very uneven. The bank argued that soft drinks, flour, and animal feeds (all developed in the NJM era) were the only industries to have expanded production to any appreciable extent during this period.[241]

(b) Agriculture
Under both the PRG and the Blaize governments, agriculture continued as the single most important sector of the Grenadian economy. While each of these regimes envisaged an entirely different role for agriculture in the development of the national economy, each recognized its primacy at least over the short and medium terms. In 1987 agriculture contributed 25 per cent of GDP, 40 per cent of total export earnings, and employed half of the labour force.[242]

Before October 1983, the priority of agricultural policy was the lowering of unemployment levels and the development of national and regional self-reliance in basic foodcrop production. The strategy thus involved land reform and crop diversification measures which resulted in an expansion of the acreage devoted to basic foodstuffs like yams, sweet potatoes, tannias, and cabbages.[243] While traditional export crops continued as the key source of foreign-exchange earnings, the PRG's reform measures were designed to wean the economy from dependence on these commodities because of their sensitivity to price fluctuations on international markets. By the end of the revolutionary period the strategy had raised the level of food self-sufficiency and had reduced unemployment tremendously in the agricultural sector relative to what it had been in 1979.

After the US invasion of the island, agricultural policy changed fundamentally. In agriculture, as in all other sectors of the economy, the

driving principle of new policy was a private sector, market orientation. Agricultural diversification continued to be an important component of this strategy, but it was a diversification unrelated to that exer-
cised under the PRG. Again, under the guidance of USAID advisors,
and with policy prescriptions often written directly into terms of agreement for economic assistance between USAID and the Grenadian government, the main emphasis was on the production of cash crops for
extra-regional markets.[244]

The policy included both traditional exports — bananas, cocoa, and
nutmeg — and new crops such as exotic fruit, flowers, and winter vegetables. All of these were destined for markets in North America and the
European Economic Community. Sales of these products were supposed to finance an increasing import bill for food items and consumer
goods. Given the linkage of US economic assistance to the country's
export trade, it was also envisaged that Grenada's import requirements
would be purchased increasingly from United States producers.[245]

As the centrepiece of the new agricultural policy, the Grenada
Model Farms Project (GMFP) epitomized the contrast with the PRG
approach to the economy. In 1987 the government began divesting
public lands in an effort to transfer control of agricultural activity back
to the private sector. When completed, this process was to involve the
sub-division of 24 estates, totalling 3 400 acres, into small land parcels
to be settled by private farmers on the basis of lease-purchase agreements.[246] In the initial phase the government hoped to establish up to
200 farms on about half of the available land. To expedite the project,
Washington funded the development and implementation of all infrastructural requirements of the private landholders selected to participate in the program, including surveys, access roads, seeding, training
in new techniques, irrigation, and drainage.[247]

The program had a major, and for the most part, detrimental
impact on the rural labour force. Because very few of those employed
in the state farm sector qualified for the GMFP, being either ineligible
for bank financing or too old (i.e., over 40), the selection process
resulted in a large increase in rural unemployment.[248] Inevitably, in
view of the private sector orientation of the program, the needs of
workers displaced by the GMFP but unable to qualify for lease-purchase arrangements were forgotten in the process. Virtually all were
older and many near retirement and thus unlikely to find similar work.
They were offered neither compensation nor training for alternative
occupations.

Farm workers also suffered in the post-revolutionary period as a
consequence of concerted, and successful, efforts to close the co-operative
farms that were established by the PRG. This policy involved both direct

methods (in which troops were used to intimidate workers and prevent them from continuing in their jobs) and indirect methods, which starved co-operative enterprises of cash and credit. Since some of these co-ops produced goods for the local market, these policies also depressed domestic food production and hence consumption levels generally.[249]

Perhaps some justification for the social dislocation caused by this restructuring could be found if the agricultural sector showed any sign of meeting expectations. It did not. It is fair to say that the successes of the agricultural sector have more to do with external factors such as the movement of international commodity prices than with the reforms themselves. In the year after the invasion, output from two of the country's four most important agricultural export earners, cocoa and bananas, fell by 10 per cent and 22 per cent, respectively. Many non-traditional food crops also made a poor showing, with production stagnating or declining during 1984.[250]

Subsequently, the international trade environment for export crops such as those produced in Grenada experienced significant improvement. After 1983 the Western economies enjoyed a long period of sustained economic growth. While the effects of this were not reflected immediately in international commodity markets, their impact soon began being felt in Grenada. The year 1985 was the first year in the 1980s that all four of the country's leading agricultural exports — from which the agricultural sector derives three-quarters of its foreign-exchange earnings — experienced a rising trend in international prices.[251]

After three years of reforms intended to revitalize agriculture, and millions of US dollars devoted to the removal of structural obstacles to private sector development, Caribbean observers were still identifying problems in this area. According to the Caribbean Development Bank, by the end of 1986 the "difficulties facing the agricultural sector such as poor marketing facilities, poor harvesting practices and inadequate extension services [had still been] only partially reversed."[252] In view of this it was fortunate that the lacklustre performance of the country's principal export crops continued to be disguised by the general upturn of international prices.

After 1986 neither productivity nor overall production levels improved to any appreciable extent. In 1987 total output grew only marginally, and production of nutmeg, Grenada's leading commodity export, actually declined. Once again, however, the crop attracted much higher prices than hitherto. Even with the fall in output, nutmeg sales earned the Grenadian economy $14.6 million, almost $5 million more than in 1986.[253]

Other export crops registered increases in output, but in all cases the expansion was slight. Cocoa producers were experiencing growing difficulties during this period, since many of Grenada's stock of trees were aging and required replacement. A cocoa rehabilitation program had in fact already begun prior to the invasion. With the help of Canadian government funding, extension services were provided to smaller growers to improve farming practices in the industry, and hundreds of new trees were planted to produce the high-priced, quality beans much favoured by European chocolate makers.[254] After 1983, however, the project was undermined by government policy. In line with its US-inspired strategy of reducing the state's role in the economy, it attempted to turn over responsibility for cocoa development to the private sector — despite the indications that private farmers were unwilling or unable to respond to the challenge.[255]

One partial exception to this gloomy economic picture was the banana industry. Here the combined effects of land reform and the withdrawal of facilities for boxing bananas began taking hold.[256] A sharp contraction in the numbers of growers registered with the Grenada Banana Co-operative Society in 1987 indicated that centralization of ownership was indeed occurring in the industry and that marginally efficient farmers were being forced out of business. A consequence of the restructuring of the banana industry was a slight increase in production. Despite a storm in late 1986 which destroyed about 60 000 trees, output rose the following year by almost 7 per cent.[257]

(c) Tourism

At the start of the post-revolutionary period, because the short-term prospects for industry and agriculture appeared to be dubious, US advisers proposed the vigorous promotion of tourism in order to bolster foreign-exchange earnings and generate employment. Given the delays in transportation between Grenada and North America, the early opening of Point Salines airport to international traffic was considered crucial to success. Hence, completion of Point Salines was treated as an infrastructural priority, and $19 million in USAID funding was devoted to it. The result was that the airport was opened to international traffic within a year of the invasion.[258]

Despite the debilitating effects of the pegging of the Eastern Caribbean dollar to the US dollar (which was then riding high on international exchange markets), prospects appeared relatively bright in 1984. The Economic Commission for Latin America and the Caribbean (ECLAC) reported healthy growth in Grenada's tourism receipts in that year. Tourism revenue rose by more than 17 per cent over 1983, accounting for roughly 35 per cent of merchandise exports and nonfactor services.[259] Major international hotel chains were also showing interest in extending tourism operations to the island.

The decision to complete the Point Salines airport reportedly prompted decisions by American, European, Caribbean, and local companies to invest a total of $55 million in the tourism industry. By 1988 these investments were expected to more than double the hotel accommodation available on the island. Plans included the rebuilding and expansion of the Holiday Inn destroyed by fire in 1983, and the construction of large hotel complexes by European companies. As in Barbados and other smaller islands in the region, hoteliers operating in Grenada wished to target upscale tourism, as opposed to the high-volume, package tour market.[260]

In large measure, the "tourism boom" experienced in 1984 was due to the presence of US military personnel and economic advisers still resident on the island. But for them, hotel occupancy rates would likely have been as low as 25 per cent.[261] This was not the case, however, after 1984. The revival of tourism-related activity was quite strong in the following year. Arrivals of stopover visitors grew by more than one-third, while the less lucrative cruise ship arrivals almost tripled.[262] In March 1986 the Ramada Renaissance Hotel opened, considerably expanding the amount of luxury accommodation. This development, combined with benefits accruing from improved access, led to a further rise in tourism earnings. Both stopover and cruise arrivals grew, increasing total revenue by 12 per cent over 1985.[263]

By 1987 both the general economic outlook and the prospects for the Grenadian tourism industry were gloomier than they had been in the initial phase of economic reconstruction. Although the number of visitors continued to grow, revenue was scarcely higher than for 1986. Contrary to expectation, the cruise ship trade rather than the more profitable stopover arrivals was turning out to be the real growth area. Numbers arriving from the United States and Trinidad — two of the most important sources — declined significantly, while those from other countries stagnated. According to one report, at the peak of the 1987 holiday season Grenada's 12 hotels were still half empty.[264]

In the opinion of the Grenada Hotel Association (GHA), the difficulties confronting the hotel industry during the 1987 holiday season were directly attributable to deteriorating political conditions.[265] In reference to the problems besetting the NNP administration throughout 1987, the GHA criticized the government for failing to establish an environment conducive to profitable accumulation in the tourism sector. "One would have thought," argued GHA President Andre Cherman in late 1987, "that after all the political problems over the years, this country would have settled down. Instead we are all confused. There is lack of discipline and respect, and Grenada is still considered to be an unsafe destination."[266]

The tourism sector was also starting to feel directly the debilitating effects of NNP economic policy. Faced with acute financial problems arising from its 1986 tax reform measures the government had already depleted many sources of funds, including the two state-owned banks and the National Insurance Scheme. The 1987 tourism budget allocation of EC$1.1 million reflected these constraints and was described by the GHA as "woefully inadequate" to the task of promoting the nation's tourism industry.[267]

4.4 Social and Political Impact of Post-revolutionary Policy

In the end, any policy or set of policies purporting to support economic development should be measured by the extent of the improvement in the living conditions of the people most affected by those policies. Under the PRG the modernization of the national economy involved the transformation of the living conditions of most Grenadians, which had remained basically unchanged since independence. Wages were improved, discrepancies between the wages of men and women lessened, children were given access to education regardless of social class, and a national health scheme was introduced. Through the Production and Discipline Committees workers had something of a say in workplace decisions. In the communities where estate workers lived substantial efforts were made to improve housing conditions and social amenities.

By 1989, more than half a decade after the US invasion of Grenada, it was still difficult to cite indicators illustrative of an improvement in living and working conditions for Grenadians. The official unemployment rate was hovering at around 30 per cent. One may take it as given that the actual figures were considerably higher, particularly among women and youth. Price ceilings on staple goods like milk, flour, and rice were long gone. Many people now complained of being barely able to afford the backs and necks of chickens at the local markets.

By 1987 the number of trade unions in existence during the revolutionary period had been almost halved. Three of these were affiliated with the right-wing AIFLD and had been since well before the invasion. As a result these unions played a leading role in the "reorientation and training of the leadership[s]" of other unions considered to be "radical." These efforts, and those directed at building a conservative union of agricultural workers in order to offset the effect of the progressive Agricultural and General Workers union, have not met with success.[268]

The Council on Hemispheric Affairs in Washington, DC, has commented on the poor human rights record of Grenada since 1983. In the period following the US invasion, opposition politicians and progressive labour leaders were harassed and their houses subject to search on a regular basis.[269] In June 1987 the government enacted legislation giving it emergency powers. These included the right of police to sweeping powers of search, detention without charge or legal representation, curfews, and house arrests.[270]

It seems likely that Grenada is set to head down a path well worn by other countries in the region, as cycles of economic restraint are accompanied by police and military measures designed to control displays of popular dissatisfaction with these policies. In a confidential report of the International Monetary Fund, leaked in January 1985, the Grenadian government was advised to maintain a policy of wage restraint because of the island's substantial debt burden. The report also suggested that restraint on social welfare expenditure in general would be important in view of the expected increase in debt servicing and the costs associated with the maintenance of the infrastructure put in place to attract private capital into various sectors of the economy.[271]

In the face of such a bleak set of prospects for the Grenadian economy, some solace can be found for the architects and proponents of the new Grenada. At the new, reconstructed airport in Point Salines one particular area of unfettered private enterprise began flourishing in the midst of growing poverty and repression. The cocaine trade is now thriving in Grenada.[272]

5   Conclusion

One theme, repeated throughout the post-war period, stands out in the history of relations between countries of the First and Third Worlds. That is the single-faceted, homogeneous view of the latter by the former. For whatever reasons, writers of left and right continue to paint countries of the Third World in the same two-tone way: black (or yellow) and poor. The CBI continues this tradition, in spades. Even in a sub-region of countries with so much in common — British colonial history, geography, language — it is the differential effects of the CBI on nations of the Commonwealth Caribbean and their responses to it which may teach observers the most.

There are, surely, commonalities in the effects of the Caribbean Basin Initiative on these nations. At a general level none has benefited from it, and most are worse off.[273] None is close to having a vibrant manufacturing sector, ostensibly one of the principal aims of the CBI. In none has the agricultural sector been effectively restructured to increase productivity and social prosperity. All are in worse fiscal straits than they were prior to the enactment of the CBI. And in all cases, living standards have deteriorated and working conditions (for those who can find work) are either unimproved or are substantially worse than they were before the installation of the CBI.

The most significant common development is the fact that the CBI has been met with almost universal disaffection by mass organizations, progressive unions, and groups of individuals in each of Barbados, Jamaica, and Grenada. This widespread mobilization against the CBI is the locus for a determined and vocal attempt to devise alternative strategies for development that accommodate the various histories and aspirations of the peoples involved.

In Barbados, traditionally a relatively high-wage country, industry is facing serious difficulties. This is most obvious in the area of non-traditional manufacturing, an area targetted for rapid expansion by the Caribbean Basin Initiative. Living standards are generally lower than in the early 1980s. As yet, however, the country has shown no significant signs of political radicalization. That is, in the lexicon of the World Bank and the International Monetary Fund, it remains a stable investment site.

In Jamaica, a national political system characterized by a violent right-left polarization has now become slightly more centrist. As in Grenada, there has been a serious erosion of human rights. The one area of marked improvement has been in the non-traditional sub-sector of manufacturing, namely, export-oriented garment production. Even here, however, the situation is not stable. The establishment of Export Free Zones and the availability of cheap, sweated, female labour attracted an influx of Asian and US capital into this sub-sector. Little of this capital tends to find its way into the pockets of Jamaicans. Maybe the most overwhelming trait of Jamaica throughout the post-war period has been the seeming permanence of the conditions of grinding poverty for most of its population. No change in political leadership has altered that fact, nor has, nor will, the CBI.

Of the three, Grenada under Gairy has come the nearest to leadership by a single individual or clique. Until the New Jewel Movement took power, no effort had been made to industrialize the economy or develop the full potential of agriculture. It is the only one of the three countries examined which has had four years of demonstrable progress in the economic, political, and social spheres of the lives of its citizens — progress which has been systematically dismantled by the CBI and its advocates. Because nothing approaching these former advances has been instituted under the Caribbean Basin Initiative, the Grenadian experience offers perhaps the clearest indication both of the potential for economic and social progress in the region (1979 83) and the limitations intrinsic in the US-sponsored development strategy currently being implemented in that country.

7

The CBI and Industrial Development in Trinidad and Tobago

Godwin Friday

1   Introduction

The US administration's Caribbean Basin Initiative has attracted a lot of academic attention. Most studies, however, have tended to be of a general nature. This chapter examines the CBI as it relates specifically to Trinidad and Tobago. Its focus is primarily empirical. Contrary to the optimism of the Reagan administration, the CBI has thus far not contributed meaningfully to economic growth in that country, specifically in the area of industrialization. Indeed, so poorly has the program performed in Trinidad and Tobago, that if tangible improvement does not occur in the short term, it may well reinforce an unfavourable reassessment there of US hegemony in the region.

2   Overview of the CBI

When US President Reagan unveiled the Caribbean Basin Initiative at the OAS meeting in February 1982, it was embraced by most Caribbean leaders as a potential economic lifeline.[1] Though somewhat more cautious in their response to the announcement, Trinidadian officials were also optimistic, hoping that the program would provide reliable markets for their country's expanding range of manufactured goods. In keeping with this, on November 16, 1983, Trinidad and Tobago officially accepted the Reagan administration's invitation to participate in the program. In its acceptance letter, the Government of Trinidad and Tobago expressed its desire for a "speedy and unfettered" implementation of the program.[2] It confirmed that Trinidad and Tobago was willing to participate in the trade regime of the CBI and "to cooperate with the United States in the administration of the program in a manner consonant with respect for the principle of sovereign equality of all States and calculated to redound to the mutual benefit of both coun-

---

Notes for Chapter 7 are on pp. 251-59.

tries."[3] Similarly, local business leaders, though lacking in ideas for concrete projects to exploit the program, were keen to show their support. The two daily newspapers raised questions about certain aspects of the program, but they too welcomed it.[4] Not everyone was so sanguine, however. Members of the academic community and several influential nationals, including William Demas, remained largely unconvinced that, in its existing form, the CBI could make any noticeable contribution to the Trinidadian economy.[5] Ultimately, the skeptical point of view would gain credibility, and even government officials and leading members of the business community would join the chorus of criticism.

Officially, the purpose of the CBI was to bolster the economies of the Caribbean and Central America (countries designated "communist" by the US government were excluded—i.e., revolutionary Grenada, Nicaragua and Cuba). By introducing this program, the Reagan administration hoped to demonstrate that it was genuinely concerned for the welfare of the peoples of the region and committed to promoting it with more than the customary military aid. All the same, military aid would remain a significant aspect of the CBI. This feature, and the fact that the program followed in the wake of the Nicaraguan and Grenadian revolutions and growing social discontent elsewhere in the region, helped to expose the predominantly political character of the program. As others have argued, these developments created a perception of eroding US hegemony in the region, and the CBI may best be understood as an attempt to reverse this process or perception.[6]

For a proper appreciation of the implications and potential of the CBI, it is necessary to situate the program within its historical context. To this end, we present an overview of the past three decades of social and economic change in Trinidad and Tobago before proceeding to analyze the performance of the CBI.

3   Development Strategy, Labour Struggles, and Economic Nationalism

During the 1950s and 1960s, Trinidad and Tobago followed a staunchly pro-capitalist development strategy which accorded a preeminent role to foreign capital.[7] This ultimately engendered a nationalistic reaction among segments of the population which was heightened in the late 1950s and early 1960s by the political rhetoric that accompanied the government's efforts to regain the Chaguaramas peninsula from US control and, shortly thereafter, the movement towards formal independence.[8]

The period 1960 to 1965 was marked by intense industrial struggle. Workers, mobilized by the attainment of formal independence, sought to make the transition tangible in their lives. Their struggle for better wages and improved working conditions often brought them into direct conflict with foreign capital, especially in the foreign-dominated sugar and petroleum industries. Similar demands were made against the state as employer, but workers generally looked to the state for support in their confrontations with foreign-owned companies. For the most part, however, this support did not materialize. Indeed, by 1965, as pressure from organized labour mounted, the state felt impelled to act decisively to contain the rising tide of demands. The main outcome was the Industrial Stabilization Act (ISA) which effectively banned strikes, except when sanctioned by the Minister of Labour. With the concurrence of the official parliamentary opposition and while the entire sugar belt had been placed under a state of emergency to counter labour unrest in the sugar industry, the Act was hastily passed (essentially in one day).[9]

The passing of the ISA confirmed that the state was more inclined to align with capital than with workers. The labour movement protested vigorously against the Act. Given the nature of the ownership of capital in the country (i.e., predominantly foreign), the reaction assumed nationalistic overtones. Anger was also directed against the local Euro-Trinidadian elite, which had managed to maintain its economic prominence even after losing direct political control. This group, which largely constituted the fledgling indigenous capitalist class, maintained its historic links with international capital. This, along with the obvious racial aspect, made it an easy target for attack as a hostile presence in the bosom of the new nation. In the wake of the ISA, there was a lull in industrial action. As economic conditions deteriorated in the late 1960s, however, the number of strikes increased again, as did demands for greater national control over the economy and for a more equitable distribution of the nation's wealth.

The main forces behind the demands were radical students and academics, organized labour (especially in the oil industry), and the growing number of unemployed. The disenchantment eventually erupted into the so-called "Black Power" uprising of 1970. This event, coupled with a mutiny among sympathetic elements of the defence force, shook the foundations of the complacent Williams administration. The government had managed to survive only after imposing a nationwide state of emergency and by subsequently adjusting its rhetoric and policies to give traditionally marginalized segments of the society a greater stake in the economy. Even so, deteriorating economic conditions in the early 1970s continued to fuel political discontent and to undermine the legitimacy of the state, and with it, the leadership role of the petty bourgeois elements who inherited state power at independence. This forced the government to reconsider its development strategy, particularly its exclusive reliance on the private sector to generate growth. A succession of documents and public speeches, beginning with the Third Five Year Development Plan (1969-73), declared the state's intention to begin to play a more active role in the economy, including direct participation in business enterprises. This was elaborated in a 1972 White Paper on state participation in the economy. Also, for the first time, attention was directed to the development of a "People's Sector," which meant promoting locally owned small businesses with government assistance.

If national political crisis provided the impetus for state capitalism, events half a world away provided the means to implement it. In late 1973, middle-eastern nations imposed an oil embargo on several Western countries, leading to a sharp increase in world oil prices. Subsequent actions by a reinvigorated OPEC cartel resulted in an escalation in oil prices throughout the rest of the decade. Being an oil exporter, Trinidad and Tobago reaped a harvest from the oil embargo and, through new taxes on the petroleum industry and equity participation in oil companies, the state secured a significant share of the new revenues. Through subsidies, reduced taxes, and higher wages, some of the new-found wealth was passed on to the general population, resulting in an unprecedented improvement in living standards for most Trinidadians. Of equal importance, however, was the fact that increased revenues enabled the country to embark on an ambitious industrialization program based on state capital and an abundant supply of natural gas, discovered some years earlier.

The oil windfall also strengthened the state's bargaining position in relation to foreign capital. This was, perhaps, especially true in the financial sector, where an ultimatum was issued to foreign-owned banks and insurance companies to permit significant indigenous ownership in their operations in the country.[10] Meanwhile, through a number of joint ventures with foreign companies in the manufacturing sector and the hiring of numerous foreign contractors and consultants under the government's massive building program, foreign capital's role in the country increased overall.

In 1982, world oil prices began a downward spiral from which they have yet to recover fully. This brought an abrupt end to the economic boom and the phase of state-led industrialization. It also set the stage for the abandonment of the policies and rhetoric of economic nationalism. With encouragement from external forces, this process would intensify.

4   Current Economic Conditions

Since 1982, Trinidad and Tobago has experienced uninterrupted economic decline. This has amounted to a fall of over 25 per cent in gross domestic product, and the failure of numerous companies, including Kirpalani's (one of the largest indigenous firms). Over 13 000 workers have been retrenched while others have been forced to accept wage and salary cuts.[11] At the end of March 1987, the number of unemployed stood at over 105 000 persons, or just over 22 per cent of the labour force. The unemployment rate was even higher (28%) among those 20-24 years old and over 50 per cent of the unemployed were in the 15-24 years age group. This harsh reality, following on the heels of a period of unprecedented economic boom and rising expectations, has produced a potentially explosive situation, in light of which the government's view that "unemployment is *one* of the most pressing economic concerns at the present time" appears as somewhat of an understatement.[12]

External debt obligations have compounded the country's difficulties. Though relative to other developing nations Trinidad and Tobago cannot be considered a high debt country, a combination of factors have made its debt burden considerably more onerous in recent years. Most of the debt is comprised of short- and medium-term loans owed to private institutions and comes due for repayment within a few years.[13] Hence, debt service payments have increased as export earnings declined. Furthermore, much of the debt (i.e., over 40%), in large part acquired during the energy-based industrialization program (1975-84), is held in currencies which rose against the US dollar (to which Trinidad and Tobago's currency is tied) during the 1980s.[14] The rise in these currencies against the US dollar amounted to an effective devaluation of the latter currency (and by extension the Trinidad and Tobago dollar) against these currencies and automatically increased the debt burden. Finally, the problem was hardly helped by the fact that most of Trinidad and Tobago's foreign earnings continued to be in US dollars. The net effect was to increase the external debt by an average of 62 per cent per annum between 1983 and 1985. In 1986, it totalled to US$1.8 billion or 37 per cent of GDP.[15] Debt service rapidly consumed much of the country's foreign reserves, bringing enormous social and economic hardship. In 1981 Trinidad and Tobago's foreign reserves stood at US$3.4 billion dollars; by the end of June 1988, they had fallen to $72.5 million, the lowest level since December 1973.[16] Meanwhile, the overall balance of payments deficit rose from 1 per cent of GDP in 1985 to 12 per cent a year later. So profound is the current economic crisis that even by 1988, after six successive years of recession, there were "no perceptible signs of imminent recovery."[17]

One commentator explained, "In the short to medium term all our options seem to be characterized by one feature — PAIN."[18]

As noted earlier, the crisis has led to a reversal of the state's role in the industrialization process and to a shift in its attitude towards foreign capital. The private sector is once again being relied upon as the principal agent of economic growth, especially in manufacturing. Furthermore, earnest overtures are being made to potential foreign investors. The investment process is being streamlined through, for example, the establishment of a "one-stop-shop" at the Industrial Development Corporation. Thus, it appears that the primary interest in foreign investment has shifted from a focus on access to technology, to one of access to capital. Although the present administration (elected in 1986) espouses a greater ideological commitment to these policies than its predecessor, the process was in fact initiated by the latter. A tangible expression of this was a visit in 1985 by a delegation led by then Prime Minister George Chambers to the Far East and Europe to court potential investors. In July 1988 another delegation, this time led by the minister of industry and enterprise and comprising several prominent local businessmen, visited the Far East. The specific purpose of the visit was to promote Trinidad and Tobago as a potential site for Export Processing Zones (EPZs).

Arguably, the most important factor in the adoption of the policy of greater reliance on the private sector, both local and international, has been the steady deterioration in government revenues since 1982. The policy shift did not occur in a vacuum, however; the economic crisis created conditions which allowed other factors to exert considerable influence over state policy. In this context, the influence of the free enterprise rhetoric which accompanied the CBI cannot be ignored, for it provided ideological reinforcement to a regime favourably predisposed to such ideas. Moreover, by dominating the ideological sphere it also served to intimidate those who would suggest alternative strategies.

The ideological campaign was relentless and pervasive. At the 1985 Miami Conference on the CBI, US Vice-President George Bush reminded regional governments that "the CBI legislation assumes that the participating countries will work hard to improve the climate for both foreign investment and for domestic entrepreneurship." For good measure, he added "For the CBI to succeed, the CBI countries need to do more than they are doing now."[19] Other emissaries from Washington have played a similar role, with specific reference to Trinidad and Tobago. In an influential publication, CBI Ombudsman Alexander Good praised the Government of Trinidad and Tobago for its new investment policy of emphasizing the private sector (discussed below), though this policy still awaits legislative action to bring it fully into effect.[20] Also, in May 1988, Dr. Erwin Geiger, a private economic consultant, visited Trinidad and Tobago under the auspices of the US Information Service.[21] His basic advice to the government was first, that it should institute policies to create confidence in Trinidad and Tobago's economic and political situation so as to attract foreign capital, and second, that it should abandon state ownership, especially in the petroleum sector. State ownership, he pointed out, is socialism and "While on the one hand it looks good and the state takes care of this and that, gradually you go down the road of a serf. No more the free individual."[22] Geiger argued not only for private capital in general, but also specifically for foreign capital. This was evident, for example, when he asked "What's so sacred" about the oil industry "that it should remain in national hands?"[23] In all of this, the local dailies have also been playing a significant supporting role.

5   Investment Policies and Priorities

Perhaps the most significant indicator of the shift in official thinking is the document *Investment Policy in Trinidad and Tobago*, published in August 1987 by the Industrial Development Corporation (IDC).[24] This publication outlines the criteria upon which new investment decisions will be based. They can be summarized as follows: (i) that the enterprise earn or save the country foreign exchange, preferably the former; (ii) that it generate "substantial employment," and (iii) that it contribute to the deepening of the manufacturing process in the country.[25]

More than ever, the current economic crisis has made Trinidadians painfully aware of the hazards of dependence on a single export commodity, even if that commodity happens to be petroleum. The suddenness and severity of this crisis appears to have created an unprecedented sense of urgency and a conviction within the state that the problem must be fixed at all costs, if its own political legitimacy and the legitimacy of its strategy of capitalist development is to be maintained.[26] Consequently, greater effort is being made to streamline and channel investment incentives "away from import substitution activity and towards support for production for export markets."[27] Along with the usual incentives of tax holidays (5 to 10 years), duty-free importation of machinery and material, and inexpensive ready-made factory shells, other inducements are offered, particularly to local companies. In an effort to stimulate private sector investment in export-oriented and high employment activities, such inducements include: (i) soft loans to small local companies whose activities support the state's investment objectives; (ii) a subsidy to train workers where necessary skills are scarce and to encourage companies to locate in areas of high unemployment and to employ more workers than the industry norm;

(iii) a tax incentive (allowance) for certain activities;[28] and, of special interest to foreign investors, (iv) double taxation relief in the form of reduced rates of Withholding Tax for individuals and companies of countries which have double taxation treaties with Trinidad and Tobago. Measures designed specifically to stimulate the production of export commodities, especially by locally owned companies, include: (i) an export allowance "computed on the basis of the per centage which export sales bear to total sales";[29] (ii) a tax-exempt grant of 50 per cent of expenditures incurred in the development of overseas markets;[30] (iii) tax deduction of 150 per cent of approved promotional expenses;[31] and (iv) easier access to foreign exchange for companies which contribute "meaningfully" to the country's foreign earnings.[32]

Specifically related to potential foreign investors is the movement towards an amendment of the Aliens (Landholding) Ordinance—a piece of legislation which restricts the activities of foreign investors in the country.[33] The local capitalist class, which has always maintained very close ties with foreign capital, has made repeated demands for the repeal of the Act. As a representative of business interests in the Senate argued, "the perpetuation of the attitude that anything that smacks of foreign ownership should be somehow penalized or severely controlled, should be halted."[34] Lately, such calls have also emanated from within the bureaucracy. Within the context of urging the creation of an investment climate conducive to private enterprise, various representatives of the US Government have been repeating similar arguments. However, instead of repealing the Act outright, the government has opted to amend it to permit "the free access of foreign investors to the stock market to acquire up to a maximum of 20 per cent of the total Issued Shares in any single enterprise without the need for an Alien Licence."[35]

Finally, certain areas of the economy have been reserved for nationals of Trinidad and Tobago, and foreign investment is permitted only in special circumstances such as when the scale of the project exceeds the capabilities of nationals or when production is exclusively for export.[36]

As noted above, the Reagan administration has applauded the Trinidadian government's efforts to liberalize the investment climate in Trinidad and Tobago, although it still expresses reservations about the pace. This is largely because, as also noted, relevant legislation is still needed to implement fully the new investment policy.[37]

The above discussion (and later analysis) suggests quite clearly that a vigorous debate over economic strategy is currently underway in Trinidad and Tobago. Moreover, it suggests that, at least at the ideological level, the CBI may have played an important role in influencing this debate. Finally, and for our purposes perhaps more importantly, the discussion demonstrates that changes (fiscal and otherwise) which theoretically should enhance the ability of Trinidad and Tobago to take advantage of economic opportunities offered by the CBI are currently being implemented by the government. It is doubtful, however, whether these measures or any set of measures will be sufficient to enable the country to benefit from the program. This is so not only or even primarily because of deficiencies within Trinidad and Tobago, but also, as Ramnarine and others have argued, because of serious deficiencies within the program itself.

At this point, it would be useful to provide a brief account of industrialization in Trinidad and Tobago, emphasizing those characteristics which may affect the country's ability to take advantage of the CBI.

6   Overview of Industrialization in Trinidad and Tobago

Trinidad and Tobago is one of the most industrialized countries in the Caribbean. Official interest in industrialization emerged there in the late 1940s, largely as a result of the efforts of St.Lucia-born economist Sir Arthur Lewis to persuade British colonial authorities of the viability and necessity of industrialization in the Caribbean. In 1950, legislation (the Aid to Pioneer Industries Ordinance and The Income Tax [in Aid of Industry] Ordinance) was enacted which provided fiscal and material incentives to attract capital and technology to the manufacturing sector. Recognizing the scarcity of capital and technology in the country, these incentives were targetted primarily at potential foreign investors. Throughout the decade, the manufacturing sector expanded rapidly. Although subsequently slowing down, this sector still maintained a respectable average annual growth rate of 4.5 per cent between 1962-66. Between 1966 and 1969 it rebounded and grew at an average annual rate of 14.9 per cent. But despite this rapid growth, unemployment continued to increase, suggesting that the manufacturing sector's capacity to absorb labour was limited. This was a consequence of the capital intensive nature of the technology adopted and, more importantly, of the fact that manufacturing consisted mainly of "mixing, blending, assembly, packaging and other final stage processes."[38] This meant that the import content in the manufacturing sector was very high and, conversely, backward and downstream linkages with the rest of the economy were very low.[39] Girvan explains the implications of this for the sector's capacity to generate employment.

> If manufacturing activities were carried backwards to the stages of processing primary or raw materials ... and the manufacture of intermediate products for final processing and packaging, then it

would increase the requirements of both labor and capital in relation to final output and correspondingly reduce the foreign exchange cost of the material of final output. In such a case, the average capital/labor ratio in manufacturing might be higher, but—and this is what is important—the average labor/final output ratio would be higher. The employment impact of the gross value of manufacturing production would be correspondingly greater.[40]

Twenty years later, the situation has changed very little in Trinidad and Tobago, especially with regard to private sector manufacturing.

The only serious attempt to expand and deepen the manufacturing process was undertaken by the state between 1975 and 1984. This was the phase of state-led, energy-based industrialization referred to above. Between 1977 and 1988 six new production facilities based on natural gas, either as energy or raw material input, were brought into operation. They included three anhydrous ammonia plants undertaken as joint ventures between the state (51%) and foreign capital (49%); an iron and steel factory; a methanol plant; and a urea plant. These three were 100 per cent state-owned. The total investment, including supporting infrastructure, amounted to an estimated US $2 billion.[41]

Table 7-1
Investment in Major Gas-based Industries

Firm	Ownership	Product	Rated capacity (metric tonnes)	Start-up date
TRINGEN I	State 51% W.R.Grace 49%	Anhydrous Ammonia	1 134 per day	1977
ISCOTT	State 100%	Sponge Iron Billets Wire Rods	860 000 per year 600 000 per year 500 000 per year	1981
FERTRIN	State 51% Amoco 49%	Ammonia Ammonia	1 500 per year 1 150 per day	1981 1982
Trinidad Urea Co.	State 100 %	Urea	1 620 per day	1984
Trinidad Methanol Co.	State 100%	Methanol	1 200 per day	1984
TRINGEN II	State 51% W.R.Grace 49%	Anhydrous Ammonia	1 400 per day	1988

Source: Adapted from National Planning Commission, *Restructuring for Economic Independence, Draft Medium Term Macro Planning Framework 1989-1995* (Port of Spain, Trinidad & Tobago: Government Printer, 1988).

Unfortunately, adverse world market conditions (especially for urea), including protectionist pressures from the United States steel lobby, prevented these investments from performing satisfactorily as foreign-exchange earners. Nevertheless, they represent simultaneously a broadening of the country's industrial base and a deepening of the manufacturing process. Also, their unsatisfactory performance as hard currency earners does not negate their considerable export *capability*, as virtually all of the methanol and nitrogenous fertilizer and most of the iron and steel produced are exported.[42] Hence, an improvement in international market conditions would reverse the foreign-exchange position of these companies and alter the general perception of failure associated with the energy-based industrialization program. An indication of this was provided by the encouraging performance of the Methanol Company and the fertilizer companies (particularly the Urea Company) in 1988.[43]

Table 7-2
The Manufacturing Sector

Manufacturing Value-added (1986) US$741 million*			
Real growth rate of MVA (%)			
1965-73	1973-84	1984	1985
6.1	4.7	−11.3	−15.7
Distribution of MVA (%)			
	1970		1983
Food products	15		26
Textiles & clothing	5		6
Machinery & transport equipment	5		15
Chemicals	5		8
Other manufacturing	69		44
Employment in manufac. (1985):	51 412		
Manufactured export (June 1986):	TT$18 411 678		
Share in total exports:	5.3%		
Manufactured imports (1984):	US$704 million		
Share in total imports**:	51.9%		

* Preliminary estimate.
** Excluding food products; including machinery and transport equipment.
Source: UNIDO, *Industrial Development Review Series, The Caribbean Region*,
September 1987.

The structural weaknesses of the manufacturing sector discussed above also hold implications for the ability of Trinidadian manufacturers to take advantage of any opportunities offered by the CBI. Specifically, the superficial nature of the manufacturing process and its high import content prevent many of the local manufactured goods from satisfying the value-added and "substantial transformation" rules necessary for duty-free treatment under the program.[44] Caribbean governments have petitioned Washington for a lowering of the value-added requirement but have thus far been unsuccessful. Also hampering Trinidadian manufacturers is the fact that most of them began operation on an import-substitution basis with generous protection behind tariff barriers and a device called the Import Negative List.[45] This protection was intended to be temporary, with the individual enterprise or industry being gradually weaned as it grew stronger. In reality, however, the weaning never occurred. Over time, this situation became self-reinforcing, as later manufacturers established enterprises, not on the basis of the stated "temporary" protection, but with the knowledge that in reality the protection would never be withdrawn. Consequently, the outlook of local manufacturing entrepreneurs and the design of their production facilities reflected this reality. Moreover, the manufacturers were substituting imports in a very small market and were essentially content to confine themselves to that domain until forced to do otherwise. Finally, indiscriminate consumer spending during the boom years (especially between 1978 and 1982) induced inefficient management practices and poor quality control, both of which also adversely affected the competitiveness of the country's manufactured goods. These factors combined to create deficiencies which continue to limit severely the ability and inclination of Trinidadian manufacturers to compete in foreign markets.[46] Even within Caricom markets, they have not always been very competitive. This was especially true during the late 1970s and early 1980s, when the excesses of the oil boom were most evident. Today, all energies are focussed on developing greater export capability in the manufacturing sector.

It is clear from the above discussion that the manufacturing sector in Trinidad and Tobago will have to undergo a substantial degree of structural change if it is to be capable of capitalizing on CBI and other export markets. The state has recognized this and has outlined a restructuring program in a seven-year development plan (published in August 1988). The plan emphasizes the development of an industrial base more appropriate for export production and the maximum utilization of local technology, skills, and material inputs. However, the fact that it relies very heavily on private capital which, as noted earlier, has never demonstrated much dynamism in the manufacturing sector, raises serious doubts about the feasibility of the restructuring program. As far as the CBI is concerned, it would be absurd to suggest that the restructuring program was predicated upon it. Indeed, unless the duration of the CBI is extended (perhaps to the year 2007 as the "CBI II"

Table 7-3
Indices of Average Weekly Earnings and Productivity for Production Workers, 1978-87
(1978 = 100)

| Year | All industries, including oil and sugar | | All industries, excluding oil and sugar | |
	Average weekly earnings	Productivity	Average weekly earnings	Productivity
1978	100.0	100.0	100.0	100.0
1979	124.0	102.5	120.4	109.8
1980	154.4	109.0	149.2	112.2
1981	180.9	107.3	174.2	117.1
1982	212.9	124.6	207.3	146.7
1983	253.1	137.6	258.4	176.0
1984	292.9	144.9	297.0	181.9
1985	307.3	159.8	307.6	212.7
1986	313.4	199.7	316.7	271.6
1986 (Jan.-June)	272.2	198.3	314.4	265.8
1987 (Jan.-June)	315.6	218.9	312.2	302.6

Source: Central Statistical Office, *Review of the Economy, 1987* (Port of Spain, Trinidad and Tobago, 1988).

bill proposed), the restructuring program will still be in process when the CBI expires as scheduled in 1995. It is, nevertheless, correct to say that the CBI has offered the development planners a modicum of encouragement, stemming largely from expectations regarding "CBI II." On the other hand, its ideological function may be of much greater significance. It is at that level that the program has provided considerable support for the liberalization policies currently being implemented.

7   The CBI: Actual Performance

Thus far, the CBI has had about as much effect on the economy of Trinidad and Tobago as a brief shower on the Sahara. The high expectations which attended the program's introduction have given way in some quarters to profound disappointment. The comments of local government officials and, to a lesser extent, members of the business community, give an indication of the level of disappointment and frustration which the program has engendered in Trinidad and Tobago. The Minister of External Affairs and International Trade Dr. Sahadeo Basdeo, in an address to business people and government officials at

Table 7-4
The Sectoral Composition of Real GDP
(percentage contribution)

	1973	1978	1983	1984	1985	1986	1987
Petroleum	20.9	15.9	9.0	10.7	12.6	12.7	12.2
Non-oil economy	79.1	84.1	90.0	89.3	87.4	87.3	87.8
Agriculture	6.3	5.3	3.1	3.3	3.6	3.6	4.1
Manufacturing	11.0	11.1	13.5	12.8	11.8	15.1	16.7
Construction	7.9	13.8	12.2	10.5	8.9	8.1	7.8
Government	8.7	8.2	7.6	8.0	8.1	7.5	7.8
Other	45.2	45.7	53.6	54.7	55.0	53.0	51.4

Source: National Planning Commission, *Restructuring for Economic Independence, Draft Medium Term Macro Planning Framework 1989-1995* (Port of Spain: Government Printer, 1988).

the Caribbean Expo '88 trade show in Port of Spain, noted that the CBI has not been living up to expectations and that it has "failed to produce the boost to regional exports which had been expected at the commencement of the program."[47] An official at the Industrial Development Corporation whose job it is to identify potentially viable CBI projects in Trinidad and Tobago commented: "the CBI is ridiculous!" The comment was motivated by his inability to find any projects resulting from the CBI that were not already covered under the General System of Preferences (GSP).[48] An analysis of the performance of the program in several areas, beginning with trade, follows.

7.1 Trade

The CBI was advertised as a vehicle to promote the economic diversification and export capability of the beneficiary countries. But as Ramnarine[49] and others have demonstrated, this has not been achieved for the region as a whole. In fact, while the CBI proponents in Washington were challenging the beneficiary countries to increase their "non-traditional" exports to the United States, regional sugar quotas were being reduced by about 67 per cent between 1983-87. The export value of other staples from the region (bauxite, coffee, and petroleum) also declined. In absolute terms, Trinidad and Tobago's experience has been worse than most countries'. Whereas several countries experienced an increase in exports to the US, the value of Trinidad and Tobago's exports to that country fell by over US $500 million between 1983-87, though the US share of its total exports increased slightly over the same period. Although the collapse in world oil prices in the 1980s accounts for most of this decline, it is worth noting that no other export commodity has been able to compensate to any significant degree for the loss in foreign-exchange earnings from oil.

Table 7-5
US Imports from Selected CBI Countries
(of all products) ($US millions)

	1983	1984	1985	1986	1988
Barbados	204.9	255.5	205.9	111.0	51.4
Jamaica	296.6	437.5	286.5	320.9	440.9
St. Vincent	4.4	3.1	10.4	8.1	13.9
Trinidad & Tobago	1 356.7	1 410.9	1 301.0	833.2	701.7

Source: Adapted from *Report by the US Department of State on the Caribbean Basin Initiative: Progress to Date*, March 1988 and November 1989.

The heavy investment in the energy-based enterprises has not resulted in the measure of diversification in foreign-exchange earnings intended. The CBI has not altered this dismal picture. In fact, despite its reassuring rhetoric regarding the program, the US government has taken actions which have compounded Trinidad and Tobago's difficulties. As is evident in the 1988 Budget Speech, this fact has not escaped the attention of Trinidad and Tobago's prime minister, who complained that "[i]n the US market growing protectionist sentiments continue to hamper entry of Trinidad and Tobago products," and that "[t]his is so even in the case of special items such as 'ethnic goods.'"[50] But of greater significance has been the experience of the state-owned Iron and Steel Company of Trinidad and Tobago (ISCOTT) in its attempt to enter the US market. It provided a sobering lesson to Trinidadians on the reality behind the rhetoric of the CBI.

When, in the mid-1970s, the Government of Trinidad and Tobago undertook to build ISCOTT, the company was hailed as the cornerstone of the country's new energy-based industrialization program. More than simply a potential foreign-exchange earner or a provider of jobs, ISCOTT became the symbol of industrialization itself. Since it began operating in 1981, however, the company has lost much of its lustre. Its operation has been marred by enormous technical, managerial and marketing problems. Consequently, it has never turned a profit and in 1989 was continuing to lose money, though at a slower rate. Moreover, ISCOTT's external debt is high, requiring an annual debt service of US $64.5 million in 1985.[51] Nevertheless, this unenviable record did not prevent the present administration from proposing to make the steel industry "one of the cornerstones of the economy's industrial sector."[52] It would appear, then, that ISCOTT, as an indigenous company, and steel as a major new manufactured product, can serve effectively as tests of the sincerity and economic importance of the CBI. As it turned out, a significant (and well-publicized) contributing factor in ISCOTT's difficulties was the tremendous opposition which the company faced in trying to sell its steel in the United States. Five US steel companies accused ISCOTT of dumping steel on the US market. Subsequently, a team of US officials visited Trinidad and Tobago to examine ISCOTT's production costs and concluded that the company was being subsidized in various ways by the state and as such was not competing fairly in the US market. Consequently, in 1984 countervailing duties assessed at 6.738 per cent *ad valorem* were imposed on Trinidad and Tobago's steel.

In 1987, in order to avoid fines of up to US $100 million, ISCOTT signed a Voluntary Restraint Agreement, limiting Trinidad and Tobago's steel exports to the US to 73 500 tons per annum.[53] Although, according to the Minister of External Affairs and International Trade, this represented a reduction of only 8 per cent of Trinidad and Tobago's steel exports to the US, it has nonetheless been regarded as a "major setback to the local steel industry."[54] ISCOTT, it should be noted, was operating at well below its rated capacity for all product lines and, under hired German management, production had increased over the 1986 level. In the first half of 1988, the total output of iron and steel products amounted to 625.9 thousand tonnes, or 25.1 per cent higher than the corresponding period in 1987. This comprised 287 000 tonnes of direct reduced iron; 204 000 tonnes of billets; and 135 000 tonnes of wire rods.[55] Hence, not only did the VRA reduce the existing level of exports, it may also have curtailed future exports to the US which would have resulted from improved productivity. Of the quota allowed, 40 000 tonnes have been reserved for ISCOTT, with the rest going to other local exporters of steel products.

ISCOTT has not been the only company affected by the VRA. Steel-products exporting companies in the private sector have also been affected. The most important of these is Central Trinidad Steel Limited (Centrin), "the only serious local private downstream industry established at Point Lisas."[56] As the *Trinidad Guardian* editorialized, Centrin had "by its own enterprise, penetrated the US market under the CBI but was halted in its tracks by a Voluntary Restraint Agreement (VRA) over which it had no control."[57] The VRA came at a time when Centrin was expanding its US market share and had set a goal of 70 000 tonnes of exports to the US. But as a company spokesman put it, the VRA "stopped the private sector in its tracks"[58] by causing the company's exports to the US to be limited to 20 000 tonnes a year.[59] The fact that Trinidad and Tobago's steel enters the US market duty-free under the CBI has apparently not been sufficient to placate Trinidadian steel exporters and state officials and restore their confidence in the CBI and the Reagan administration generally. Nevertheless, they are publicly hopeful that a revised version of the CBI legislation which has come before the US Congress (often referred to as CBI II) will provide some redress, if enacted. Of particular interest is a proposal to introduce a separate injury-determination basis for CBI beneficiary countries in countervailing duty and antidumping cases. This presumably will be less punitive than existing arrangements and may benefit the local steel industry. The future of the bill is, however, uncertain. The experience with steel has made Trinidadian officials wary of the CBI. It prompted one official of the IDC to caution that duty-free concessions under the program do not prevent import quotas from being imposed on any product.[60]

Finally, as was noted in the introductory essay of this volume, the CBI was enhanced in 1986 by the introduction of Guaranteed Access Levels (GALs, also referred to as "Super 807") which provided for the export of garments to the US at negotiated levels above "807" quotas. Since Trinidad and Tobago already possesses a fairly well-developed textile and garment industry dominated by local capital, this measure appears more promising than any other aspect of the CBI. However, although the Government of Trinidad and Tobago has already negotiated GALs with the US government, this has not yet yielded any significant benefits to the local textile and garment industry. During the first quarter of 1987, Trinidad and Tobago's production of textiles and garments fell by over 30 per cent, compared with the third quarter of 1986. It fell by a further 19 per cent during the second quarter of 1987. Although the industry had recovered somewhat by the end of 1987, production still remained below the level attained at the end of 1986.[61] Moreover, the recovery, which continued into 1988, has resulted primarily from domestic sales, which increased substantially after the government, in a desperate attempt to arrest further decline in the industry, imposed a ban on the importation of garments in mid-1987.[62] Nevertheless, exports have also increased from a modest TT$6 million in 1986 to TT$11 million by the end of 1988.[63] Although part of this increase may be attributable to Caricom markets, it is also likely that the "807" trade accounts for a portion.[64]

7.2 Investments

Alexander Good, the CBI Ombudsman in the Reagan administration, has noted that 12 companies have signed Letters of Intent for new investments in Trinidad and Tobago. The proposed projects included an ammonia plant, a resort complex, a merchant bank, and a rice production facility.[65] Attributing these developments to the CBI is, to say the least, highly problematic. Certainly, local officials at the IDC and the TTMA were not as sanguine as the Ombudsman.[66] But even if the Ombudsman's information is reliable, it would still be in reference to potential rather than actual investment. This would hardly be a departure for the CBI, since the program has always tantalized regional capitalists and state officials with its potential.[67] While this position may have had some credibility when the program was introduced, today, as the CBI approaches the mid-point of its statutory duration of 12 years, it is much less defensible. Clearly, the actual impact and not the theoretical potential of the program must now be the focus of any assessment.

It was suggested that at least one company, Colourclad, may have had its origin in the CBI.[68] This company is a joint venture between a local conglomerate, Neal and Massy Holdings (60%) and a French company, TREFIMA (40%). Currently, Colourclad constitutes a relatively small investment of about US $2 million and employs only six people.[69] The company makes colour-coated corrugated metal roofing sheets. The sheets are imported pre-coated from the foreign partner and Colourclad simply presses them into corrugated sheets. This process adds very little value to the product and transforms it only marginally. Hence, the product does not presently qualify for duty-free treatment under the CBI because it fails to meet the "substantial transformation" and value-added requirements of the program. Consequently, 80 per cent of the output is sold on the local market, with the rest going to other Caricom countries. The aim of the investors is to perform both the colour-coating and the corrugation processes in Trinidad and Tobago. Since the colour-coating treatment is a high value process, it is expected that its addition will enable the product to meet the CBI's value-added requirements and place the company in a position to export to the US under the program. Access to the US is by no means assured, however, for there remains the danger of import quotas being imposed by US authorities.[70] When, or if, the company becomes ready to export to the US, it will most likely be constrained by the VRA. Since ISCOTT has already laid claim to 40 000 tonnes of the steel quota negotiated under the VRA and Centrin has also been awarded 20 000 tonnes, this obviously leaves very little to be divided among remaining affected companies. It would appear, then, that there is little scope for Colourclad in the US market, irrespective of the CBI.

The above discussion notwithstanding, it is nevertheless evident that the investors in Colourclad saw potential access to the US market through the CBI as an incentive for their investment (it should be noted that the investment decision was taken prior to the VRA). Yet, it cannot be said that that was the only, or even the primary, motivation behind the investment. In fact, the feasibility study for the venture undertaken by the foreign partner included the scenario of an inaccessible US market. It was found that such a situation would not jeopardize the viability of the enterprise because Latin American and Caribbean markets would be adequate.[71] It is thus likely (and this is the view of a local representative of the company) that the venture would have been undertaken even in the absence of the CBI.[72]

The existence of Colourclad does little to contradict the basic argument that the CBI has had no significant impact on the economic development of Trinidad and Tobago. The venture is singular and, furthermore, may not even have originated from the CBI. Moreover, it currently constitutes a relatively small investment, employs very few people and, having created no backward linkages with the rest of the economy, contributes very little to the deepening of the manufacturing process in the country. There are, obviously, forward linkages with the local construction industry, but since other local companies were already producing similar products for the domestic market, these linkages represent essentially a quantitative rather than a qualitative enhancement of manufacturing in the country. Finally, Colourclad has had very little impact on the country's export position and is not a hard currency earner. Thus, it would appear that on all criteria the operations of this company contravene the government's new investment policy and its expectations of the manufacturing sector, as outlined in the IDC's investment document (cited earlier) and the government's new development plan.[73]

One phenomenon which has the potential to boost a country's exports (especially of manufactured goods) is the Export Processing Zone (EPZ), and increasingly regional governments are turning to them as a way of capitalizing on the CBI. Trinidad and Tobago is no exception. For this reason, we now turn to a discussion of EPZs as they relate to the CBI and industrial development in Trinidad and Tobago.

7.3   Export Processing Zones

In the summer of 1988, Export Processing Zones (EPZs) became the most widely discussed economic issue in Trinidad and Tobago. The idea had in fact already received some governmental attention as early as 1985, when a committee was appointed to study its prospects in Trinidad and Tobago. The present administration (which came to power in December 1986) has embraced EPZs as the only realistic solution to the current unemployment crisis in the country and has been actively promoting it at home and abroad. Prior to 1985, this type of investment was not given serious attention by the Government of Trinidad and Tobago.[74] So the enthusiasm with which it is currently being pursued gives some indication of the profundity of the country's current economic crisis and the level of desperation, if not panic, which has seized the ruling classes there. One official captured this urgency when he noted, "it is very good that Trinidad and Tobago should be going into this [i.e., EPZs] at this time," and went on to explain, "this is the only saviour for providing jobs and to [sic] providing them quickly, because this country is fast going into a state of anarchy, caused mainly by unemployment."[75] Another contributor to the national debate on the issue felt the establishment of EPZs would give Trinidad and Tobago "a breathing space to avoid social disorders and revolution while the longer term economic strategic plans are waiting to bear fruit."[76] The Minister of Industry and Enterprise (under whose portfolio this issue falls) has expressed a similar view. He argued that "export processing zones are not to be seen as the total industrialization package but as a short term measure intended to alleviate the crushing unemployment problem."[77] Support for the strategy comes from the local business community (especially the conglomerates), the bureaucracy, the middle and upper levels of the state enterprises, and a segment of organized labour.[78]

In July 1988, the Trinidad and Tobago Parliament passed the Free Zones Bill, officially inaugurating the policy. The plan was to establish at least five EPZs in various parts of the country, with the first to be located at Point Lisas, where most of the necessary infrastructure already exists.[79] Over TT $500 000 have been allocated for the further preparation of the Point Lisas site.[80]

The 1985 committee which examined the prospects offered by EPZs concluded that because of the relatively high wages in the country "there is no real opportunity for attracting to the country enclave-type industries which depend on low wage labour."[81] The government, too, has argued that the "sweatshop" variety EPZs trumpeted by critics of the policy are not viable in Trinidad and Tobago, but that the country will be able to attract investment in the technologically advanced industries to develop the "more sophisticated" types of EPZ.[82] Vehement opposition to the EPZ policy has come from women's groups, from several academics, and most vociferously, from the militant Council of Progressive Trade Unions. Objections are made on four basic grounds: (i) that EPZs will lead to "sweatshops" being established in Trinidad and Tobago, to the detriment of rights won by workers in past struggles; (ii) that they will attract footloose investors who will leave as soon as workers begin to organize and make industrial demands; (iii) that EPZs can never be the panacea they are portrayed to be; and most importantly, (iv) that if EPZs become established in Trinidad and Tobago, a dependence on this type of industrial development may ensue, thereby jeopardizing more sound, long-term, national industrial and economic planning and development. Denis Pantin, for example, argues that while there may be some benefit from the "more sophisticated" types of EPZs, nevertheless, "the place to start . . . is not with EPZs but with overarching economic strategies for survival in the 1990s and 21st century." He adds, "Any attempted shortcut to this slow but vital and unavoidable process of strategic planning . . . will be the equivalent of playing 'scratch lottery' with the future of the country."[83]

It has also been argued that the EPZ strategy is essentially a return to the failed "industrialization by invitation" strategy of the 1950s and 1960s. In reality, the EPZ strategy is more liberal than the earlier strategy in the concessions it offers to foreign capital. Moreover, there is no stipulated time limit on the concessions. Largely because of this, some critics have argued that the EPZ policy signifies a lack of faith within the political leadership in the capacity of indigenous capitalists to bring about economic change, as the policy proposes to "surrender" the country's trade advantages under the CBI, Lomé, and Caribcan "to Hong Kong based entrepreneurs."[84] Hence, they conclude that after nearly 40 years of effort at industrialization, the present administration, by instituting this policy, will have brought the country full circle. If indeed the state chooses to rely on Export Processing Zones as a strategy of industrialization, the validity of this argument will become undeniable. At this stage, the state defends itself, as we have seen, by arguing that EPZs are merely an emergency measure, not a long-term economic strategy. Nevertheless, doubts persist.

Export Processing Zones existed in the region for some time prior to the advent of the CBI, but they have increased rapidly since the program was introduced.[85] The US administration played an important role in this increase, as its CBI-related offices have periodically exhorted regional governments to "adopt legislation allowing privately run free-trade zones."[86] The connection between the EPZs and the CBI becomes even clearer when we note that Trinidadian officials have used the CBI as one of the main selling points for the proposed EPZs, especially to potential Asian investors. For example, the chairman of the Trinidad and Tobago Export Processing Zone company opportunistically observed that, because the US (traditionally the largest market for Asian exports) had indicated that in 1989 it would begin removing preferential tariffs extended to these exporters, "The Far Eastern countries are [sic] . . . looking for new places to manufacture with preferential entry arrangements into USA which we [i.e., Trinidad and Tobago] can supply under the Caribbean Basin Initiative."[87]

Yet it is by no means certain, or even likely, that even with EPZs Trinidad and Tobago will be able to take advantage of the CBI. This is mainly because the competition for EPZs among CBI beneficiary countries is fierce and there is every likelihood that, as the economic crisis in the region intensifies, it will become more so. Despite repeated devaluation of its currency in recent years (most recently in August 1988),[88] Trinidad and Tobago enters the competition with the significant disadvantage of having one of the highest wage rates in the region.[89] The disadvantage is even greater in relation to low-wage Asian countries.

Furthermore, the Trinidadian trade union movement is stronger than in most of the other CBI countries, and the militant Congress of Progressive Trade Unions has already given notice that it will fight for EPZ workers' rights to union representation as well. The danger of this, from the point of view of the state and local capitalists, is that foreign investors will be frightened away by the prospect of having to contend with a well-organized labour force. This situation is not without precedent in Trinidad and Tobago. Rhoda Reddock has cited the case of Trindata, an export-oriented company based on female labour which "ceased operations after the female staff had joined a radical trade union and concluded a favourable (to the workers) industrial agreement."[90] However, there are signs that the current economic crisis has made organized labour in the country more vulnerable to attacks from opposing forces for, as one businessman put it, "the unemployed have no Union and some may feel that a low salary is better than none at all."[91] This cynical comment is an indication of a basic anti-union/anti-working class sentiment which has been intensifying in Trinidad and Tobago in recent years, especially within the upper levels of the bureaucracy, state enterprises, and the private sector. One implication suggested by this statement is the possibility that those controlling the state may have taken the view that the current economic crisis offers an opportunity to recapture for capital some of the ground lost to workers during the boom years. In this light, EPZs would appear to provide one avenue through which to accomplish this. They would serve this end even more effectively if most of the enterprises established in them are foreign owned, for it is felt that foreign investors are likely to be less tolerant of, and vulnerable to, the demands (which are invariably deemed to be unreasonable) of Trinidadian workers.

Finally, the competition for EPZs may jeopardize efforts towards regional economic integration such as Caricom. This compounds a divisive tendency already inherent in the CBI at the political level, resulting from the fact that the program is administered on the basis of bilateral negotiations and agreements between individual governments of participating countries and the US government. Trinidad and Tobago, as the most industrialized member of Caricom, stands to lose

Table 7-6
Hourly Compensation Costs for Semi-skilled Production Workers in Export Manufacturing Industries, Selected Countries, 1987

	US$/hr*	US = 100	Low wage Asia = 1**
United States	13.66	100.0	52.3
Hong Kong	1.98	14.5	7.6
Thailand	0.35	2.6	1.3
Sri Lanka	0.29	2.1	1.1
Philippines	0.26	1.9	1.0
China	0.15	1.1	0.6
Mexico	0.84	6.1	3.2
CBI Beneficiary Countries			
Costa Rica	0.95	7.0	3.6
Guatemala	0.88	6.4	3.4
Honduras	0.53	3.9	2.0
Dominican Republic	0.79	5.8	3.0
Haiti	0.58	4.2	2.2
Jamaica	0.63	4.6	2.4
Barbados	1.72	12.6	6.6
Trinidad-Tobago	1.66	12.2	6.4
Antigua	1.40	10.2	5.4
St. Vincent	1.15	8.4	4.4
Dominica	0.92	6.7	3.5

* Including estimated payroll taxes, fringe benefits and year-end or equivalent bonuses.

** Average of Thailand, Sri Lanka, Philippines, and China.

Source: Adapted from the World Bank, *The Caribbean: Export Preferences and Performance* (Washington, DC, 1988).

a great deal from any disruption of trading relations within that group. Proponents argue that Trinidad and Tobago has much to offer potential investors. One official outlined the following attractions: (i) the country's workforce has one of the highest literacy rates in the region (98%) which makes it well-trained and easily trainable; (ii) the national language, English, is one with which Asian investors tend to have greater facility than other regional languages (Spanish, Dutch, and French); (iii) the presence of excellent transportation and telecommunication facilities in Trinidad and Tobago; (iv) the country's location at "the crossroads between North and South America with air and shipping facilities available in all directions"; and finally, (v) the availability of adequate electricity at favourable rates and abundant natural gas to be used directly as a raw material or as an energy feedstock.[92] It is interesting to note, however, that other regional countries advertise themselves on virtually the same basis, with the significant addition of "a positive investment climate" and the availability of cheap labour.[93] This suggests that even with the dubious strategy of Export Processing Zones, as the situation presently exists, Trinidad and Tobago stands to gain very little from the CBI. As is evident in the case of Jamaica, the Dominican Republic, Haiti, and to some extent Barbados, EPZ investors appear to be primarily in search of cheap labour.[94] Furthermore, if in order to attract foreign capital the state is to relinquish further control over investment strategy and abandon economic management to the "invisible hand" of private capital (especially foreign capital) through, for example, privately-run Export Processing Zones; and if, as well, the Trinidadian working class is to relinquish rights it has won through earlier struggles against capital, then the "benefit" to be derived from any resulting investment is obviously questionable.

7.4   936 Funds and Twin-Plant Projects

In August 1988, the Government of Trinidad and Tobago signed a Tax Information Exchange Agreement with the Government of the United States, the sole purpose of which was to make the country eligible to benefit from the use of 936 funds. In October 1988, an investment mission sponsored by the Overseas Private Investment Corporation (OPIC), an institution which is very closely associated with the CBI, and the US embassy (Port of Spain) visited Trinidad and Tobago to assess the prospects for investment, especially in the form of joint ventures, in "twin-plant" activities.[95] It is too soon to tell whether or not any concrete projects will emerge from this mission. Nevertheless, at this stage, it appears that prospects may not be particularly bright, for "Puerto Rico has indicated that qualifying projects are likely to be 'twin-plants' in which a CBI country operation is established to do labor-intensive production of semifinished goods for final processing and quality control procedures in Puerto Rico."[96] This obviously raises once more the question of Trinidad and Tobago's ability to profit from these funds, given that country's wage structure. That the government is, nevertheless, avidly pursuing these funds may suggest one of two things: either that it is not aware of the conditions which are attached to their use (which seems unlikely); or that it is aware of them but anticipates that its policies for reducing wages will eventually make wages in Trinidad and Tobago competitive with those of other countries in the region, thus enabling the country to compete for the labour-intensive twin-plant projects. The latter position, which appears more likely, conforms to the logic of American policy in the region, which holds that it is in the workers' interest to receive lower wages so as to expand employment. Either way, the prospects for the majority of the people in the country remain unattractive.

8 Conclusion

Chinese historians apparently take the view that it is still too soon to tell what impact the Renaissance has had on Europe. The proponents of the CBI might make similar claims with regard to the effect that program has had on the economies of the Caribbean and Central America. But, for the most part, they have opted for the more aggressive posture of defending the program, not simply on the basis of its potential, but also on its performance thus far. For example, the US Department of State reported that despite disappointing results in terms of overall export earnings, "the fundamental purpose of the CBI broadening and diversifying the production and export base of the region is being fulfilled."[97] We have seen also that the CBI ombudsman even attempted to include the program's performance in Trinidad and Tobago in his own optimistic appraisal. However, we have demonstrated that in the case of Trinidad and Tobago such optimism is unwarranted. The CBI has brought no significant new investments and has led to no noticeable increase in the volume, value, and diversity of the country's exports to the United States. On the contrary, since 1984 when the CBI came into operation, trade between Trinidad and Tobago and the US has shifted in the latter's favour, although Trinidad and Tobago still has a surplus of visible trade with the US. Finally, given that there have been no significant new investments and no noticeable increase in exports ("non-traditional" or otherwise), there cannot have been many new jobs created, either.

Currently, a great deal of attention is being devoted to Export Processing Zones but our analysis suggests that it is not at all clear that even the minimum expectation of this policy, the creation of employment, will be fulfilled. Furthermore, any employment which results is likely to be of a highly oppressive nature.[98] The latter would signify a substantial deterioration in the position of workers in the country. Finally, even if significant new investments do eventually materialize, it would still be necessary to examine the enterprises established to see what implications they hold for the country's overall industrialization before a judgment about their utility to the country can properly be made. Needless to say, in such an analysis the mental and physical cost to workers would have to be taken into account. If the evidence gathered in studies of existing EPZs in the region (e.g., in the Dominican Republic and Jamaica) and in other developing countries is suggestible, then overall, the odds are not in Trinidad and Tobago's favour.[99] Of major concern also is the danger that the considerable attention which the state is currently giving to Export Processing Zones will result in the relative neglect of more integrated, long-term industrial and overall economic planning. Meanwhile, the instant industrialization and ready-made export capability promised by EPZs may prove to be no more than a mirage, or at best they may become pit-stops for international capital in its relentless quest for that elusive quantity, the competitive edge. In this light, the fears of Pantin and other local critics of the policy cannot be ignored.

So completely has the CBI failed in Trinidad and Tobago that there is the distinct possibility of it backfiring on the US administration. In Trinidad and Tobago, the initial high expectations generated by the program have already given way in some quarters to profound disappointment. This in turn may already be giving way to cynicism and anger as frustrated government officials and, to a lesser extent, local business people, see little reward from their efforts, while they must constantly defend themselves against accusations from Washington that they are not doing enough to give effect to the program. Trinidadians may be more predisposed to such a reaction than other "beneficiaries" of the program, for several reasons. First, the memory of the "victimization" of ISCOTT (a company which has contributed significantly to the country's economic problems) is still very much alive and has made some people, especially in the state apparatus and the business community, wary of initiatives emanating from Washington — CBI-related or otherwise.[100] Second, Trinidadians have found it extremely difficult to accept that the boom years are really over, and many continue to look for instant or short-term solutions to return them to prosperity. The CBI may have been seen as potentially contributing to such a solution, but it has not delivered. Disillusionment with the CBI may compel Trinidadians and other CBI participants to turn elsewhere for solutions. Where they turn will depend on the outcome of current and future social struggle. Finally, for most of the post-colonial period, Trinidad and Tobago has acknowledged, but never fully embraced, US hegemony in the Caribbean. Consequently, it has tended to regard US initiatives (especially of a military nature) towards the region with some degree of reservation.[101] The failure of the CBI may very well reinforce this attitude.

It would appear, then, that not only has the CBI failed at the economic level, but that this failure may jeopardize its political objective as well. In the case of Trinidad and Tobago, the final outcome will depend particularly on the ability of the working class to defend itself against the heightened pressures being exerted upon it by a constellation of forces consisting of the local bourgeois stratum, the state, and US imperialism currently manifest in the CBI. Given the weakened position of organized labour brought about by the economic crisis, however, and the absence of a coherent project involving the entire labour movement, this defence constitutes an extremely formidable task at present. Nevertheless, regardless of its limitations, such opposition represents a challenge to the state and capital and as such an implicit rejection of the US administration's cynical attempt to buttress the fragile ruling classes of the region under the guise of an economic recovery program. As the preceding analysis has demonstrated, the program turned out to be not the economic medicine advertised, but a placebo.

8

The CBI and the Caribbean Community: The Implications of the CBI for the Regional Integration Movement

Fauzya Moore

1 Introduction

Analyses of the Caribbean Community (CARICOM) in the early 1980s usually begin with a litany of the Community's failures and end on a note of surprise because of its tenacity. Many developments in the early 1980s suggested that CARICOM had failed to fulfil its mandate. The Treaty of Chaguaramas,[1] which brought the Caribbean Community into being in July 1973, endows it with three functions: to promote integration amongst member states through arrangements for a common market and an economic community; to promote functional co-operation (co-operation in the social sectors); and to co-ordinate the foreign policies of the member states. The overarching task of the Community is to strengthen the historical ties of the peoples of the region and deepen them into a movement for further integration of the constituent countries.[2]

However, by 1980 intra-regional trade had not increased for several years, regional institutions experienced difficulty in obtaining financing for regional programs, and in 1983 the heads of government, in a highly public failure, did not reach a consensus on policy towards Grenada before the American intervention. The impetus to integrate slowed as a result of economic and political differences between Caribbean governments. The future success of Caribbean regional integration appeared to be in some doubt.

This chapter explores the difficulties facing the integration movement in the early 1980s. The inherent limitations of the regional integration scheme were severely exacerbated by the Caribbean Basin Initiative. The offer of the CBI (if such it may be called) placed a severe strain on

---

Notes for Chapter 8 are on pp. 259-60.

the regional institutions, since governments were called upon to choose between support for regionalism and a rival approach to development, based on bilateral ties to the United States. The fact that the integration movement survived the challenge of the CBI, which had its ultimate manifestation in the Grenada crisis, is due in no small measure to the flexibility of the regional arrangements. It is also due to the failure of the CBI to take into consideration regional priorities and therefore its inability to promote the development of the participating countries.

To evaluate the impact of the CBI on CARICOM it is first useful to look at developments within CARICOM at the beginning of the 1980s.

2   The Emerging Regional Crisis, CARICOM

It is usually argued that a "crisis of inertia" had developed within the regional integration arrangements by this date. Most of the ministerial committees of the Community, including the Common Market Council (CMC) and the Standing Committee of Ministers Responsible for Foreign Affairs (SCMFA), met regularly, but a conference of the heads of government had not taken place since 1976. The movement appeared to lack political direction.

The trade regime had also failed to produce a significant overall growth in intra-regional trade; on the contrary, such trade had diminished. In 1973, intra-regional exports accounted for approximately 10.3 per cent of all exports. Yet in constant (1975) values intra-regional trade declined every year between 1975 and 1980, except in 1978, when it increased by 1.5 per cent over 1977. The real value of intra-regional imports fell to 8 per cent in 1979-80.[3]

The difficulties of intra-regional trade stymied the development of other intra-regional arrangements. The Caribbean Multilateral Clearing Facility (CMCF) collapsed in 1982, and the Caribbean Investment Corporation (CIC) and the Agricultural Marketing Protocol (AMP) were both terminated in the same year.

As a result of economic difficulties in several CARICOM countries, contributions towards financing regional integration schemes derived primarily from Trinidad and Tobago, the only oil exporter of the group. Between 1973-81 it was estimated that Trinidad provided at least $400 million to CARICOM countries to finance regional projects and for balance of payments support.[4]

Without active financial participation by Guyana and Jamaica, both of which experienced an economic crisis during this period, the regional infrastructure lacked the necessary resources to implement many of its programs. The secretariat experienced some limited success in attracting support from donor agencies; but in so doing, the regional integration movement became increasingly subject to external influences.[5]

The expectation that CARICOM would contribute to the development of its member states was also called into question. Progress in regionalism was adversely affected by the two oil shocks of the 1970s, the emerging debt burden, and the increasing need for structural adjustment. The common market contributed very little to the development of member states. With the exception of Trinidad and Tobago, the region's countries experienced declining rates of growth.[6] Between 1970 and 1979 Guyana experienced zero growth in its real per capita GNP, and five countries, Antigua and Baruda, Dominica, Grenada, Jamaica, and St. Vincent, experienced negative rates of growth.[7] The external debt of all the region's more developed countries (again excluding Trinidad and Tobago) also grew considerably during this period.[8] Regional arrangements appeared unable to counter this decline or to encourage intra-regional dynamism. A CARICOM working group recognized in 1981 that "in the face of its limited achievements — particularly when measured against . . . great hopes and expectations . . . CARICOM has suffered a serious loss of faith and hope by the regional public and international community. . . . Thus while both the regional and international situations demand fresh commitment to and indicate an increased role for CARICOM, there is at the same time a more urgent need for renewal of confidence in the regional movement itself."[9]

There were mitigating aspects to this economic picture. In the area of institution building, a great deal of "functional federalism" had taken place.[10] Most of the standing committees of the Community met regularly and had promoted integration through the technical co-operation of the member states. The Associate Institutions of the Community, such as the Caribbean Development Bank and the University of the West Indies, continued to function effectively. The existing network of regional institutions was considerably expanded and new areas of functional and technical co-operation developed. For example, a Caribbean Examinations Council and a Caribbean Food Corporation were created, and a regional food and nutrition strategy was developed. The West Indies Shipping Corporation was redefined and in 1975 Leeward Islands Aviation Travel (LIAT) was designated a regional carrier. Considerable progress was made in health manpower development, epidemiological surveillance, establishing national programs for women and development, and so on.[11] In the important area of international economic relations, three agreements were collectively negotiated — the Lomé Convention, the Mexico-CARICOM agreement, and the updated Canada-West Indies agreement of 1979. Some non-official initiatives also reinforced the tradition of multi-island co-operation. For example, in the area of information the Caribbean News

Agency (CANA) was created, and several non-governmental organizations were organized to serve the CARICOM constituency.

Even in the "Cinderella" aspect of the treaty, the co-ordination of foreign policy, a significant level of co-operation had taken place. The Standing Committee of Ministers Responsible for Foreign Affairs (SCMFA) had met regularly since its creation. It co-ordinated regional positions on, *inter alia*, the Law of the Sea, the decolonization of the non-independent Commonwealth Caribbean countries, and the Guyana/Venezuela and Belize/Guatemala territorial disputes. The SCMFA also served as an introductory forum for new countries to the international arena.

Thus, as a result of this extensive technical and functional co-operation, the Community built a fund of "political capital," and the system of standing committees institutionalized a habit of joint consultation and co-operation on issues of policy, both intra-regional and international. CARICOM in 1980, while in need of revitalization, had developed both a technocratic and political culture, based largely on the pragmatic need for co-operation between small island states. It had become both a support for and a focus of national policy amongst the countries of the region.

3   The Impact of the CBI

The CARICOM group had established procedures for the negotiation and implementation of international economic agreements with third countries. Negotiations were conducted jointly by CARICOM countries after they had established collective negotiating positions. The CARICOM group also participated in the joint review of established international agreements. The Common Market Council considered the implementation of the Lomé Convention and the Canada-West Indies agreements and usually reviewed changes to the agreements. The slate of regional projects was in both instances submitted to council.

Hall has argued that three principles governed the role of regional institutions in the management of international economic agreements.[12] They were that;

- international economic agreements should respect the integrity and autonomy of regional organizations;
- external economic programs should utilize regional institutions, resources, and expertise; that external economic agreements should strengthen regional integration and co-operation and encourage more intensive exchange in the industrial, financial, and trade areas in order to maximize economic and developmental benefits and respect the commitment of regional states to regional objectives;
- external economic agreements should reflect regional priorities.

The CBI paid no regard to these emerging traditions. The governing assumptions of the CBI were that the "incipient radical alliance" of Cuba, Nicaragua, Grenada, Guyana, and Suriname posed a threat to the peace and security of the area. The non-radical Caribbean countries were in a state of decline and therefore subject to political (i.e., Communist) disruption. This process could be reversed if the private sector were permitted to initiate the development thrust of the area and governments developed free market economies. Exports from these countries would be allowed preferential access to the American market. Conversely, American enterprise would be given free rein in the "Basin."

The "package" to be offered to the countries of the area was therefore an integrated proposal with trade rather than aid as the locomotive of growth, and free enterprise as the basis for development. The economic policies of any country were an important indication of its political orientation and therefore a criterion of eligibility for beneficiary status. Security assistance could be provided to countries which felt themselves under threat from Communist subversion.

Despite early consultations with Prime Minister Seaga of Jamaica by the Republican administration on an economic recovery plan for the region, no Commonwealth Caribbean country appears to have been fully involved in the early discussions on the form and substance of the CBI. The US administration instead concentrated its efforts on co-opting Canada, Venezuela, and Mexico as partners in the "plan." In July 1981, a meeting of representatives of the four governments was held in Nassau during which President Reagan outlined his plans for the area and sought the collaboration of the three governments. While sympathetic to the initiative, the three governments moved away from joint sponsorship when its geopolitical implications became clear. The CARICOM countries, in search of development, did not have the same option.

In 1981, therefore, the Commonwealth Caribbean was confronted with a situation in which an entire agenda for its economic and political development had been created without its input, knowledge or collective behest. The key to the United States' Commonwealth Caribbean strategy was the situation in Central America and concern over the "importation" of Communism into the region. American hostility to Grenada was sufficiently pronounced to attract denunciation at the 1981 meeting of CARICOM foreign ministers.[13]

Notwithstanding (and perhaps because of) the CBI's disregard of the area's regional institutions and its governments, the secretariat, at the request of the CARICOM foreign ministers, began to study the CBI and to design a strategy to address the impact of the proposed American munificence. The developing momentum of the CBI also facilitated the work of the secretary-general in convening a meeting of the conference of heads of government of the Community, in 1982, the first such conference since 1976. In other words the regional movement, following what was by now a classic pattern, responded with consultative and technical activity to anticipated changes in the external environment.

4   Preliminary Considerations

By September 1981 several standing committees and technical working groups had been convened to study the question of the CBI. Consultations were subsequently held with the Dominican Republic, Suriname, and Haiti. These meetings developed guidelines which became the centrepiece for the emerging regional position on the CBI. They were announced in the communiqués of CARICOM meetings held during the negotiations for the CBI.[14] They included stipulations that
- the plan be open to all countries of the region;
- the principles of ideological pluralism be respected;
- the national goals should be respected and aid should not be granted or denied for military or political considerations;
- regional institutions should be utilized wherever reasonable;
- the principle of non-interference in the internal affairs of countries of the area be respected.

In keeping with the expectations raised by the Lomé process, some Caribbean countries expressed concern that
- development assistance should be provided in grant form
- it should be provided for both the public and the private sectors
- consideration should be given to Caribbean "regional value added" criteria
- the region as a whole should be designated a single beneficiary for the purposes of negotiating a bilateral investment treaty
- the "basin" would require about 4.7 billion between 1982 and 1985, and $580 in emergency aid in 1982 to meet its development needs.[15]

But no procedure, or forum, was established for joint negotiations with the United States. There was, moreover, no institution which could facilitate the development of a joint negotiating position between the Central American and Caribbean countries; and as a result of the haste of the Republican administration to usher the CBI through Congress, the creation of any joint negotiating structure within the Caribbean to achieve consensus on Caribbean concerns, and then to negotiate with the US, proved impossible.

While such regional consultations as did occur continued, the draft legislation for the Caribbean Basin Economic Recovery Act (CBERA) was under consideration by Congress. The bill was supported by other legislative provisions, including provisions for increased economic and security assistance and bilateral investment treaties. Yet the "package" making its way through committee did not recognize regional concerns. The bilateral investment treaties even contained clauses that were arguably in violation of the sovereignty of the individual member states. In a region seeking a unified approach to foreign investment in order to obviate competition between its numerous small states, the CBI provided only for treaties between the USA and individual countries. No support was to be provided for regional production schemes, and little recognition was given to potential co-operation in agro-industry. The CBERA also excluded many of the exports in which the Caribbean had a potential comparative advantage and allowed for inspection of the agricultural policy of CBI beneficiaries, a duplication of the existing regional strategy on food and nutrition. The "package" even envisaged the creation of new, externally sponsored, regional institutions, such as a proposed private sector development bank.[16]

It was also made clear that there was to be no regional or sub-regional dialogue between the United States and the beneficiaries. The concerns of the regional integration movement were not considered, since the movement contained the suspect regimes of Guyana and Grenada. Negotiations took place on a bilateral basis, and the smaller countries of the area were thus placed at a severe numerical and technical disadvantage in their discussions with US officials.

Under the CBI, competition became possible between CARICOM states for financial benefits from the United States. The smaller countries of the group participated in the negotiations without the benefit of regional advice and were unable to make any headway in their efforts to stress the priority they attached to their urgent need for support for basic infrastructure.

The CBI offered an apparently unprecedented opportunity for access to the American market and for American assistance both in economic development and security. The choice was either to abandon its regional institutions to marginalization (and to the non-beneficiary member states) or to insist on regional treatment in the face of American resistance. Acceptance of the CBI meant that the region was to be redefined in Cold War terms between the acceptable and the isolated.

Despite the early cohesion of the CBI member states, when confronted with a "take it or leave it" attitude on the part of the administration they began to weigh their options. On the one hand was a Community that had yet to prove its economic worth, on the other a plan for access to a lucrative market. Several countries outside CARICOM, and a few within, had already signalled their interest in the plan;

should the others be left out in the cold with their principles, or join the group?

5 The Heads of Government Conferences

The emerging challenge to regional integration was discussed at the heads of government meeting in 1982 in Ocho Rios, Jamaica. The successful convening of the meeting was in part due to the concern about the CBI and the question of a redefinition of the Caribbean. Faced with the possibility of a region divided, the heads re-affirmed their support of the Caribbean Community, but stopped short of criticizing the CBI.

In fact, the heads somewhat meekly hoped "that the legislative process would soon be completed . . . [and] requested the United States government, in addition to evolving bilateral programmes, to give consideration to contributing on a grant basis to the Unified Special Development Fund of the Caribbean Development Bank."[17]

The heads also reaffirmed the right of the Community countries to "ideological pluralism," i.e., the ability of each member state to pursue its choice of political orientation without judgment or sanction from others. Having done so, the countries of the region then proceeded with bilateral negotiations on the CBI in the vain expectation that the guidelines established in joint consultation and the pronouncements of the heads of government would be sufficient to protect regional unity and perhaps to influence the nature of the CBI.

Caribbean attitudes towards the CBI were further influenced by the promise of supplementary economic assistance from the US. When the Supplemental Assistance Bill of 1982 was finally approved, however, only the Eastern Caribbean received a small amount of supplemental funding. More significantly, in October 1982 Barbados and some members of the Organization of Eastern Caribbean States (OECS) group — Grenada's neighbours — signed a Memorandum of Understanding which provided for joint co-operation in some areas of security. The Regional Security System (RSS) was created, and financing for it was obtained from the American government.[18] Grenada was not a signatory to the Memorandum. The possibility of security assistance remained an incentive to the CARICOM LDCs to accede to the provisions of the CBI.

Thus the objections of the Caribbean to the CBI were muted, and a collective negotiating approach never emerged, even when American policy appeared to be to the disadvantage of the Caribbean. It was not until mid-1983 that reservations about the CBI began to be collectively expressed. When, in 1983, the United States introduced countervailing duties on Trinidadian steel imports and the future of Caribbean rum under the CBI became questionable, the CARICOM group once again sought strength in cohesion.

In July 1983 the heads of government met in Port-of-Spain, Trinidad and Tobago, almost on the eve of the final passage of the CBI legislation through Congress. At that meeting a comprehensive discussion of the provisions of the legislation took place, and the communiqué indicated the growing regional frustration at the intransigence of the United States.

> In taking note of progress in the implementation of the CBI Conference expressed its conviction that participation in the benefits under the CBI should be open to all CARICOM states. It was agreed that Member States in their bilateral discussions with the United States Administration on the trade aspects of the CBI Bill should press for simultaneous designation of all Member States of CARICOM as beneficiaries so as to preserve the integrity of the regional common market arrangements.[19]

Notwithstanding the above, the CBI legislation was passed by Congress on August 5, 1983, without consideration of CARICOM concerns. For the first time, the offer of the CBI divided CARICOM states over a question of international economic relations. In so doing it weakened the fabric of the integration movement. Despite attempts to co-ordinate negotiations, bilateral discussions ensured that there was no collective co-ordination of effort and therefore no means of putting forward a CARICOM position other than announcements at heads of government meetings. And the importation of ideological considerations into the negotiations meant that the political relations between CARICOM countries were adversely affected. The extent of the disunity was not fully recognized until the Grenada crisis of October 1983.

It is not the intention of this chapter to discuss the details of the Grenada crisis. However, the disunity in the CARICOM group over Grenada resulted in part from the loss of faith in the regional consultative process to address the problem. This in turn was a result of the emerging alignment of CARICOM states into opposing ideological camps and disagreement over the interpretation of the nature of the "threat" posed by Grenada to the peace and security of the region.

Although the CBI was primarily an economic agreement, its geopolitical underpinnings and the US insistence on bilateral designation thus had far-reaching implications for CARICOM, the region's political community. Acceptance of the CBI by all but two member states damaged procedures for consensus on economic issues among the group and made respect for the principle of ideological pluralism impossible. The CBI also created a second institutional nexus within the region, calling into question established loyalties and alignments.

6   The Post-Nassau Environment

Yet the regional integration movement weathered the storm of the CBI and the Grenada crisis. How did this happen? Several responses are possible. At the level of *process*, the Nassau Summit, convened in July 1984 after several months of intensive intra-regional diplomacy, brought to an end the official rancour over Grenada by re-establishing the Community as an option for economic development. With the change of government in Grenada, member states were able to put aside ideological questions and address the problem of the regional economy. Barriers to intra-regional trade were removed, and in subsequent years intra-regional trade grew significantly. A Community response to the problem of structural adjustment was developed, and negotiations on structural adjustment have tended to consider regional as well as national concerns. In general, Community arrangements for export-led development were updated.

The Community discovered rather quickly that the gains under the CBI were modest and that a revitalization of intra-regional trade would provide as much if not more developmental benefit than integration on CBI terms with the North American market. In political terms the "implosion" of the NJM regime, followed by intervention in Grenada and the American rapprochement with Guyana, removed the "problem" of radical regimes from the optic of the CBI and therefore improved the internal cohesion of the CARICOM group. And in global terms, the Caribbean Community had simply built up too many regional arrangements and too great an inter-sectoral dependency on regional co-operation—functional, economic, and political—to allow external penetration significantly to damage the movement.

However, some issues have not been addressed by the Community since 1983. The issue of regional security was until 1990 relegated to the polite ruminations of the Commonwealth Small States Report.[20] Pronouncements on ideological pluralism have disappeared from CARICOM communiqués, and a CARICOM approach to the emergence of any new "radical" government in the Community awaits clarification. The joint management of international economic relations has acquired renewed credibility in view of the obvious shortcomings of the CBI, but the Caribbean has not yet tried to achieve an agreement on a joint negotiating process with the United States on the CBI. As a result, Caribbean countries remain subject to the vicissitudes of the American political process and subordinate partners in a paternalistic, and at times, inappropriate agreement.

7 Conclusion

The impact of the CBI on the regional integration movement is a story of both weakness and strength. The governments of the CARICOM movement appeared to give up far too easily the hard-won principles of nearly a decade of integration for the short-term gains of the CBI. The negotiating centre could not hold. And there was a redefinition of the region on ideological principles, and a consequent waning of the regional integration effort. But the problems caused by such redefinition also demonstrated some of the strengths of the movement, including its apparent ability to "ratoon" (spring back) in the face of overwhelming odds. These include the flexibility of the regional movement to adapt regional programs where necessary; the resistance to dismantling longstanding institutions for reasons of political or ideological expediency; and finally, the existence of a regional fund of expertise on the region, worthy of greater utilization. On balance, even the CBI might become more effective if regional — and national — concerns were given due consideration: but in order for this to happen the CARICOM group would have to signal its collective unwillingness to proceed with a process so completely dominated in Washington by political and domestic considerations.

Notes

Chapter 1

1 Maurice Bishop of Grenada, however, denounced it as "the biggest confidence game of the century" (*Sunday Express*, Caribbean Basin supplement, March 28, 1982). Revolutionary Grenada was excluded from the program.

2 President Reagan, Address to the OAS, February 24, 1982, cited in D. Ramnarine, *The Philosophy and Developmental Prospects of the United States Caribbean Basin Initiative*, Occasional Paper Series, Group for Studies in National and International Development, Queen's University, Kingston, Canada, 1989, p. 42 (a revised version of which appears under the same title in this volume).

3 Stephen Lande, former Assistant US Trade Representative and considered by some the father of the original CBI and an important contributor to CBI II (see below), has argued that the "CBI now has the potential to evolve from a modest success into a program creating vigorous export economies." See Stephen Lande and Nellis Crigler, "CBI: The Bermuda Triangle of Trade?," *The International Economy* (March/April 1989): 54. See also "Economic Development in the Caribbean Basin Region," CBI Embassy Group, Washington, DC, January 1989.

4 The eligible countries/territories are: Anguilla, Antigua-Barbuda, The Bahamas, Barbados, Belize, Dominica, Dominican Republic, El Salvador, Grenada, Guatemala, Guyana, Haiti, Honduras, Jamaica, Nicaragua, Panama, St. Lucia, St. Vincent and the Grenadines, Suriname, Trinidad-Tobago, Cayman Islands, Montserrat, Netherlands Antilles, St. Kitts-Nevis, Turks and Caicos Islands, and the British Virgin Islands. 98th Cong. 2nd sess., 1984, H. Doc. 98-151 (Washington, DC: US Government Printing Office, 1984), p. 39.

5 Anguilla, Cayman Islands, Suriname, and Turks and Caicos Islands have not yet requested beneficiary status.

6 This provision was used to exclude Nicaragua and Grenada from the program until the leftist governments in those countries had been removed.

7 Panama's beneficiary status was withdrawn in April 1988, following the indictment of its leader, General Manuel Noriega, for drug-trafficking.

8 The president of the US may waive several of the above conditions for reasons of "national, economic, or security interests" (US Department of Commerce, *1989 Guidebook Caribbean Basin Initiative*, Washington, DC, October 1989, p. 14).

9 Ibid., pp. 14-15.

10 W.I. Robinson and Kent Norsworthy, *David and Goliath* (New York: Monthly Review Press, 1987) provide an excellent account of US strategic

assessments of the Nicaraguan situation. On the general history of American interests in the region, see Jenny Pearce, *Under the Eagle: US Intervention in Central America and the Caribbean* (Boston: South End Press, 1982). See also John Holmes and Colin Leys, eds., *Frontyard/Backyard: The Americas in the Global Crisis* (Toronto: Between the Lines, 1987).

11 US Department of Commerce, *1989 CBI Guidebook*, p. 32.
12 Ibid., pp. 32-33.
13 Richard C. Schroeder, "Congress Moving Slowly on CBI-2," *The Times of America*, September 6, 1989, p. 14.
14 Testimony of J. Paul Sticht, Vice-Chairman of the Caribbean/Central American Action, to the Senate Committee on Finance Sub-committee on International Trade, February 9, 1990. Mr. Sticht is a former chairman of RJR Nabisco. Caribbean/Central American Action is a lobby group which represents economic interests in the respective regions.

Chapter 2

1 Robert Manning, "Reagan: Sights on a New Order," *South* (September 1983): 9.
2 The method of impressing this point of view on other developed countries consisted of a reminder that the US was responsible for their collective security. President Reagan saw the economic decline as "the decline of Western security" and argued that the policies of the allies "undermined free markets and compromised our collective security" (Address by President Reagan to the Commonwealth Club of California, March 4, 1983, *Weekly Compilation of Presidential Documents* 19 [1983]: 338).
3 Inherent in this prescription is the assumption that the US, the locomotive, was being stalled by the protectionist weight of other countries. This interpretation, by vindicating the US economy, might have given comfort to the administration, but it evaded the still persistent structural determinants of the crisis and their manifestations in the US economy.
4 President Reagan made clear this strategy when he declared: "We're working with the International Monetary Fund to keep a firm focus on the role of effective domestic policies in the growth and stability of the world economy" and disclosed that the US had taken a leading role at the November 1982 GATT Ministerial meeting in "resisting protectionism, strengthening existing institutions, and addressing the key issues of trade in the future" (Ronald Reagan, Address, pp. 341-42).
5 In 1984, $1.2 billion in imports were released from duty-free treatment, bringing total exclusions to $11.9 billion. For the first time in the 10-year history of the GSP, the value of exclusions (based on 1983 trade) exceeded the value of GSP imports ($10.8 billion). The countries most affected have been Taiwan, Korea, Hong Kong, and the debt-ridden Brazil, and Mexico (US International Trade Commission, *Operation of Trade Agreements, 1984* [Washington, DC: USITC, 1984], p. 218).
6 US economic assistance fell from $13.1 billion in 1985 to $8 billion in 1986 (US Congress, Senate Committee on Appropriations, *Related Programs Appropriations Bill, 1987* [Report], 99th Cong., 2nd sess. [Washington, DC: US Government Printing Office, 1986], pp. 5-7).
7 Manning, "Reagan," p. 10.

8 Net external borrowing by the seven major Latin American countries (Argentina, Brazil, Chile, Colombia, Mexico, Peru, and Venezuela), for example, declined from about $48 billion in 1981 to about $16 billion in 1984, owing to a decline in official lending (Inter-American Development Bank, *Economic and Social Progress in Latin America. External Debt: Crisis and Adjustment* [Washington, DC: IDB, 1985 Report], p. 18).

9 Ibid. In 1984, for example, interest payments for the seven major Latin American countries averaged 38 per cent of export earnings, and investment dropped from 24 per cent of GNP in 1980 to 17 per cent in 1984.

10 See D. Ramnarine, "The Philosophy and Development Prospects of the Caribbean Basin Initiative," in this volume.

11 The familiar "evil empire" characterization was rendered at an address by President Reagan to the Annual Convention of the National Association of Evangelicals in Orlando, Florida on March 8, 1983. See *Weekly Compilation of Presidential Documents* 19 (1983): 369.

12 The view that the Soviet Union was becoming more expansionist was widely articulated by US officials at a number of public forums. See, for example, Ronald Reagan, Annual Convention, and Casper Weinberger, Address before the Council on Foreign Relations, New York, April 20, 1982 (*American Foreign Policy* [AFP] [1982]: 5). This assertion was convincingly refuted in a widely acclaimed study by the Centre for Defense Information, "Soviet Geopolitical Momentum: Myth or Menace? Trends of Soviet Influence Around the World from 1945 to 1986," *The Defense Monitor* 15, 5 (1986).

13 "Communist Interference in El Salvador," Report by the Department of State, February 23, 1891. *AFP: Current Documents*, Document 670, pp. 1230-36.

14 "Documents Demonstrating Communist Support of the Salvadoran Insurgency," Documentary Annex to a Report prepared in the Department of State, February 23, 1981, *AFP*, Supplement, 1981, Chapter 30, Part B, Document 1218.

15 Former US ambassador to El Salvador Robert White testified before a Subcommittee of the House Appropriations Committee just two days after the appearance of the White Paper that, *inter alia*, most of the 10 000 civilian executions were committed by members of the security forces in the pay of the oligarchy, and that the Salvadoran government was therefore not neutral, nor had it stabilized in view of this fact.

16 "Tarnished Report," *Wall Street Journal*, June 8, 1981, p. 1; "White Paper on El Salvador is Faulty," *Washington Post*, June 8, 1981, p. 1A. The perspective of a one-time insider on the role of the CIA in fabricating "evidence" such as is presented in the White Paper is given in Warner Poelchau, ed., *White Paper Whitewash: Interview with Philip Agee on the CIA and El Salvador* (New York: Deep Cover Books, 1981).

17 Defense Secretary Casper Weinberger argued that "a victory of [the] guerrilla factor, would constitute a basic threat to the United States . . . actually on the mainland, that has been traditionally resisted in this country since the Monroe Doctrine was promulgated" (*AFP*, 1981, Document 682, March 11, 1981, p. 1282).

18 The undersecretary of state for political affairs (Stoessel), when pressed for an explanation for direct US involvement replied that "it was an incident, an isolated thing" (*AFP*, 1981, Document 702, p. 1358).

19 Ibid.
20 Cited in Peter Kornbluh, *Nicaragua: The Price of Intervention* (Washington, DC: Institute of Policy Studies, 1987), p. 4.
21 Under the Carter administration, $75 million were appropriated for the new Sandinista government.
22 Statement by the Department of State, April 1, 1981, *AFP*, 1981, Document 687, p. 1298.
23 Ibid.
24 For a detailed examination of how this tactic was used against countries on a political "hit list," see the three-part findings of the Centre for International Policy, Washington, DC, published in issues of the *International Policy Report*; Caleb Rossiter, "The Financial Hit List," February 1984; Caleb Rossiter and Anne-Marie Smith, "Human Rights: The Carter Record, The Reagan Record," September 1984; and W. Frick Curry and Joanne Royce, "Enforcing Human Rights: Congress and the Multilateral Banks," February 1985.
25 For a revealing account of the CIA's role, see the article by former Contra leader Edgar Chamorro, "Confessions of a Contra," *New Republic*, August 5, 1985. The atrocities committed by the Contras against civilians are carefully documented by the Washington Office on Latin America (*Nicaragua: Violations of the Laws of War by Both Sides*, February-December, 1985); and the First Supplement of this report, January-March, 1986.
26 See report by this title, US Department of State Special Report No. 90, December 14, 1981, *AFP* 1981, Document 663, pp. 1207-23.
27 Ibid., p. 1212.
28 In February 1982, 54 members of Congress signed a letter to the president claiming, *inter alia*, that "the Certification you have just submitted to Congress that human rights standards specified in the Foreign Assistance Act have been met is contrary to the documented facts." See US Congress, House Committee on Foreign Affairs, Subcommittee on Inter-American Affairs, *Presidential Certification of El Salvador*, vol. 1. Hearings, February 2, 23, 25; March 2, 1982. 97th Cong., 2nd sess. (Washington, DC: US Government Printing Office, 1982).
29 Jeanne Kirkpatrick, "Dictatorships and Double Standards," *Commentary* 68, 5 (November 1979).
30 Ibid., p. 40.
31 Ibid., pp. 40-41.
32 Ibid., p. 36.
33 Ibid., p. 37. The author observed that the Carter administration was therefore wrong when it interpreted insurgency "as evidence of popular discontent and a will to democracy."
34 Ibid., p. 38.
35 Ibid., p. 37.
36 Ibid., p. 44.
37 Ibid., p. 34; p. 44.
38 Testimony before the Subcommittee on Foreign Operations and Related Agencies, of the Committee on Appropriations, House of Representatives, 97th Cong., 1st sess. Reprinted in *AFP*, 1981, Document 672, p. 1241.

39 William Leo Grande, *Central America and the Polls*, Washington Office on Latin America (WOLA) Special Report, March 1987 (revised) p. 20.

40 Remark during testimony by Secretary Haig before the Senate Foreign Relations Committee, March 19, 1981. Reprinted in *AFP*, 1981, Document 685, p. 1294.

41 Leo Grande, *Central America*, Table 4.

42 Robert White testified that the Salvadoran government had in fact requested economic rather than military aid.

43 February 27, 1981, *AFP*, 1981, Document 675, p. 1276. Transcript of a press conference with President Reagan, March 6, 1981, *AFP*, 1981, Document 679.

44 For a sample of statements in which the administration denied plans of future direct involvement in Central America, see Documents 671, 673, 674, 679, 683, 684 in *AFP*, 1981. With regard to assertions that no options were being ruled out, see Documents 674, 684, 685.

45 Remarks during testimony by Secretary Haig before the House Foreign Relations Committee, March 2, 1982, *AFP: Current Documents*, Document 6773, p. 1392.

46 Ibid., p. 1393.

47 Ibid., p. 1257.

48 This had become a familiar tactic of Secretary Haig when pressed for clarification of important policy issues regarding Central America. See, for example, *AFP*, 1981, Document 707, p. 1354.

49 Jim Lehrer, on the "MacNeil-Lehrer Report" of March 13, 1981, appropriately reminded Secretary Haig that it was he who had made the Salvadoran issue "a pretty big deal by choosing it as a symbol and virtually saying so" (*AFP*, 1981, Document 683, p. 1288).

50 Leo Grande, *Central America*, Table 21.

51 Documents corresponding to these events are featured in Robert S. Leiken and Barry Rubin, eds., *The Central American Reader: The Essential Guide to the Most Controversial Foreign Policy Issue Today* (New York: Summit Books, 1987), text, p. 619; Documents 1 & 2 (pp. 626-27).

52 A more "neutral" position was, however, taken in March when the Duarte government seemed to be winning control over the conflicts.

53 Ibid., Document 3, pp. 627-28.

54 Ibid., p. 629.

55 This was done by Assistant Secretary of State for Inter-American Affairs Thomas Enders, during his visit to Bonn in June 1981. A senior German official explained his government's capitulation: "We are very exposed in Berlin, and we can't risk recognizing the FDR as France and Mexico have done. It's not that we would not like to, just that we have not got the independence to do it" (quoted in *Latin American Weekly Report*, WR-81-37, September 18, 1981, p. 2).

56 Quoted by senior US administration official (unidentified) (*AFP*, 1981, Document 690, p. 1314).

57 *AFP*, 1981, Document 671, p. 1380.

58 Ibid., pp. 1379-80.

59 *AFP*, 1982, Document 694, September 7, 1982, p. 1463.

60 Kornbluh, *Nicaragua*, p. 117.

61 *Latin American Weekly Report*, WR-82-28, July 16, 1982, p. 11.

62 Address by the President to the OAS, February 24, 1982, *AFP*, 1982, Document 672, p. 1385.

63 Ibid., p. 1383.

64 Ibid., p. 1384.

65 July 14, 1983, *Congressional Record*, vol. 129, no. 98. p. H5147. The *Congressional Record* (*CR*) is printed in two formats. The original format indicates, by the letters "H," "S" or "E" before the page number, whether the member of Congress made the relevant statement in the House of Representatives (H), in the Senate (S), or by extension of remarks (E) later through a printed submission. The other, newer, format, which uses the original as its source and is therefore published later, dispenses with the alphabetical component of the page number. Both these sources have been consulted, so that page numbers listed refer to the version which was available in the respective libraries where research was conducted.

66 February 24, 1982, *CR*, p. 2206.

67 July 14, 1983, *CR*, vol. 129, no. 98, p. H5147.

68 August 10, 1982, *CR*, p. 20072.

69 "Transmittal of the Proposed Caribbean Basin Economic Recovery Legislation," March 17, 1982, *AFP*, 1982, Document 681, p. 1434.

70 July 13, 1983, *CR*, p. H5110.

71 March 23, 1982, *CR*, p. 20072.

72 Reagan, Address to the OAS, p. 1383.

73 Message of transmittal of the CBI to Congress, p. 1431.

74 July 13, 1983, *CR*, p. H5109.

75 Ibid., p. H5112.

76 Message to Congress, p. 1434. Emphasis added.

77 Address to the OAS, p. 1384.

78 The relevant committee reports are: US House, Committee on Foreign Affairs, *Caribbean-Central American Economic Revitalization Act of 1982*, Report No. 97-665, Part 1, July 26, 1982, 97th Cong., 2nd sess. (Washington, DC: US Government Printing Office, 1982); US Congress, Senate Committee on Foreign Relations, *Caribbean-Central American Revitalization Act of 1982*, Calender no. 781, Report no. 97-541, September 10, 1982, 97th Cong., 2nd sess. (Washington, DC: US Government Printing Office, 1982).

79 Reagan, Address to the OAS, p. 1385.

80 Ibid., p. 1385.

81 Testimony before the US Senate Committee on Finance, April 13, 1983, 98th Cong., 1st sess., 1983, p. 55.

82 Ibid., p. 55.

83 July 14, 1983, *CR*, p. H5143.

84 Ibid., p. H5146. Emphasis added.

85 Reagan, Address to the OAS, p. 1384.

86 Testimony before the House Ways and Means Committee, Subcommittee on Trade, March 17, 1982, 97th Cong., 2nd sess. (Washington, DC: US Government Printing Office, 1982), p. 22.

87 March 17, 1982, *CR*, p. 4602.

88 Reagan, Address to the OAS, p. 1383.

89 Lars Schoultz, *National Security and United States Policy Toward Latin America* (Princeton, NJ: Princeton University Press, 1987), p. 109.

90 Reagan, Address to the OAS, pp. 1384-85.

91 Ibid., p. 1385.

92 Ibid.

93 "Remarks of the President at the Caribbean Basin Ceremony," inserted in the *CR*, March 17, 1982, p. 4602. Emphasis added.

94 For a good discussion of the network of US bases and installations in the Caribbean Basin, see Schoultz, *National Security*, pp. 160-222. This issue is also discussed by officials of the Department of Defense in their annual presentations to Congress during hearings on "Foreign Assistance and Related Programs."

95 Schoultz, *National Security*, pp. 160-62.

96 Since President Reagan came to office, the facilities here have been increased. Guantanamo accommodates the Fleet Training Group (FTG) and the Intermediate Maintenance Activity (SIMA) facilities.

97 The most important facility is the modernized air force base at Palmerola. Other significant installations include radar sites and the US operated Regional Military Training Centre (CREM) for the training of personnel from the armed forces of the region.

98 Reagan, Address to the OAS, p. 1386.

99 Testimony before the Senate Committee on Finance, April 13, 1983, p. 53.

100 The original CBI proposal was formulated by the administration. In the process of congressional deliberations, the House of Representatives and and the Senate evolved their own versions of the CBI. From these, the final CBI bill was agreed upon through a process of negotiations or "conferencing" between the two bodies of Congress.

101 Testimony, p. 78.

102 Remarks during hearings on the CBI by the Senate Committee on Finance, August 2, 1982, p. 2.

103 August 10, 1982, *CR*, p. 20073.

104 CBI II represents an attempt by several members of Congress to extend certain provisions of the CBI and to add new ones, so as to make the program more effective. See "Introduction," this volume.

105 July 13, 1982, *CR*, p. H5115.

106 Ibid., p. H5112.

107 Ibid., p. H5116.

108 Committee on Foreign Relations, US House of Representatives, 97th Cong., 2nd sess., Report No. 97-665, Part I, July 26, 1982.

109 "Remarks by President Reagan and Jamaican Prime Minister Seaga," January 28, 1982, *AFP*, 1982, Document 667, p. 1229.

110 Transcript of a White House briefing by Richard V. Allen, national security adviser, and David Rockefeller, chairman, US Business Committee on Jamaica, *AFP*, 1981 Supplement, Document 1229, p. 2.

111 Ibid., p. 3.

112 Ibid., p. 6. Cited by senior administration official (Richard Allen) in background briefing.

113 Ibid., p. 7. Senior administration official.

114 There is no evidence of the degree to which the *private* initiative for the region was thereafter pursued. It seems, however, that it was either abandoned in favour of, or superseded by, the *official* initiative.

115 Transcript of a White House press briefing, conducted on background by two administration officials, June 9, 1981, *AFP*, 1981, Document 690, p. 1308.

116 Ibid., p. 1312.

117 Ibid., pp. 1312-13.

118 July 11, 1981, *AFP*, 1981, Document 692, pp. 1323-24.

119 Transcript of a press conference by the Secretary of State (Haig) and the US Trade Representative (Brock), Nassau, July 12, 1981, *AFP*, 1981, Document 693, p. 1324.

120 Prepared statement before a Subcommittee of the House Foreign Affairs Committee, July 28, 1981, *AFP*, 1981, Document 695, p. 1330.

121 Committee on Foreign Relations, US Senate, 97th. Cong., 2nd sess., Calender No. 781, Report No. 92-541, September 10, 1982, p. 2.

122 February 24, 1982, House of Representatives, *CR*, p. 2230

123 Ibid., p. 1331.

124 See Chapter 1, D. Ramnarine, "The Political Significance of the United States Caribbean Basin Initiative" (Ph.D. thesis, Queen's University, 1988), for a description of the various programs of the donor countries.

125 US Congress, House, "Title II: Caribbean Basin Economic Recovery Act . . . ," in *Interest and Dividends Tax Withholding Repeal*, 98th Cong., 1st sess. (Washington, DC: US Government Printing Office, July 27, 1983), p. 18. The House version of the bill had included Cuba as one of the potentially eligible countries but later followed the Senate, during the conference negotiations, to exclude this country.

126 Author's interview with Jonathan Ferrar, Office of Regional Economic Policy, Department of State, December 10, 1987.

127 Testimony before the US Senate Committee on Finance, 98th Cong., 2nd sess., August 2, 1982, p. 84.

128 Kornbluh, *Nicaragua*, p. 174.

129 Author's interview with Jonathan Ferrar.

130 Author's interview with Melissa Coyle, Division of Caribbean Affairs, Office of the United States Trade Representative, December 15, 1987.

131 Author's interview with Richard Holwill, deputy assistant secretary for the Caribbean, US Department of State, December 9, 1987.

132 Testimony before the US Senate Committee on Finance, August 2, 1982, p. 84.

133 Ibid., p. 77.

134 Ibid., p. 84.

135 For the original administration's proposal on recipients and the amount of assistance earmarked for each, see the President's letter of transmittal of the CBI to Congress, March 17, 1982, *AFP*, 1982, Document 681.

136 Reagan, Address to the OAS, p. 1386.

137 Address before the Foreign Policy Association, New York, January 1984, *Current Policy*, US Department of State Bureau of Public Affairs, No. 539, p. 3.

138 Ibid., p. 3. Emphasis added.

139 For a well-argued and documented refutation of the premises of these demands, see Kornbluh, *Nicaragua*. The author quotes former US ambassador to Nicaragua, Lawrence Pezzullo, as recalling that "Every bit of evidence we had, every indicator showed there was a cutoff" of arms flow

from Nicaragua to El Salvador after 1981. This conclusion was supported by David MacMichael, an analyst for the CIA's National Intelligence Council. Nicaragua's military forces (60 000) were assessed by the London-based International Institute for Strategic Studies (IISS) as inferior to the combined forces of Guatemala (40 000), El Salvador (44 000), and Honduras (22 000) which could be expected to co-operate against Nicaragua in the event of hostilities. In addition, a classified CIA assessment stated that Nicaragua's military buildup was "primarily defense-oriented" and devoted to improving "counter-insurgency capabilities." Lastly, the Nicaraguan government's human rights record has always been incomparably superior to those of El Salvador and Guatemala which, the US government insisted, were emergent democracies. It is also worth noting that barely one month after the Nicaraguan government had dismantled civil rights restrictions in December 1983, CIA operatives took advantage of this opening to mine the country's harbours.

140 See Caleb Rossiter, "The Financial Hit List: Part One of a Series on Human Rights and the International Financial Institutions," *International Policy Report*, February 1984 (Centre for International Policy, Washington DC). In part three of this series, "Enforcing Human Rights: Congress and the Multilateral Banks" (February 1985), the authors, W. Frick Curry and Joanne Royce, pointed out that under the Reagan administration, US representatives on international financial institutions rejected 31 per cent ($130 million) of total funds requested ($426 million) by "leftist countries," as opposed to only 3 per cent ($204 million) of the total request ($6.3 billion) by "rightist countries." This, incidentally, contrasted with a balanced voting record by officials under the Carter administration.

141 See the president's letter of transmittal of the CBI to Congress, March 17, 1982, for the proposed distribution of the supplemental funds.

142 This estimate is calculated from figures presented in "Background on the Caribbean Basin Initiative" (March 1982), Special Report, No. 97. US Department of State, Bureau of Public Affairs, Washington, DC, p. 347).

143 Calculated from ibid., p. 347.

144 President's letter of transmittal of the CBI to Congress, p. 1432.

145 August 10, 1982, *CR*, p. 20070.

146 Walter LaFeber, *Inevitable Revolutions: The United States in Central America* (New York and London: W.W. Norton & Company, 1984), p. 283.

147 Robert Pastor, "Sinking in the Caribbean Basin," inserted as testimony before the US Senate Committee on Finance, Hearings on the Caribbean Basin Initiative, April 13, 1983. 98th Cong., 1983, p. 208. This article first appeared in *Foreign Affairs* (Summer 1982): 1038-58.

148 Letter of transmittal of the CBI to Congress, p. 1432. Emphasis added.

149 Representative Long, August 18, 1982, *CR*, p. 22025.

150 August 18, 1982, *CR*, p. 22030.

151 Ibid.

152 August 18, 1982, *CR*, p. 20070.

153 Ibid.

154 Ibid.

155 August 10, 1982, *CR*, p. 20070.

156 Cited by the Committee on Foreign Affairs, US House of Representatives, 97th Cong., 2nd sess., Report No. 97-665, Part 1, July 26, 1982, p. 13.

157 Ibid.

158 See, for example, the testimony of former ambassador to El Salvador Robert White on the presidential certification of El Salvador: "US Policy toward Central America: Past, Present and Future," before the Subcommittee on Inter-American Affairs of the Committee on Foreign Affairs, US House of Representatives, 97th Cong., 2nd sess., 1982, Washington, DC. White's testimony is perhaps the most passionate appeal, from a Washington "insider," for a change in US policy toward the region.

159 Committee of Foreign Relations, US House of Representatives, p. 7. Emphasis added.

160 Ibid.

161 The human rights policy was so described by the deputy assistant secretary of state for Inter-American Affairs (Bosworth) in his testimony before the subcommittees on Human Rights and International Organizations, and on inter-American affairs, of the Committee on Foreign Affairs, US House of Representatives, 97th Cong., 1st sess., 1981, Washington, DC. Reprinted in *AFP*, 1981, Document 696, pp. 1332-34. For the opposing (and better-informed) view that the Guatemalan government and military were responsible for "the great majority of the illegal executions," see testimony by White, "US Policy toward Central America," pp. 121-22.

162 Additional views of Hons. Benjamin S. Rosenthal, Sus Yatron, Stephen J. Solarz, Don Bonker, Gerry E. Studds, Sam Gejdenson, and Mervyn Dymally (Committee on Foreign Affairs, US House of Representatives, p. 18).

163 Ibid., p. 9.

164 Ibid.

165 Testimony before the US Senate Committee on Finance, Hearings on the Caribbean Basin Initiative, 98th Cong., 1st sess., April 13, 1983 (Washington, DC, 1983), p. 53.

166 US Congress, *Public Law 97-257*, September 10, 1982 (96 STAT. 833-834) (Washington, DC: US Government Printing Office, 1982).

167 The amendment was proposed as SJ Resolution 158 and was meant to reaffirm SJ Resolution 230 of 1962, which defined US policy toward Cuba.

168 August 10, 1982, *CR*, p. 20086.

169 Ibid., p. 20095.

170 Ibid., p. 20097.

171 Ibid., p. 20085. Emphasis added.

172 Ibid., p. 20086. Emphasis added.

173 Ibid., p. 20090-91. Emphasis added. The statement was included in the record at the request of Senator Symms, but the author was not identified.

174 The original text of the letter cannot be located. This recollection of the substance of the letter was given in a conversation between the assistant secretary for Inter-American Affairs, Thomas Enders, and his deputy, Stephen Bosworth, on April 15, 1982. The text of the conversation is reprinted in *CR*, August 10, 1982, p. 20089.

175 Ibid.

176 Reprinted in ibid., p. 20086.

177 Ibid., p. 20088. Emphasis added.

178 See statements by William P. Clark, on behalf of the White House, and Fred C. Ikle, undersecretary of defense. Reprinted in ibid., p. 20086.

179 See ibid., p. 20097. The passage of the amendment occurred by way of the defeat of another amendment (no. 1201) intended to "lay it on the table" or reject it. Those who expressed opposition to the Symms amendment did so only on this issue of whether it would imply that Congress relinquished its power to declare war to the President. Only Senator Percy was concerned that the amendment would, by its "war mongering" rhetoric, further isolate the US in the context of a legitimacy crisis of US foreign policy. See ibid., p. 20094 for Senator Percy's comments.

180 For a useful account of the Caribbean socioeconomic context of the CBI, which strongly confirms the analysis advanced in this volume, see Carmen Diana Deere et al., *In the Shadows of the Sun: Caribbean Development Alternatives and US Policy* (Boulder: Westview Press, 1991, esp. Chapters 5 and 6).

Chapter 3

* Preliminary research for this paper was done by Elizabeth Grace, to whom I am greatly indebted.

1 Interview, 2 December 1988.

2 Interview, 28 November 1988.

3 D. Ramnarine, "The Political Significance of the United States Caribbean Basin Initiative" (Ph.D. thesis, Queen's University, 1988).

4 Tony Thorndike, "The Militarisation of the Commonwealth Caribbean," in Peter Calvert, ed., *The Central American Security System: North-South or East-West?* (Cambridge: Cambridge University Press, 1988).

5 Interview with David Winslade, Department of Trade and Industry (DTI), December 1988. The latest information offered was for 1984 (see *British Business*, May 22, 1987).

6 Interview with Mr. Poduval, DTI, November 29, 1988; aid to Belize and Honduras had been higher in the mid-1980s (see *DAC, OPEC and Multilateral Aid: Geographical Distribution 1980-86*, Statistics Division, Overseas Development Administration).

7 Anthony Payne, *The International Crisis in the Caribbean* (London: Croom Helm, 1984), p. 99.

8 Ibid.

9 Ibid., p. 91.

10 Ibid., p. 92.

11 Tony Thorndike, *No End to Empire*, Department of International Relations and Politics, Staffordshire Polytechnic, November 1988, pp. 4-5 (a report commissioned by the Foreign and Commonwealth Office).

12 Payne, *International Crisis*, p. 94.

13 *Fifth Report from the Foreign Affairs Committee, Session 1981-82: Caribbean and Central America* (London: HMSO, 1982), pp. lii and liv. The chairman of the committee, Sir Anthony Kershaw, was a traditional Tory, sympathetic to the nationalist leadership of the former colonies, who also felt obliged to stand by a report that was much more critical of government policies than most of his Conservative colleagues on the committee would have agreed—had they attended the committee's meetings more assiduously (Interviews with Mr. George Foulkes, MP, a member of the com-

mittee; Dr. Anthony Payne, a specialist adviser to the committee; and Mr. George Gelber, Catholic Institute for International Relations, November-December 1988).

14 Christopher Stevens, "The Single European Market: Implications for Caribbean Agricultural Exports," paper presented to "1992 and the Caribbean," conference organized by the West Indian Committee at Lancaster House, London, September 30 -October 1, 1988, Table 2.

15 Calculated from data in *British Business*, May 22, 1987, p. 28. The dramatic scale of this increase is only partly accounted for by inflation. It was primarily due to the lifting of controls on capital outflows by the Thatcher government.

16 Interview with Mr. Poduval, DTI, November 29, 1988.

17 Interviews with Mr. Winslade and Mr. Poduval, cited above, nn. 5 and 6.

18 Data supplied by the Overseas Development Administration.

19 A. J. Fairclough, Deputy Director General for Development, Commission of the E.C., "Address" to the West Indian Committee 1992 Conference, September 30, 1988, p. 7.

20 "Caribbean Survey," *The Economist*, August 6, 1988, p. 13.

21 Interview with Mr. Neville Linton, December 2, 1988.

22 Thorndike, "Militarisation," p. 136; this section relies heavily on Thorndike's succinct and judicious analysis.

23 The OECS included Grenada, but not Barbados, and could only take decisions affecting defence and security unanimously; hence the establishment of the RSS which excluded Grenada and hinged on Barbados: see Humberto Garcia Muniz, *Boots, Boots, Boots: Intervention, Regional Security and Militarisation in the Caribbean* (Puerto Rico: Projecto Caribeno de Justicia y Paz, 1986), p. 6.

24 Ibid; and Thorndike, "Militarisation."

25 Ibid., pp. 147-48.

26 Muniz, *Boots,* pp. 18 and 19.

27 On the so-called "national security doctrine" developed with US support by Brazil and other Latin American states in the 1960s, see the interesting statement in the Canadian House of Commons by Mr. Bob Ogle MP, *Commons Debates*, March 9, 1985, pp. 1943-45.

28 Quoted in Muniz, *Boots,* p. 16. Muniz also shows how the US military explicitly aims to secure long-run political influence for the US through its military training programs, including keeping a careful count of the numbers of heads of state, cabinet ministers, chiefs of staff, and generals in foreign countries who have been trained in US military schools (p. 20).

29 Thorndike, "Militarisation," pp. 150-52.

30 Anthony Payne, "The Grenada Crisis in British Politics," *The Round Table* 292 (1984): 407.

31 Payne, *The International Crisis*, p. 92.

32 Even after three black MPs were elected in 1987, however, it was not clear that this would ever make a significant impact on British policy towards the Caribbean. As Neville Linton, a Guyanese, put it, "The new MPs are black, not Caribbean, even if a couple are Caribbean-born. The issues are Black Britain. On foreign policy issues they would interest themselves in the Caribbean but they would have absolutely no weight. . . . For them to have weight they must have status in the Labour Party and this is still an issue —

how to operate in the Labour Party? Also the Caribbean States have not tried to use the diaspora to get the things that they want, because the diaspora over here is not organized in the way other groups are in the US, and the system doesn't allow such a group to be influential in that way" (interview, December 2, 1988).

33 Thorndike, *No End to Empire*, p. 4. The fact that independence had been granted to Grenada in 1974 when people had *not*, arguably, expressed the wish for it clearly and constitutionally, and that this had ended with the NJM revolution of 1979, was one of the considerations that led to the proviso quoted here.

34 Thorndike, *No End to Empire*, p. 7. The refusal of Mr. John Strong as governor of the Turks and Caicos Islands to intervene to prevent the drug-related scandals that eventually led to the suspension of elected government was a notorious case. Strong "regarded his posting like so many before him as a pre-retirement haven" (ibid., p. 53).

35 Ibid., p. 7.

36 In his 1988 speech to the Annual General Meeting of the West Indian Committee Mr. Tim Eggar, the Minister of State at the FCO responsible for the region, said that the government was studying "how the role of small businesses could be enhanced" — a possible reference to enlisting West Indian businessmen in the UK in some form of co-operation with the Caribbean. His main stress, however, was on the need for Caribbean governments to co-operate on a regional basis to attract foreign investment: "There is a selling job to be done by the governments of the region if investment is to be attracted. Let us not forget that Britain was last year the second largest investor overseas (after Japan and ahead even of the United States). Too little of this, in my view, is going into the Caribbean. I know that our investors are looking with particular interest at the evolution of CARICOM and the more ambitious plans in the Eastern Caribbean. . . . We would not wish to try to second guess the region's leaders . . . but where the economies are so small, cooperative effort must be at a particular premium. . . . [I]t cannot be in the region's interest to rely wholly on crops which in turn rely for profitability on specially protected status. Economies must aim to stand competition in the marketplace."

Chapter 4

1 Quoted in "Canada Puts No Price on Caribbean Involvement," *Journal of Commerce* 29 (November 1988).

2 Latin American Working Group, *LAWG Newsletter* 7, 1/2 (1982): 4-5.

3 T. Barry, B. Wood, and D. Preutsch, *The Other Side of Paradise: Foreign Control in the Caribbean* (New York: Grove Press, 1984), p. 221.

4 Conference Board of Canada, *Impact of Canada-United States Free Trade on Commonwealth Caribbean Countries* (A Report Prepared for the Department of External Affairs), October 1988, p. 5. All dollar figures refer to Canadian values. Also, on Canada's linkages with the region, see Brian Douglas Tennyson, ed., *Canadian-Caribbean Relations: Aspects of a Relationship* (Sydney, NS: Centre for International Studies, 1990). Note, in particular, James J. Guy, "The Caribbean: A Canadian Perspective," in this collection.

5 In 1990, Canadian trade with the world totalled $284.9 billion (148.7 billion in exports, $136.2 billion in imports). In the same year, trade with

CARIBCAN beneficiary countries amounted to $629.2 million (comprising $325.5 million in exports and $303.7 million in imports).

6 The Windward and Leeward Islands refers to Anguilla, Antigua, and Barbuda, the British Virgin Islands, Dominica, Grenada, Montserrat, St. Kitts-Nevis, St. Lucia, St. Vincent and Grenadines.

7 B. Carty, V. Smith, and LAWG, *Perpetuating Poverty: The Political Economy of Canadian Foreign Aid* (Toronto: Between the Lines, 1981), p. 51. For a more general statement on the determinants of Canadian-American relations during the Trudeau era, see also J.F. Petras and M.H. Morley, "The United States and Canada: State Policy and Strategic Perspectives on Capital and Central America," in J. Holmes and C. Leys, eds., *Frontyard / Backyard: The Americas in the Global Crisis* (Toronto: Between the Lines, 1987), especially pp. 164-74.

8 Cited by Stephen Clarkson in "Why Bother to Debate Canada's Foreign Policy?" *The Globe and Mail*, May 1985. For critiques of the Mulroney government's first review of Canadian foreign policy, see also "Two Missing Foreign Policy Issues Weaken Clark Review," *The Globe and Mail*, May 15, 1985; and Tom Axworthy, "We Must Pay Latin America More Heed," *The Globe and Mail*, March 31, 1985.

9 E. Regehr, *Arms Canada: The Deadly Business of Military Exports* (Toronto: James Lorimer and Co., 1987); "Canadian Munitions Sales to Latin America Taking Off," *The Globe and Mail*, September 9, 1988.

10 Cited in J. Leonard, "Canadian Links to the Militarisation of the Caribbean and Central America," Canada-Caribbean-Central America Policy Alternatives, May 1985, p. 1.

11 Ibid., pp. 2-4; E. Regehr, "Canadian Arms Sales," *Ploughshares Monitor*, 1985; and Regehr, *Arms Canada*, p. 148.

12 Department of External Affairs Press Release 84/139, "Police Assistance to Grenada," October 11, 1984; "$800,000 in Aid Promised by RCMP for Grenada Force," *The Globe and Mail*, October 13, 1984.

13 This policy is designed to "tie" a rising proportion of official development assistance to purchases of Canadian goods and services. At the present time, about 80 per cent of Canada's bilateral aid must be spent on Canadian exports. This represents one of the highest levels of tied aid among major donor nations. See "Jamaican Critical of Canadian Help," *Montreal Gazette*, June 1, 1984; North-South Institute, *Review '84/Outlook '85: The Mulroney Program in the Third World* (Ottawa: North-South Institute, 1985), p. 8; and Barry, *Paradise*, p. 224.

14 Canada, Senate, "Speech from the Throne," *Debates of the Senate*, 1st sess., 33rd Parliament, November 5, 1984, p. 7.

15 Canada, Standing Committee on External Affairs and National Defence, *Canada's Relations with Latin America and the Caribbean* (Final Report to the House of Commons), November 1982, p. 12, paragraph 32. The Trudeau government promised to back the special relationship by doubling aid to the region to $350 million between 1982 and 1987. See also Department of External Affairs, *Communiqué*, No. 45 (February 17, 1986), announcing Caribcan. Bill C-111 became law on June 26, 1986.

16 The main economic provision of the CBI is the granting of duty-free status, originally for 12 years but subsequently extended indefinitely, to most categories of products from over 20 designated countries in Central Amer-

ica and the Caribbean. Commodities excluded from duty-free treatment include textiles and apparel, sugar, canned tuna, petroleum and petroleum products, certain leather goods, and luggage. To qualify, 35 per cent of the value of imports must have been added in the Caribbean Basin. In addition, the US government expanded economic and military assistance to the Caribbean Basin and provided credit security for exporters and importers of US products, financing for export-oriented investment, and a variety of forms of technical and other material support. See US Department of Commerce, *Caribbean Basin Initiative: 1987 Guidebook* (Washington DC: International Trade Administration, 1986) for details.

17 "Seaga Puts Trade Deal Case to Mulroney: WI Calls for Canadian Plan," *Daily Nation*, February 26, 1985; *Barbados Advocate*, February 26, 1986.

18 The 13 territories are: Antigua and Barbuda, the Bahamas, Barbados, Belize, Dominica, Grenada, Guyana, St. Kitts-Nevis, St. Lucia, St. Vincent and the Grenadines, and Trinidad and Tobago. In this paper the terms, English-speaking Caribbean and Commonwealth Caribbean are used interchangeably to refer to Caribcan beneficiary nations.

19 Institute of Research on Public Policy, *Caribcan: Canadian Programs for Commonwealth Caribbean Trade, Investment and Industrial Cooperation* (Ottawa: Department of External Affairs, 1988), p. 4.

20 "Speech by B. Mulroney at the Canada/Commonwealth Caribbean Conference," Kingston, Jamaica, February 25, 1985, p. 2, and Canada, Department of External Affairs, *Communiqué*, No. 45, February 17, 1986, p. 1.

21 See *Canadian Customs Tariff*, Appendix A, for rates of duty applied to non-exempt items.

22 External Affairs, *Communiqué*.

23 Canada, Ministry of National Revenue, *Caribcan Rules of Origin Regulations*, 1986-543 (SOR/DORS), pp. 1-4.

24 This ruling allows the costs of production (research and development, design, inspection, and other costs related to the particular item), overheads (administrative expenses and insurance), profits, and packaging to be included as part of the 60 per cent limit.

25 External Affairs, *Communiqué*, p. 2, and Canadian International Trade Tribunal, *Import Safeguard Complaints Concerning the General Preferential Tariff (GPT) or Caribcan* (Ottawa: CITT, 1990).

26 For more detailed information on Agriculture Canada and Department of Fisheries regulations, refer to Institute for Research on Public Policy, *Caribcan*, pp. 15-24.

27 Canada, Canadian International Development Agency, *1984-1984 Annual Report* (Ottawa: Ministry of Supplies and Services, 1985), p. 41.

28 *Canada-Caribbean Monthly Business Letter*, June 1986.

29 For more information on international prices for traditional Caribbean exports, see United Nations, *Economic Survey for Latin America and the Caribbean* (Santiago, Chile: United Nations, 1985-90).

30 Canada, Statistics Canada, *Trade of Canada, Imports by Commodity*, 1980-90, Table 1, and Canada, Statistics Canada, *Trade of Canada, Exports by Commodity*, 1980-90, Table 1.

31 Ibid.

32 Cited in *Journal of Commerce*, November 29, 1988.

33 Canada, Statistics Canada, *Trade of Canada*.

34 *Imports by Commodity*, Tables 1 and 2, and *Exports by Commodity*, Tables 1 and 2.

35 The increase consisted mainly of oil and natural gas exports, as well as timber, electrical equipment, and aircraft. Much of the growth in demand for Canadian energy and other products during 1990 was linked to US military requirements during the Persian Gulf war. Official trade data for 1991 indicate a falling back in Canadian export sales to the United States.

36 *Journal of Commerce*, November 29, 1988.

37 U.S. Public Law 98-67, August 5, 1983, Section 212 — Beneficiary Country. Section 212 established the criteria for countries to be designated as beneficiaries. The president cannot designate a country if it is "communist" or if it fails to meet a number of other requirements relating mainly to property expropriation and co-operative agreements with the United States.

38 "Leaders in Caribbean Unhappy over Ottawa's Special Trade Plan," *The Globe and Mail*, July 4, 1986.

39 Quoted in, "Mulroney Lifts Trade Hopes in the Caribbean," *Financial Times*, November 6, 1985.

40 Ibid.; and "Mulroney: We'll Study Proposal," *Barbados Advocate,* February 27, 1985. See also interview with the president of the Antigua and Barbuda Chamber of Commerce in *Canada-Caribbean Monthly Business Letter*, June 1986. To put the debate about access levels in context, it should be noted that the combined imports of Commonwealth Caribbean countries represent less than one-half of one per cent of Canada's total imports.

41 For discussions of the nature of these problems from differing perspectives, see A. Maingot, *Journal of Commerce*, August 26, 1985, and A.P. Gonzales, "The Future of CARICOM: Collective Self-Reliance in Decline?" *Caribbean Review* 13, 4 (Fall 1984): 8-10, 40.

42 Cited in "Caribbean Aid Plan a Disappointment," *The Toronto Star*, January 2, 1987.

43 That is, 1986, when the reduced-duty program was introduced. This program also guaranteed access to the American market for clothing assembled in the Caribbean from material manufactured and cut in the United States. For more information, see, US Department of Commerce, *Annual Report on the Impact of the Caribbean Basin Economic Recovery Act on U.S. Industries and Consumers: Third Report, 1987* (Washington, DC: International Trade Administration, 1988), p. 11.

44 "Caribbean Exporters Wary of Canada-US Trade Pact," *The Globe and Mail,* January 16, 1988. For an optimistic assessment of the possible effects of the Canada-US trade agreement, see also Conference Board of Canada, *Impact of Canada-United States Free Trade on Commonwealth Caribbean Countries.*

45 Refer, for instance, to The Development Group for Alternative Policies, Inc., *Prospects and Reality: The CBI Revisited* (Washington, DC: The Development Gap, 1985); and Council on Hemispheric Affairs, *COHA's Washington Report on the Hemisphere*, June 1985. For more recent critiques, based on more than half a decade of experience of the CBI program, see Carmen Diana Deere (co-ordinator), *In the Shadows of the Sun: Caribbean Development Alternatives and U.S. Policy* (Boulder, CO: Westview Press, 1990), especially pp. 153-86; and Kathy McAfee, *Storm Signals: Structural Adjustment and Development Alternatives in the Caribbean* (Monroe: South End Press, 1991).

46 See evidence presented by E. Pantojas Garcia, "The Caribbean Basin Initiative and the Economic Restructuring of the Region," in Caribeno de Justicia y Paz, *The Other Side of U.S. Military Policy Towards the Caribbean: Recolonization and Militarization,* pp. 23-33.

47 Ibid. Refer also to US House of Representatives, *The Caribbean Basin Initiative: A Congressional Study Mission and Symposium* (Hearings before the Subcommittees on International Economic Policy and Trade and on Western Hemisphere Affairs of the Committee on Foreign Affairs) 100th Cong., 1st sess., September 18 and 19, 1987, particularly pp. 27-28.

48 See "Statement by Atherton Martin of the Development Group for Alternative Policies before the House Subcommittee on Western Hemisphere Affairs and Human Rights and International Organisations on the Caribbean Regional Development Act of 1988 (H.R. 4943)," July 28, 1988.

Chapter 5

1 The Central American population, for example, experienced an annual growth of 3 per cent between 1960 and 1980 and nearly doubled from 12 million to 23 million (testimony by Alan Stoga before the National Bipartisan Commission on Central America). See Henry Kissinger et al., *Report of the National Bipartisan Commission on Central America* (Washington, DC: US Government Printing Office, 1984), Appendix, p. 158.

2 It is estimated that 1983 exports from Central American economies could purchase only 70 per cent of the imports of 1978 (The Kissinger Commission, p. 24).

3 Ibid.

4 Testimony by John Jeane before the Hearings on *Demographic Impact of Immigrants to the US,* conducted by the Subcommittee on Census and Population, of the House Committee on Post Office and Civil Service, Hearings, March 19, 26, May 3, 1985, 99th Congress, 1st. sess. (Washington, DC: US Government Printing Office).

5 Kenneth Dam, *Current Policy* 529 (September 14, 1983): 1 (Bureau of Public Affairs, US Department of State).

6 Ibid., p. 2.

7 George Schultz, *Current Policy* 641 (December 1984): 2.

8 J. William Middendorf, II, Ambassador to the OAS, *Current Policy* 609 (August 30, 1984): 2.

9 The Kissinger Commission (pp. 43-44) estimated that capital flight amounted to about $3 billion in the several years preceding the report. More recent assessments put this figure at $5 billion.

10 Dam, *Current Policy,* p. 2; Ronald Reagan, Address to the Joint Session of Congress, April 27, 1983, *American Foreign Policy: Current Documents,* US Department of State, Bureau of Public Affairs, Document 623, 1983, p. 1315.

11 The two speeches by the president were the address to the Organization of American States on February 24, 1982, and the address to the Joint Session of Congress on April 27, 1983. A four-pronged strategy was outlined: (1) support for democracy, reform, and human freedom (2) resolution of conflicts through dialogue and negotiations (3) support for economic development and (4) military assistance to provide a "shield" so that the above three may be achieved.

12 Middendorf, *Current Policy*, p. 4; and Schultz, *Current Policy*, p. 2.

13 Dam, *Current Policy*, p. 4. Scott Wylie (*Business America*, July 22, 1985, p. 3) notes that a 40-foot container shipped from Haiti to Cincinnati costs less than half ($2200) the same shipped from a major Far-East port ($4800).

14 Middendorf, *Current Policy*, p. 1.

15 Peter Johnson, Testimony before the House Committee on Ways and Means, Subcommittee on Trade, *Caribbean Basin Initiative*, Hearings, March 17, 23-25, 1982, 97th Cong., 2nd sess. (Washington, DC: US Government Printing Office, 1982), pp. 128-29.

16 Alexander Wolf, Jr., Address to the House Committee on Ways and Means, ibid., p. 441.

17 Middendorf, *Current Policy*, p. 4.

18 Ibid., p. 5.

19 Ibid.

20 Schultz, *Current Policy*, p. 2.

21 Dam, *Current Policy*, p. 3.

22 Schultz, *Current Policy*, p. 2.

23 Ibid., p. 3.

24 Langhorne Motley, Assistant Secretary for InterAmerican Affairs, "Address to the Council of the Americas, December 8, 1983," *Current Policy*, 532: 4.

25 Schultz, *Current Policy*, p. 2.

26 Ibid., p. 5.

27 United States International Trading Commission, *Annual Report on the Impact of the Caribbean Basin Economic Recovery Act on US Industries and Consumers*, Second Report, 1986, USITC Publication 2024, September 1987, Washington, DC. The data presented by the USITC was compiled from the statistics of the US Department of Commerce.

28 *The Caribbean Basin Initiative: Progress to Date*, Report by the US Department of State, November 1987, Washington, DC.

29 Unless otherwise indicated, the statistical data given in this section are drawn from the Second Report of the USITC, 1986, pp. 4-8.

30 Caribbean Basin exports to the US for the first half of 1986 and 1987, compared, showed a decrease from $3 443 419 to $3 228 914. "The Caribbean Basin Initiative: Progress to Date," p. 9. These figures have not been fully reproduced here, since the 1987 figures are both tentative and incomplete.

31 Ibid., p. 4. Lawrence Theriot of the Caribbean Basin Information Centre explained that the closure was due to the introduction of new technology which rendered INTEL's products obsolete. Interview with author, December 16, 1987.

32 *The Caribbean Basin Initiative: Progress to Date*, p. 3.

33 Second Report of the USITC, 1986, p. viii.

34 Ibid., p. 14.

35 Ibid., p. 15.

36 Ibid. The product-specific analysis which follows is summarized from pp. 15-16 of this report.

37 See "Introduction" to this volume for elements of the proposed expansion of the CBI.

38 This survey was first published in *Business America*, July 22, 1985, p. 4.

39 The figures conforming to these claims are reproduced in United States General Accounting Office, "The Caribbean Basin Initiative: Need for More Reliable Data on Business Activity Resulting from the Initiative," Briefing Report to the Chairman, Subcommittee on Oversight, Committee on Ways and Means, House of Representatives, August 1986, Washington, DC, p. 11.

40 Ibid., p. 3.

41 Ibid., p. 13.

42 United States International Trade Commission, *Annual Report on the Impact of the Caribbean Basin Economic Recovery Act on US Industries and Consumers*, First Report, 1984-85, USITC Publication 1897, September 1986, Washington, DC.

43 Second Report of the USITC, 1986, pp. 20-25.

44 Ibid., p. 20.

45 Ibid., p. 21.

46 Ibid.

47 Fuel-grade ethanol is used mainly as a "gasoline extender and octane enhancer" and must compete with substitutes derived from petroleum and natural gas (ibid., p. 23).

48 Ibid.

49 OPIC usually provides political risk insurance as well as financial assistance to US investors, but cannot do so for projects that would adversely affect US labour or the US economy.

50 To qualify for the convention benefit a country must meet two conditions. First, it must be a beneficiary of the FTA provision. Second, it must sign *either* a bilateral Tax Information Exchange Agreement (TIEA) with the US Department of Treasury, *or* be certified by Treasury as having an effective tax information exchange program under the terms of a bilateral income tax treaty. This benefit was extended to Bermuda despite the fact that it is not a CBI-beneficiary country.

51 Remarks by Richard Holwill, deputy assistant secretary of state for InterAmerican Affairs to the Miami Conference on the Caribbean Basin Initiative, December 1, 1987, p. 8.

52 Interview with the author, December 16, 1987.

53 Ibid.

54 Holwill, *Remarks*.

55 Non-traditional exports are all CBI-eligible exports except (1) petroleum and petroleum products, (2) coffee, (3) sugars, syrups, and molasses, (4) fresh bananas, (5) gold or silver bullion, (6) beef and veal, (7) cocoa beans and butter, (8) bauxite, (9) tobacco products, (10) ferronickel, and (11) rum ("The Caribbean Basin Initiative: Progress to Date," p. 4).

56 See Chapter 1 for a description of these two additions to the CBI.

57 Lawrence Theriot, Testimony on "The Caribbean Basin Initiative and Minority Participation," p. 23.

58 Ibid., p. 42.

59 Alexander Good, Director General of the US and Foreign Commercial Service, Department of Commerce, "Caribbean Basin Initiative: Diagnosis and Prescriptions," *Washington Report*, Council of the Americas, October 1987, p. 4.

60 Ibid.

61 Ibid.

62 Ibid.

63 Holwill, *Remarks*, p. 4.

64 Theriot, Testimony on "The Caribbean Basin Initiative and Minority Participation," p. 43.

65 Good, "Caribbean Basin Initiative: Diagnosis and Prescriptions," p. 4.

66 Ibid.

67 Ibid.

68 William Cline, testimony to the US Senate, Committee on Foreign Relations, *Caribbean Basin Initiative*, Hearings, March 31, 1982, 97th Cong., 2nd sess. (Washington, DC: US Government Printing Office), p. 206. The problem with such an economic projection is that its "numerate" emphasis displaces a more appropriate understanding of the historical specificities of the CACM and the CBI. No account is taken of the health of the world economy, the vacillating, and now downward-spiralling fortunes of primary commodities, the huge debt-repayment burdens, the deteriorating political climate and its impact on investment, and the political problems which would confront efforts to renew economic integration.

69 See International Trade Commission (ITC) (1984), "Operation of the Trade Agreements Program, 1983," Washington, DC, p. 34.

70 Ibid., p. 32.

71 As part of the US Economic Recovery Act of 1981, the domestic sweetener industry was granted protection from import competition. In order to raise the guaranteed domestic price for sugar from 19.08 cents per pound in 1981 to 19.88 cents in mid-1982, tariffs were increased from 2.1875 to 2.8125 cents, and later, to 4.0703 cents per pound. These add up to a 185 per cent increase over the pre-1981 level.

72 From 1934 to 1974 the federal sugar program, through quotas, divided the US market between foreign and domestic suppliers in a 45/55 per cent split. Congress did not renew this program in 1974, due largely to a strong world market and high domestic prices. Quotas were implemented again in 1982, but only on foreign sugar, so as to keep supplies low and to sustain domestic prices. Each country is given a fixed share of the US market, calculated as the average share of US market between 1975 and 1982. A country is assured, however, a minimum quota of 7500 short tonnes ("Report of the Committee Delegation Mission to the Caribbean Basin and Recommendations to Improve the Effectiveness of the Caribbean Basin Initiative," Subcommittee on Oversight of the Committee on Ways and Means, US House of Representatives, 100th Congress, 1st sess., May 6, 1987 [Washington, DC: US Government Printing Office, 1987], Appendix A, p. 70 [CRS-17]).

73 Ibid., p. 69 (CRS-16).

74 J. Pelzman and D. Rousslang, "Effects on US Trade and Employment of Tariff Eliminations among the Countries of North America and the Caribbean Basin" (Washington, DC: US Department of Labour, January 1982). The authors estimate the displacement of a relatively small number (15 000) US workers in these industries, had more liberal treatment been granted to these products.

75 Richard Newfarmer, "Economic Policy toward the Caribbean Basin: The Balance Sheet," *Journal of InterAmerican Studies and World Affairs* 27, 1

(1985): 68. The concept of "models of democratic development" is more accurately a euphemism used to describe countries friendly to the US.

76 Economic Support Funds (ESF) are balance of payments assistance, available mainly in the form of lines of credit to the private sector in the region to finance imports from US exporters.

77 Albert Fishlow, testimony before the US Senate, Committee on Foreign Relations, *Caribbean Basin Initiative*, Hearings, March 31, 1982, 97th Cong., 2nd sess. (Washington, DC: US Government Printing Office, 1982), p. 201.

78 Ibid.

79 The Kissinger Commission, p. 65. External financial requirements for individual countries for 1984-90 were estimated thus: Costa Rica, $5.1 billion; Honduras, $2.3 billion; Panama, $3.2 billion; Nicaragua, $3.4 billion.

80 The Commission advised that its estimates of Central American needs were based on the assumptions that violence is reduced, and the flight of investment capital reversed; economic policies are changed to minimize the role of the public sector; bilateral and multilateral assistance be made available from other sources; and international economic and financial conditions continue to improve (ibid., pp. 64-65). Given the persistence of most of these conditions the estimates must therefore be regarded as very conservative, and US assistance so far all the more modest.

81 Newfarmer, "Economic Policy," pp. 75-76.

82 Ibid., p. 81. The proposal by the World Bank management to furnish the IDA with $16 billion was met with a US counter proposal for a $7 billion reduction, to $9 billion, amidst the near unanimous objections of the other industrialized countries.

83 Newfarmer, "Economic Policy," pp. 76-78. The multiplier depends on how much of the additional income goes into imports or savings. If much goes into these areas, the multiplier is lower. For example, savings rates of 25 per cent and import propensities of 50 per cent will yield a multiplier of 1.3; if these are lowered to 15 per cent and 20 per cent respectively, a higher multiplier of 2.9 comes into play. Growth of GNP is calculated in terms of the impact of the multiplier on initial, additional export earnings stimulated by a 1.6 per cent growth of the US economy.

84 See country data in International Monetary Fund, *International Financial Statistics: Supplement on Economic Indicators*, Supplement Series, No. 10 (Washington, DC: IMF, 1985).

85 InterAmerican Development Bank, *Economic and Social Progress in Latin America. External Debt: Crisis and Adjustment*, 1985, p. 110.

86 For Latin America in general, the export growth rate of major commodities is expected to average 11 per cent for 1986-90. But with annual inflation of 6 per cent, this growth will be brought below historical standards by at least 2.5 per cent (ibid., p. 103, p. 132).

87 The InterAmerican Development Bank notes that the structure of debts for Latin America in general has changed such that the debt owed to official creditors dropped from 22 per cent at the end of 1975 to 12 per cent in 1981, while the share for private banks increased from 69 per cent to 82 per cent. In addition, there has been a sharp rise in obligations with maturities of less than one year. These increased sixfold from 1965 to

1981, compared with a threefold increase in medium- and long-term debts (*External Debt and Economic Development in Latin America*).

88 Representative Mollahan summarized this concern with a pointed pun: "This bill is indeed an export initiative, for it would export American jobs and American capital to the Caribbean area" (July 14, 1983, *CR*, p. H5144).

89 Representative Applegate, for example, referred to the CBI as a "kick in the pants to the American taxpayer and the American worker" and urged the administration to act on the principle that "charity begins at home" and to give assistance to domestic industries which were trying to survive (July 14, 1983, *CR*, p. H5147).

90 Senator Heinz, who repeatedly raised this concern, referred to the possibility that Asian countries, such as Japan and Taiwan, which have been graduated out of the US GSP program, might use the Caribbean Basin as a "pass-through" to the US market (Hearings on the CBI by the Committee on Finance, US Senate, 97th Cong., 2nd sess., August 2, 1982, Washington, DC).

91 July 13, 1983, *CR*, p. H5108.

92 Testimony before the Senate Committee on Finance, Hearings on the CBI, US Senate, 97th Cong., 2nd sess., August 2, 1982, Washington, DC, p. 47.

93 Testimony before the Senate Committee on Finance, Hearings on the CBI, US Senate, 98th Cong., 1st sess., 1983, Washington, DC, p. 55.

94 US Congress, House Committee of Foreign Affairs, "Caribbean Basin Economic Revitalization Act of 1982," 97th Cong., 2nd sess., Report No. 97-665, Part 1, Washington, DC, p. 6.

95 Testimony before the Senate Committee on Finance, April 13, 1983, p. 57. Representative Gibbons concurred that petroleum could be so excluded since it was "just a pass-through product and is usually American-owned" (July 13, 1983, *CR*, p. H5102).

96 Representative Moody, ibid., p. H5103.

97 Testimony before the Senate Committee on Finance, April 13, 1983, p. 86.

98 Testimony before the House Committee on Ways and Means, Subcommittee on Trade, March 17, 1982, p. 132.

99 Testimony before the House Committee on Ways and Means, March 17, 1982, p. 281.

100 R. Reich, *The Next American Frontier* (New York: NY Times Books, 1983), p. 117.

101 Ibid., pp. 117-18.

102 Banu Helvacioglu, "The New Right in the US" (Ph.D. thesis, Queen's University, Kingston, Ontario, 1988), p. 31.

103 Reich, *The Next American Frontier*, p. 121.

104 "Overseas Private Investment Corporation," p. 1. No additional bibliographical information is provided in this booklet.

105 Overseas Private Investment Corporation (OPIC), *Development Report 1986* (Washington, DC), p. 15.

106 Ibid.

107 Address by Craig Nalen, president and chief executive officer, OPIC, before the 1987 Conference of American Chambers of Commerce in Latin America, Washington, DC, April 29, 1987, p. 3.

108 OPIC, *Development Report 1986*, p. 9.

109 Ibid.

110 Submission by Cameron Clark, President of the Committee on 806.30 and 807, to the House Ways and Means Committee, Subcommittee on Trade, Table 2, p. 284.

111 See ibid. and USITC 1986 Report, Table 8, p. 8.

112 Kenneth Boodhoo, "The Economic Dimension of US Caribbean Policy," in H. Michael Erisman, ed., *The Caribbean Challenge: US Policy in a Volatile Region* (Boulder, CO: Westview Press, 1984), p. 86.

113 Hilbourne A. Watson, "The Caribbean Basin Initiative and Caribbean Development: A Critical Analysis," *Contemporary Marxism* 10 (1985).

114 Emilio Pantojas-Garcia, p. 115.

115 Additional views of Hon. Richard T. Schulz, Caribbean Basin Economic Recovery Act, Committee on Ways and Means, US House of Representatives, 97th Cong., 2nd sess., Report No. 97-958, December 10, 1982, p. 37.

116 "Caribbean Basin Economic Recovery Act," Committee on Ways and Means, p. 9. Emphasis added.

117 Ibid., p. 8.

118 July, 13, 1983, *CR*, p. H 5117.

119 Author's interview with Lawrence Theriot, Director of the Caribbean Basin Information Centre, Department of Commerce. Wednesday, December 16, 1987.

120 *Business America*, US Department of Commerce, Washington DC, September 28, 1987, p. 35.

121 *807 Textile Reporter*, New York Regional Informational Pipeline, No. 1083, Supp. #1 (undated), pp. 24-25.

Chapter 6

1 Caribbean Development Bank (CDB), *Annual Report, 1986* (St Michael, Barbados: CDB, 1986), Tables, pp. 18-19. In the years 1970-87 Barbados invested 6.6 per cent of GDP in education and 4.5 per cent in health services. Figures for other Latin American and Caribbean countries indicate that Barbados has consistently devoted a higher proportion of total public spending for health and education than any other country. See Inter-American Development Bank (IDB), *Economic and Social Progress in Latin America and the Caribbean*, 1988 Report, (Washington, DC: IDB, 1988), Tables IV-6 and IV-8, pp. 70 and 75.

2 For additional information regarding the process of economic diversification in Barbados see D. Worrell, ed., *The Economy of Barbados, 1946-1980* (Bridgetown, Barbados: Central Bank of Barbados, 1982).

3 During the period 1951 to 1974 the Barbadian government enacted a series of laws extending the tax holidays and other forms of governmental assistance available to investors in industry. See W. Cox, "The Manufacturing Sector in the Economy of Barbados, 1946-80," in Worrell, ed., *The Economy of Barbados*, pp. 47-80, for further details.

4 World Bank, *Economic Memorandum on Barbados*, Report No. 3487-BAR (Washington, DC: World Bank, 1981), pp. i-ii; IDB, *Economic and Social Progress*, various issues.

5 F. Long, "Industrialization and the Role of the Industrial Development Corporations in the Caribbean Economy: A Study of Barbados, 1960-80," *Inter-American Economic Affairs* 37, 3 (Winter 1983): 36.

6 IDB, *Economic and Social Progress*, 1979 Report, pp. 165-67.

7 Ibid., p. 164.

8 World Bank, *Economic Memorandum*, p. i; and IDB, *Economic and Social Progress*, 1988 Report, p. 343.

9 N.A. Graham, and G.L. Edwards, *The Caribbean Basin to the Year 2,000: Demographic, Economic and Resource Trends in 17 Countries* (Boulder and London: Westview Press, 1984), pp. 28-30.

10 Cox, "The Manufacturing Sector," p. 74; and IDB, *Economic and Social Progress*, 1983 Report, p. 158.

11 A. Lipietz, "The Globalization of the General Crisis of Fordism, 1967-84," in J. Holmes and C. Leys, eds., *Frontyard/Backyard: The Americas in the Global Crisis* (Toronto: Between the Lines, 1987), pp. 23-56; and A. Lipietz, "Monetarism and the Third World," *New Left Review* 145 (May/June 1984): 71-87.

12 *Latin American Regional Report-Caribbean* (hereinafter *LARR-C*), RC-86-07, August 28, 1986.

13 Long, "Industrialization and Industrial Development Corporations," p. 36; and IDB, *Economic and Social Progress*, various issues.

14 IDB, *Economic and Social Progress*, 1987 Report, p. 230.

15 Ibid., 1983, 1984, and 1985 Reports.

16 Ibid., 1984 and 1985 Reports.

17 Ibid., 1984 Report, pp. 229-31.

18 United Nations, Economic Commission for Latin America and the Caribbean, *Economic Survey of Latin America and the Caribbean, 1984*, vol. 2 (Santiago, Chile: ECLA, 1986), p. 52; and IDB, *Economic and Social Progress*, 1988 Report, p. 343.

19 CDB, *Annual Report*, 1985-87.

20 This compares quite favourably with annual GDP growth of industrialized countries. The average rate of growth for the 24 OECD nations in the years 1984-87 was 3.3 per cent, with three of the seven leading economies (Italy, France, and Germany) achieving growth rates substantially lower than that of Barbados (OECD, *OECD Economic Outlook* [Paris: OECD, various years]).

21 *Latin American and Caribbean Review, 1986* p. 156; and CDB, *Annual Report, 1986*, p. 24.

22 *Latin American and Caribbean Review*.

23 M. Raymond, "Barbados 1984," *Business Week*, Industrial/Technology Edition, 2838 (April 16, 1984), p. 35; *The Globe and Mail*, August 7, 1986, p. B18.

24 According to *The Globe and Mail* correspondent Cecil Foster, in only one year (Fall 1984-85) 16 US businesses were given licences to establish captive insurance companies in Barbados. See *The Globe and Mail*, September 23, 1985.

25 IDB, *Economic and Social Progress*, 1988 Report, Table D-13, p. 573.

26 *Business Week*, April 16, 1984, p. 33.

27 Ibid.

28 Ibid.

29 Ibid., pp. 33-34, p. 39.

30 *The Globe and Mail*, August 7, and October 6, 1986.

31 United States Commerce Department, Office of Trade and Investment Analysis, *1986 US Foreign Trade Highlights* (Washington, DC: Office of Trade and Investment Analysis, 1986), p. 10; and United States Commerce Department, Office of Trade and Investment Analysis, *1987 US Foreign Trade Highlights* (Washington, DC: Office of Trade and Investment Analysis, 1987), p. A-007.

32 Ibid., and IDB, *Economic and Social Progress*, 1988 Report, p. 346.

33 *1986 US Foreign Trade Highlights*, p. 10; and *1987 US Foreign Trade Highlights*, p. PA-007.

34 *1986 US Foreign Trade Highlights*, p. 10; and *1987 US Foreign Trade Highlights* pp. PA-007 and PA-012. As the 1987 report indicates, in that year the US secured a positive balance of trade with Barbados amounting to $71 million (almost double that for the previous year. It should also be borne in mind that while the United States is now by far the largest market for Barbadian commodity exports, according to the US International Trade Commission all Caribbean merchandise exports to the US represent less than one-fifth of one per cent of total US trade. Cited in United States House of Representatives, Committee on Foreign Affairs, *The Caribbean Basin Initiative: A Congressional Study Mission and Symposium* (Washington, DC: US Government Printing Office, 1988), p. 87.

35 *1986 US Foreign Trade Highlights*, p. 10.

36 CDB, *Annual Report*, 1987-88; and IDB, *Economic and Social Progress*, 1987-88 Reports; and *Sunday Advocate* (Barbados), February 7, 1988.

37 *1986 US Foreign Trade Highlights*, p. 10.

38 Ibid.; and *1987 US Foreign Trade Highlights*, p. PA-022.

39 In 1987, exports of Barbadian manufactured goods to the United States' market earned $48 million, or 79 per cent of total commodity sales ($61 million) to that country.

40 Cox, "The Manufacturing Sector," p. 71.

41 Ibid.; World Bank, *Economic Memorandum*, p. 2; and United States International Trade Commission, *Background Study of the Economies and International Trade Patterns of the Countries of North America, Central America and the Caribbean*, Report on Investigation No. 332-119 Under Section 332 of the Tariff Act of 1930, Publication 1176 (Washington, DC: International Trade Commission, 1981), Table A-5, p. 170.

42 *Business Week*, April 16, 1984, p. 40.

43 United States Commerce Department, "Caribbean Basin: CBI Attracts Investment, Boosts Trade with US," *Business America* 8, 5 (March 4, 1985); *LARR-C*, RC-85-08, September 29, 1985, p. 5; and IDB *Economic and Social Progress*, 1985 Report, p. 195.

44 IDB, *Economic and Social Progress*, 1988 Report, p. 62. The IDB estimates that output in the electronics sub-sector fell by 10 per cent in 1986.

45 *LARR-C*, RC-86-10, December 11, 1986; IDB, *Economic and Social Progress*, 1987 Report, p. 232; and IDB *Economic and Social Progress*, 1988 Report, pp. 344-46.

46 United States International Trade Commission, *Annual Report on the Impact of the Caribbean Basin Economic Recovery Act on US Industries and Consumers*, First Report, 1984-85, p. 3, 30.

47 Cox, "The Manufacturing Sector," p. 54.

48 Caribbean/Central American Action, *Caribbean Action*, Summer 1985, p. 7. In the case of garments, one of the most important US fiscal concessions was that provided by TSUS 807.00, exempting US inputs (which can constitute between 75 per cent and 80 per cent of total value) from import duty.

49 Cox, "The Manufacturing Sector," pp. 71-76.

50 Ibid.

51 C. Sunshine, *The Caribbean: Survival, Struggle and Sovereignty*, (Washington, DC: EPICA, 1985), p. 141; "Barbadian Textiles Look for Way over Protectionist Wall," *The Globe and Mail*, December 16, 1987, p. B18.

52 *Caribbean Action*, Summer 1985, p. 6.

53 *The Globe and Mail*, August 7, 1986, p. B18; and IDB, *Economic and Social Progress*, 1986-88 Reports.

54 T. Barry, B. Wood, and D. Preusch, *The Other Side of Paradise: Foreign Control in the Caribbean* (New York: Grove Press, 1984), p. 264; and IDB, *Economic and Social Progress*, 1984 and 1985 Reports.

55 IDB, *Economic and Social Progress*, 1983 and 1985 Reports.

56 Barry et al., *Other Side of Paradise*, pp. 264-65.

57 IDB, *Economic and Social Progress*, 1987 Report, p. 231, and 1988 Report, pp. 345-46.

58 *1986 US Foreign Trade Highlights*, p. 6 and p. 249; and *1987 US Foreign Trade Highlights*, p. A-042 and p. A-047.

59 Calculated from ibid.

60 The Barbados Labour Party was led by Tom Adams, who died in May 1985, and later Bernard St. John. In May 1986, after a landslide victory which gained the party 24 of 27 legislative seats, the Democratic Labour Party gained office under the leadership of Errol Barrow.

61 IDB, *Economic and Social Progress*, 1985-88 Reports; and *LARR-C*, RC-87-04, May 14, 1987, p. 7.

62 Ibid.

63 Ibid.

64 See report of the reaction of Leroy Trotman, former head of the Barbados Workers Union (ibid.).

65 *The Globe and Mail*, August 7, 1986, p. B18.

66 IDB, *Economic and Social Progress*, 1988 Report, p. 448.

67 For example, during the 16 years ending 1985 Barbados spent on average 11.1 per cent of GDP on health and education services while Jamaica invested only 8.7 per cent (IDB, *Economic and Social Progress*, 1988 Report, Tables IV-6 and IV-8, pp. 70 and 75.

68 CDB, *Annual Report, 1985*, pp. 18-19.

69 Political violence reached a climax during the 1980 general election in which more than 700 people were killed.

70 M.A. Ayub, *Made in Jamaica: The Development of the Manufacturing Sector* (Baltimore: Johns Hopkins University Press, 1981), pp. 16-29. The JDIC was established in 1952.

71 Ibid.

72 O. Jefferson, "Some Aspects of the Post-War Economic Development of Jamaica," in N. Girvan and O. Jefferson, eds., *Readings in the Political Economy of the Caribbean* (Kingston, Jamaica: New World Group, 1971), p. 109.

73 Ibid.

74 S. Reid, "An Introductory Approach to the Concentration of Power and Notes on its Origin," in C. Stone and A. Brown, eds., *Essays on Power and Change in Jamaica* (Kingston, Jamaica: Jamaica Publishing House, 1978).

75 T. Lacey, *Politics and Violence in Jamaica, 1960-70* (Manchester: Manchester University Press, 1977).

76 It should be noted that during the 1972 general election the party never referred to "democratic socialism" as a PNP principle. The party officially adopted democratic socialist objectives only after a lengthy internal debate was concluded in late 1974. The PNP then published its first official document on the subject. Entitled *Democratic Socialism: The Jamaican Model*, the publication outlined the party leadership's somewhat idiosyncratic understanding of the term.

77 The various incentive programs and services offered to companies locating in the Kingston Export Free Zone were outlined by the Jamaica Chamber of Commerce in *Jamaica Chamber of Commerce Journal* 33, 1 (1977): 4-5.

78 Ayub, *Made in Jamaica*, pp. 32-41; and W. James, "The Decline and Fall of Michael Manley: Jamaica, 1972-1980," *Capital and Class* 19 (Spring 1983): 153-55.

79 These gains are all the more remarkable, given other developments. This period coincides with both the early 1970s international recession, and with the marked cooling of economic and political relations with the United States. See W. James, "Decline and Fall," pp. 158-66, for an analysis of these events.

80 Ayub, *Made in Jamaica*, p. 42.

81 Ibid., citing Paul Chen-Young, "A Study of Tax Incentives in Jamaica," *National Tax Journal* 20, 3 (September 1967).

82 Ibid.

83 Ibid., pp. 42-43.

84 See James, "Decline and Fall." In this article James offers a persuasive interpretation of Jamaica's political and economic decline during the 1970s and the relative importance of the IMF, Carter administration, Bauxite/Alumina companies, and local business classes in the downfall of the Manley government.

85 Ayub, *Made in Jamaica*, p. 46, Table 3-6; and James, "Decline and Fall," p. 170.

86 Ibid.

87 IDB, *Economic and Social Progress*, 1980-81 Report, p. 299; James, "Decline and Fall," pp. 166-67; and Ayub, *Made in Jamaica*, p. 47. Ayub notes that the Jamaican dollar was devalued by almost 50 per cent, from US$1.10 to US$0.56, between April 1977 and mid-1979. The government also removed subsidies from almost 60 of the list of 100 basic items previously under price control, and adjusted prices of public utilities to reflect increased costs. These actions, combined with the effects of devaluation on prices of imports, pushed inflation up to 48 per cent in 1978, at the same time as the PNP government was limiting wage increases to 15 per cent.

88 The Resource Center, *Jamaica: Open for Business* (Albuquerque: The Resource Center, 1984), p. 27; and C. Stone, "Jamaica in Crisis: From Socialist to Capitalist Management," *International Journal* 60, 2 (Spring 1985): 293.

89 One of the most serious obstacles to economic development was the explosive political climate generated in the run-up to the 1980 general election, which inhibited any recovery in investment spending. In addition, Hurricane Allen wreaked havoc in the agricultural sector, affecting output of all export crops, with the exception of coffee.

90 IDB, *Economic and Social Progress*, 1979-82 Reports.

91 IDB, *Economic and Social Progress*, 1980-84 Reports; CDB, *Annual Report*, 1980-84; and T. Bogues, "Jamaica Today," *Caribbean Contact* (August 1984).

92 The main factors were: the emergence of a number of low-cost producers elsewhere in the Third World, economic problems faced by a number of US refineries processing Jamaican bauxite, and the slow rate of recovery of international markets for aluminum after the recession. These problems led to the closure of two major US mining operations owned by Reynolds Metals and ALCOA in 1984 and 1985, respectively (The Private Sector Organization of Jamaica [PSOJ], *Jamaican Economy Review, 1984* [Kingston, Jamaica: PSOJ, 1984], p. 11; IDB, *Economic and Social Progress*, 1985 Report, pp. 298-301; and CDB, *Annual Report*, 1983, p. 38).

93 CDB, *Annual Report, 1983*, p. 38; and IDB, *Economic and Social Progress*, 1984 Report, p. 333.

94 At that time Mexico and Canada were the only other countries enjoying this privilege.

95 IDB, *Economic and Social Progress*, 1984 Report, p. 333.

96 Ibid., 1980-81 Report, p. 298.

97 Ibid., p. 299.

98 M. Kaufman, "Sitting in Limbo," *The Nation*, December 27, 1986, and January 3, 1987; PSOJ, *Jamaican Economy Review, 1984*, p. 9; IDB, *Economic and Social Progress*, 1979-84 Reports; and Stone, "Jamaica in Crisis," p. 304.

99 IDB, *Economic and Social Progress*, 1980-81 Report, p. 299.

100 *LARR-C*, RC-82-06, July 16, 1982, pp. 1-2; and Kaufman, "Sitting in Limbo."

101 Ayub, *Made in Jamaica*, p. 47.

102 IDB, *Economic and Social Progress*, 1984 Report, p. 333.

103 Barry et al., *The Other Side of Paradise*, Table IIC, p. 346.

104 "Jamaica's Human Rights Body on Police Brutalities," *Caribbean Contact* (September 1983); and T. Hector, "The Caribbean in Crisis," *Race Today* 16, 1 (September-October 1984): 14.

105 K. Polanyi-Levitt, "The Origins and Implications of the Caribbean Basin Initiative: Mortgaging Sovereignty?" *International Journal* 60, 2 (Spring 1985): 275-76.

106 PSOJ, *Jamaican Economy Review, 1984*, p. 9.

107 IDB, *Economic and Social Progress*, 1985 and 1988 Reports.

108 Stone, "Jamaica in Crisis," pp. 298-99.

109 IDB, *Economic and Social Progress, 1985 Report*, p. 301.

110 Ibid.; 1980-1988 Reports; and CDB, *Annual Report*, 1980-87.

111 PSOJ, *Jamaican Economy Review, 1984*, Table A1, pp. 25-27.

112 Ibid., p. 23; IDB, *Economic and Social Progress*, 1980-88 Reports; and "The Agony of Jamaica," *Caribbean and West Indies Chronicle*, August/September 1985.

113 Calculated from IDB *Economic and Social Progress*, 1980-88 Reports; and United States International Trade Commission (USITC), *Annual Report on*

the Impact of the Caribbean Basin Economic Recovery Act on US Industries and Consumers, Second Report (1986) (Washington, DC: USITC, 1987), p. 4, Table 5.

114 Ibid.; and USITC, *Third Annual CBERA Report*, p. 73.

115 United States Department of Commerce, Office of Trade and Investment Analysis, *US Merchandise Trade Position at Mid-Year 1987* (Washington, DC: International Trade Administration, 1987), pp. 11 and 57; USITC, *Second Annual CBERA Report*, p. 3, Table 4; and US Department of Commerce, *1987 US Foreign Trade Highlights* (Washington, DC: International Trade Administration, 1987), PA-012.

116 Calculated from United States Bureau of International Labour Affairs, *Trade and Employment Effects of the CBERA Act*, First Annual Report to the Congress Pursuant to Section 216 of the CBERA (Washington, DC: United States Department of Commerce, National Technical Information Service, 1985), Table 23; and USITC, *Annual Report on the Impact of the Caribbean Basin Economic Recovery Act on US Industries and Consumers*, Third Report (1987) (Washington, DC: USITC, 1988).

117 USITC, *First Annual CBERA Report*, p. 3; USITC, *Second Annual CBERA Report*, p. 2, Table 3; and *1987 US Foreign Trade Highlights*, PA-012.

118 IDB, *Economic and Social Progress, 1985 Report*, p. 300.

119 *1987 US Foreign Trade Highlights*, PA-027.

120 The "807" program allows entry to the United States of imported items of apparel assembled from US-made materials (PSOJ, *Jamaican Economy Review, 1984*, p. 11).

121 Ex-Prime Minister Edward Seaga, cited in the *Sunday Gleaner*, February 15, 1987. See "Free Zone Jobs to Double Soon," *Daily Gleaner*, April 15, 1985, for a full list of benefits available to Free Zone Investors.

122 USITC, *First Annual CBERA Report*, p. 3-30.

123 Ayub, *Made in Jamaica*, pp. 94-96. The 807A program was announced by Reagan in February 1986 and went into effect the same year. Under the 807/A programs most garments assembled in the Caribbean Basin enter the US under liberalized "guaranteed access limits" and pay duty only on Caribbean Basin content.

124 Centre for Caribbean Dialogue, "Free Trade Zones: Development for Caribbean?" (Toronto: Centre for Caribbean Dialogue, 1987), p. 9.

125 USITC, *Third Annual CBERA Report*, p. 76.

126 Ibid.; and *1987 Foreign Trade Highlights*, PA-163.

127 Joint Trade Unions Research Development Centre (JTURDC) and CUSO, *Women in Industry: Garment Workers in Jamaica*, pp. 4 and 12-13; "Unprecedented Opportunities for Export Growth," *Daily Gleaner*, June 18, 1986; and IDB, *1988 Report*, p. 450.

128 *Sistren* 9 (January 1987): 1.

129 JTURDC/CUSO, *Women in Industry*, Appendix 2.

130 Ibid., pp. 63-64.

131 "Labour Time Bomb Ticking in the Free Zone," *Sunday Gleaner*, May 12, 1985; and "Free Zones and Labour Relations: A Case for Caution," *Daily Gleaner*, October 26, 1986.

132 JTURDC/CUSO, *Women in Industry*, pp. 32-35; *Daily Gleaner*, June 18, 1986; and "News of Industry," *Sunday Gleaner*, May 18, 1986.

133 Ibid.; and *Daily Gleaner*, June 18, 1986.

134 JTUDRC/CUSO, *Women in Industry*, pp. 33-34.

135 "Big Garment Order Secured," *Daily Gleaner*, February 24, 1987, p. 32.

136 Centre for Caribbean Dialogue, "Free Trade Zones."

137 "Vaz Claims Success Record Is Confounding His Critics," *Daily Gleaner*, March 31, 1986; and "807 and Free Zone," ibid., February 3, 1987.

138 Ibid.

139 Latin America Bureau, *Green Gold: Bananas and Dependency in the Eastern Caribbean* (London: Latin America Bureau, 1987), pp. 80-81.

140 Friends for Jamaica, *Newsletter* 3, 12 (December 1983); S. L. Driever, "Structural Adjustment in Jamaican Agriculture," unpublished paper presented at the 1987 Annual Meeting of the Association of American Geographers, April 23-26, 1987, Portland, Oregon, p. 2.

141 Friends for Jamaica, *Newsletter*; and Driever, "Structural Adjustment," pp. 2-3.

142 IDB, *Economic and Social Progress, 1988 Report*, pp. 448-50.

143 In the opinion of Driever the main problem was not the government's willingness to divest to large private investors, but its inability to attract them with the Agro 21 program (Driever, "Structural Adjustment," p. 3).

144 Ibid., p. 5.

145 *1987 US Foreign Trade Highlights*, PA-163.

146 Driever, "Structural Adjustment," pp. 5-6; and D. Robotham, "An Approach to the Severe Economic Crisis Facing Our Nation," *Socialism* 1, 1 (February 1986): 35-36.

147 Spraying to control spot leaf disease was discontinued, and boxing plants on the north coast of the island were closed (Driever, "Structural Adjustment," p. 6).

148 US imports of Jamaican agricultural products increased in 1984 but dropped in each year thereafter up to 1987 – an overall decline of 24 per cent. Vegetable exports to the US more than doubled between 1983-86. Since then they have also declined (*1987 US Foreign Trade Highlights*, pp. PA-047 and PA-163).

149 *The Globe and Mail*, September 19, 1986, p. B22.

150 IDB, *Economic and Social Progress, 1987 Report*, pp. 46-49, Tables iv.3(a)-iv.3(c); and IDB, *Economic and Social Progress, 1988 Report*, pp. 54-59, Tables iv.2-iv.4.

151 *1987 US Foreign Trade Highlights*, PA-052.

152 "NCL Views Steep Increases with Grave Concern," *Daily Gleaner*, October 1, 1984, p. 3.

153 *Sistren* 9, 2 (1987): 1.

154 *NACLA Report on the America's*, 22, 3: 11.

155 New Jewel Movement, "Progress in Grenada: Accomplishments of the People's Revolutionary Government," October 1982.

156 World Bank, *Grenada: Economic Report* (Washington, DC: World Bank, 1985), p. 55, Table 2.1.

157 Refer to, T. Barry et al., (*Other Side of Paradise*, pp. 309-10), for information regarding PRG policy towards the private sector.

158 F. Ambursley and W. James, "Maurice Bishop and the New Jewel Revolution In Grenada," *New Left Review* 142 (Nov.-Dec. 1983): 191; and EPICA Taskforce, *Grenada: The Peaceful Revolution* (Washington, DC: EPICA, 1982), p. 42.

159 Ibid., pp. 36-51.
160 Ibid., p. 44; and Ambursley and James, "New Jewel Revolution," p. 197.
161 Ibid., pp. 194-95, Tables 9.1 and 9.2.
162 *Union Farmer*, April/May 1981; Ambursley and James, "New Jewel Revolution," p. 195.
163 Ibid., p. 196.
164 *Union Farmer*, April/May 1981; and C. Searle, ed., *In Nobody's Backyard: Maurice Bishop's Speeches 1979-1983* (London: Zed Books, 1984), p. 70.
165 Ambursley and James, "New Jewel Revolution," p. 194, Table 9.1.
166 Searle, *Nobody's Backyard*, p. 155.
167 EPICA, *Peaceful Revolution*, pp. 43-44.
168 NJM, "Progress," p. 3.
169 C. Henfrey, "Between Populism and Leninism," *Latin American Perspectives* 11, 3 (Summer 1984): 19-20 (Issue 42).
170 EPICA, *Peaceful Revolution*, pp. 44-45.
171 Ambursley and James, "New Jewel Revolution," pp. 199-201; and Henfrey, "Between Populism," pp. 21-24.
172 Ibid.
173 Ambursley and James, "New Jewel Revolution," p. 191.
174 H. O'Shaunessy, *Grenada: Revolution, Invasion and Aftermath* (London: Hamish Hamilton, 1984), p. 79; and Ambursley and James, "New Jewel Revolution," pp. 199-201.
175 Searle, *Nobody's Backyard*, p. xvii; and Caribbean Development Bank (CDB), *Annual Report, 1985*, p. 19.
176 C. Searle, *Grenada: The Struggle Against Destabilisation* (London: Writers and Readers, 1983); and "Maurice Bishop on Destabilisation: An Interview with Chris Searle," *Race and Class* 20, 3 (Winter 1984): 1-13.
177 B. Coard (Deputy Prime Minister and Minister of Finance and Trade), "Report on the National Economy for 1981 and the Prospects for 1982," St. Georges, Grenada, 1982.
178 The NJM's economic, social and political programs were outlined in 1973 in the *Manifesto of the New Jewel Movement for Power to the People and for Achieving Real Independence for Grenada, Carriacou, Petit Martinique and the Grenadian Grenadines*, no date. See also, Prime Minister M. Bishop, *West Indian Digest* (March 1980): 11-12.
179 Coard, *West Indian Digest*, p. 24.
180 "Grenada Then and Now," *West Indian Digest* (March 1980): 22.
181 Searle, *Nobody's Backyard*, pp. 69-71; and Ambursley and James, "New Jewel Revolution," p. 205.
182 Searle, *Nobody's Backyard*, p. 71.
183 Henfrey, "Between Populism," p. 25; and NJM, "Progress," p. 2.
184 Ibid., p. 1; and Ambursley and James, "New Jewel Revolution," pp. 205-206.
185 *Friends for Jamaica* 13, 9 (September 1983); NJM, "Progress," p. 1; B. Coard, *Revolutionary Grenada: A Big and Popular School* (London: 1985), p. 28.
186 CDB, *Annual Report, 1980-1983*.
187 Ibid.; and NJM, "Progress," p. 2.
188 Coard, *Revolutionary Grenada*, p. 38.
189 Ibid., pp. 27, 38; and CDB, *Annual Report, 1981*.
190 Coard, *Revolutionary Grenada*, pp. 39-40; and NJM, "Progress," p. 2.

191 Coard, *Revolutionary Grenada*, p. 27; NJM, "Progress."
192 Ibid.
193 *Latin American Regional Report: Caribbean (LARR-C)*, RC-82-03, March 26, 1983, p. 2; and World Bank, *Grenada*, p. 6.
194 *New York Times*, July 29, 1984; and Barry et al., *Other Side of Paradise*, p. 306.
195 *The Militant*, January 23, 1987, p. 9; World Bank, *Grenada*, p. ix; CDB, *Annual Report, 1985*; and J. Heine, ed., *A Revolution Aborted: The Lessons of Grenada* (Pittsburgh: University of Pittsburgh Press, 1990), chap. 3.
196 Coard, *Revolutionary Grenada*, pp. 28, 41.
197 NJM, "Progress," p. 3.
198 Ibid.
199 Ibid.
200 Searle, *Nobody's Backyard*, pp. 55-58; and NJM, "Progress," p. 3.
201 Ibid., pp. 3-4.
202 R. Thomson, *CUSO Forum* (January 1984): 21; *Militant*, January 23, 1987, p. 9; and *LARR-C*, RC-82-03, March 26, 1983, p. 2.
203 Ambursley and James, "New Jewel Revolution"; Henfrey, "Between Populism"; and M. Marable, *African and Caribbean Politics: From Kwame Nkrumah to Maurice Bishop* (London: Verso, 1987).
204 Henfrey, "Between Populism," pp. 26-31.
205 See Marable (*African and Caribbean Politics*, pp. 240-62), for an analysis of the PRG and its changing relationship with the mass organizations in the 1979-83 period.
206 *Latin America and Caribbean Review*, p. 178.
207 Quoted in "Grenada: Easy Triumph Turns to Disintegration and Despair," *Los Angeles Times*, October 13, 1985.
208 United States Agency for International Development (USAID), "Summary Highlights of Grenada A.I.D. Program" (Washington, DC: Office for Press Relations, 1986), p. 1; and *LARR-C*, RC-88-07, August 25, 1988, p. 8.
209 The conditionality of US financial assistance on radical economic restructuring was made explicit in the "Summary Highlights" published by USAID. See, for example, p. 1, referring to the linkage between Economic Support Fund (ESF) grants and "fiscal and other reforms" to be implemented by the government of Grenada.
210 Ibid., pp. 2-8.
211 Ibid., p. 8; *Business America*, Issue 22, October 29, 1984, pp. 6-9; "Grenada Hopeful Despite Early Setbacks," *Miami Herald*, July 8, 1985.
212 *Fortune*, February 6, 1984, p. 36; and *Maclean's*, March 3, 1986.
213 "Grenada Being Transformed by AID from the United States," *The Globe and Mail*, August 26, 1986; and "Frustration Pervades in Grenada," *Caribbean Contact* (October 1985).
214 E. Oakes, "Grenada under Occupation: US Economic Policy 1983-87," William Trotter Institute for the Study of Black Culture, University of Massachusetts, Boston, November 1987, p. 10; and *The Globe and Mail*, August 25, 1986.
215 Ibid. According to this report, USAID commissioned a Washington, DC company, Alternatives Inc., to advise the Grenadian Finance Ministry on the proposed tax reforms.
216 *Caribbean Insight* 10, 10 (October 1987); *The Globe and Mail*, August 25, 1986.

217 *Caribbean Insight* 10, 11 (November 1987); "Defections, Deficit Threaten to Destroy Grenadian Coalition," *The Globe and Mail*, September 8, 1987, p. A13.

218 *Latin America Weekly Report* (LAWR), WR-87-17, May 7, 1987, p. 5; and *Time*, November 23, 1987.

219 T. Burley, ed., *Caribbean Handbook*; "The US Finds Few Takers in Its Efforts to Draw Business," *New York Times*, July 29, 1984.

220 US International Trade Commission, *Annual Report on the Impact of the Caribbean Basin Economic Recovery Act on US Industry and Consumers*, First Report (1984-85) (Washington, DC: USITC, 1986).

221 USAID, "US Economic Assistance to Grenada" (Washington, DC: Office of Press Relations, 1986), p. 1.

222 United Nations Economic Commission for Latin America and the Caribbean (ECLA), *Economic Survey of Latin America and the Caribbean, 1984*, vol. 2, Tables 6 and 7, pp. 87-88.

223 Ibid.

224 USITC, *First CBERA Report*.

225 CDB, *Annual Report, 1985-87*.

226 Ibid.; and *LARR-C* RC-87-03, April 2, 1987, p. 3.

227 See remarks of the Grenadian Prime Minister, cited in *Caribbean Contact* (October 1985) in which Blaize argued that the "main economic thrust" of his government was the creation of "an industrial base."

228 ECLA, *Economic Survey*, pp. 84-88; and World Bank, *Grenada Economy*, p. 21. The ECLA report estimates that manufacturing output rose by a healthy 18 per cent in 1982.

229 Ibid. According to ECLA, garment exports were destined mainly for Trinidad and Tobago. Dominica and Jamaica were the most important external markets for flour. Flour exports were also seriously depressed as a result of CARICOM trade restraints beginning in 1983.

230 USAID, "US Economic Assistance," p. 7; and World Bank, *Grenada Economy*, pp. 22-24.

231 *Business America*, October 29, 1984, pp. 3 and 11; *New York Times*, July 29, 1984; and World Bank, *Grenada Economy*, p. 24.

232 US InterAgency Team on Commercial and Private Sector Initiatives, "Prospects for Growth in Grenada: The Role of the Private Sector" (Washington, DC: 1983), pp. 20-21.

233 *New York Times*, July 29, 1984; *The Globe and Mail*, August 25, 1986; *LARR-C*, RC-87-03, April 2, 1987, p. 4; and *Time*, November 2, 1987.

234 *Fortune*, February 6, 1986, p. 36; and *New York Times*, July 29, 1984.

235 *Business America*, Issue 22, October 29, 1984, p. 7.

236 World Bank, *Grenada Economy*, pp. 20-23; and *Business America*, October 29, 1984, pp. 14-16.

237 ECLA, *Economic Survey*, pp. 84-85; and World Bank, *Grenada Economy*, p. 55. The ECLA report indicates negative growth rates in both 1983 and 1984 of 2 per cent and 1.6 per cent, respectively. The ECLA data indicate also that output was declining in most manufacturing industries. World Bank figures for the same period show marginal growth in 1984.

238 *Caribbean Insight* (November 1987); "Defections, Deficit Threaten Grenadian Coalition," p. A13. In addition to leading to growing fiscal problems, the restructuring of public finances contributed to a political crisis in April

1987. Education Minister George Brizan, Attorney-General Francis Alexis, and Junior Minister for Legal Affairs Tilman Thomas defected from the government to form the National Democratic Congress (NDC). The NDC also gained the support of two earlier defectors from the NNP and from the only non-NNP MP to be elected in 1984.

239 *Maclean's*, March 3, 1986; and *Caribbean Contact* (October 1985).

240 Ibid. In February 1986 President Reagan announced an improved 807 (Super807) program for CBI designates and encouraged participants to take advantage of funds made available in Puerto Rico to promote production-sharing arrangements.

241 CDB, *Annual Report, 1986-1987*.

242 USAID, "US Economic Assistance," p. 6.

243 ECLA, *Economic Survey*, p. 85.

244 USAID, "US Economic Assistance," especially p. 2.

245 *LARR-C*, RC-87-03, April 2, 1987, p. 3.

246 Oakes, "Grenada under Occupation," pp. 20-24.

247 Ibid., p. 25; and USAID, "US Economic Assistance," pp. 6-7.

248 Oakes, "Grenada under Occupation," p. 24.

249 *CUSO Forum*, January 1984, pp. 18 and 20.

250 ECLA, *Economic Survey*, pp. 83-85.

251 World Bank, "Summary and Conclusions," *Grenada Economy*; and CDB, *Annual Report, 1985*, p. 34.

252 CDB, *Annual Report, 1986*, p. 27.

253 CDB, *Annual Report, 1987*, p. 31.

254 "Stirring Up the Cocoa in Grenada," *The Globe and Mail*, August 23, 1986.

255 Ibid.

256 Latin America Bureau, *Green Gold*, p. 82.

257 CDB, *Annual Report, 1987*, p. 31.

258 *Business America*, October 29, 1984, p. 5; and USAID, "Summary Highlights," p. 1.

259 ECLA, *Economic Survey*, p. 86.

260 *The Globe and Mail*, June 4, 1984; *Miami Herald*, July 8, 1985; and *Business America*, October 29, 1984, p. 10.

261 *New York Times*, July 29, 1984.

262 CDB, *Annual Report, 1985*, p. 34.

263 CDB, *Annual Report, 1986*, p. 28.

264 CDB, *Annual Report, 1987*, pp. 31-32; and *Time*, November 23, 1987.

265 *Caribbean Insight* (November 1987): 1.

266 Ibid.

267 Ibid.

268 Oakes, "Grenada under Occupation," pp. 13-14.

269 "Grenada Placed Hight on List of Human Rights Violators," *New York Times*, December 31, 1985.

270 *LARR-C*, RC-87-06, July 23, 1987, p. 8.

271 "IMF Recommends Grenada Practice Wage Restraint," *Contrast*, January 18, 1985.

272 *Time*, November 23, 1987.

273 One overview of the local responses to this general impact in the Eastern Caribbean is presented by Aaron L. Schneider, "Grass Roots Development in the Eastern Caribbean," in *Canadian-Caribbean Relations: Aspects of a*

Relationship, edited by Brian Douglas Tennyson (Sydney, NS: Centre for International Studies, 1990), pp. 173-255.

Chapter 7

1 As was noted in the "Introduction" in this volume, Grenada's Prime Minister, Maurice Bishop, was among the very few regional leaders to denounce the CBI immediately as yet another US political ploy.

2 98th Cong., 2nd sess., House Document No. 98-151, *Designating Eleven Caribbean Basin Countries as Beneficiaries of CBERA* (Washington, DC: US Government and Printing Office, 1984), p. 39.

3 Ibid.

4 The *Sunday Express* published a special supplement on the CBI in its March 28, 1982 issue. To date, support for the CBI from the dailies (especially the *Trinidad Guardian*) remains largely undiminished.

5 William Demas was at that time president of the Caribbean Development Bank. He is currently governor of the Central Bank of Trinidad and Tobago. He explained in an interview with *Business Wave*, a publication of the Caribbean Association of Industry and Commerce, that when he suggested the CBI "would take long to bear results," he was criticized for being "too pessimistic and against the private sector." "And now," he continued, "all the private sector people and governments who most enthusiastically hailed the CBI as something that would apparently give immediate benefits, have changed their minds and have even stronger reservations than I do" (quoted in *Daily Express*, June 4, 1988).

6 Hilbourne A. Watson, "The Caribbean Basin Initiative and Caribbean Development: A Critical Analysis," *Contemporary Marxism* 10 (1985). For a more thorough discussion of this position, see Devanand Ramnarine, "The Political Significance of the United States Caribbean Basin Initiative," Ph.D. thesis, Department of Political Studies, Queen's University, Kingston, Canada, 1988; and "The Philosophy and Developmental Prospects of the CBI," in this volume.

7 This is also referred to as the "Lewis Model," so called after its principal architect, Sir Arthur Lewis. It was pursued throughout the British Caribbean and, more famously, in Puerto Rico. The main features of the strategy will be discussed later.

8 The Chaguaramas peninsula and several other parts of Trinidad had been alienated from indigenous control since WW II, when they were given over for use as US military bases as part of the destroyers-for-bases deal between the US government and the British government.

9 Other measures were also taken to control labour. In 1963, a commission of inquiry was set up to examine the degree of communist penetration in the trade union movement; in the early 1970s, radical labour leaders were imprisoned for political activities; a labour march in 1975 which attempted to unite agricultural and oil industry workers (hitherto an elusive goal) was suppressed by police; and finally, industrial action by BWIA pilots in 1978 was met with a state of emergency (imposed at Piarco International Airport) and subsequently with the denial of the right to strike in future (this was done by making BWIA an essential service).

10 See Leslie Scotland, "The Localization Process in the Banking Industry in Retrospect," in Selwyn Ryan, ed., *Trinidad and Tobago: The Independence Experience, 1962-1987* (St. Augustine, Trinidad and Tobago: Institutes of Social and Economic Research, University of the West Indies, 1988).

11 A local periodical noted that in 1986, "[t]he receivership industry . . . became the only growth sector in the economy, as creditors scrambled to obtain some lien on the assets of unviable debtors" ("Introduction," *Asset* 6, 1 [October 1987]: vii).

12 National Planning Commission, *Restructuring for Economic Independence: Draft Medium Term Macro Planning Framework, 1989-1995* (Port of Spain: Government Printer, July 1988). My emphasis.

13 At the end of 1986, 64.5 per cent of Trinidad and Tobago's external debt was owed to private institutions. As to repayment, 64 per cent of the debt had an original maturity of less than five years and the remainder between five and 10 years (The World Bank, *Trinidad and Tobago: A Programme for Policy Reform and Renewed Growth* [Washington, DC: World Bank, 1988]).

14 The figure is for 1986, when only 56.8 per cent of the external debt was held in US currency (NPC, *Restructuring for Economic Independence*).

15 The Central Bank of Trinidad and Tobago, *Quarterly Economic Bulletin* 13, 2 (June 1988). For the period 1977-82 it had averaged a mere 8 per cent of GDP per annum.

16 NPC, *Restructuring for Economic Independence*.

17 Gale Moneypenny, *Sunday Express*, May 8, 1988. This is also the view of University of the West Indies lecturer in economics, Patrick Watson. In an interview (summer 1988) on local television he rejected Prime Minister Robinson's more optimistic forecast that the economy would begin to turn around by the end of 1988 as being utterly without foundation.

18 Karl Theodore, lecturer in economics at the University of the West Indies, writing in the *Trinidad Guardian*, June 16, 1988.

19 The *Sunday Guardian*, February 28, 1988, section 2, p.3.

20 See A.H. Good, "Progress in the Caribbean Basin: A Special Report by the CBI Ombudsman," *Caribbean Affairs* 1, 1 (January-March 1988).

21 Dr. Geiger is also a member of the American Enterprise Institute and the Cato Institute in the US.

22 *Trinidad Guardian*, May 8, 1988.

23 Ibid.

24 Many of the measures included in this document were taken from the "Report of the Committee to Examine Export Development in the Non-Oil Sector," submitted to Parliament in April 1982. The committee comprised state officials and leaders of the local private sector.

25 See Industrial Development Corporation (IDC), *Investment Policy in Trinidad and Tobago*, Port of Spain, Republic of Trinidad and Tobago.

26 The "Mighty Sparrow" (the country's most successful calypsonian) has perceptively observed in song that Trinidad and Tobago appears to be a case of "capitalism gone mad!" The depth of the political crisis becomes clearer below.

27 IDC, *Investment Policy*, p. 6.

28 This is an allowance of 30 per cent on new plant and machinery acquired after December 31, 1987, 100 per cent on approved locally designed and

built machinery and equipment, and 150 per cent for petroleum exploration and new mining operations. An allowance of up to 100 per cent is also to be made available to companies which reinvest profits in manufacturing or service industries or expand their existing operations.

29 IDC, *Investment Policy*, p. 8. An export allowance was first introduced in 1966 and has been amended over the years to make it more attractive to investors.

30 The expenditures may be on activities such as overseas market research, the testing of local products in overseas markets or by foreign agencies for quality and technical standards, and for product design and consultancy.

31 These may include costs for the following: advertizing in overseas markets; attending overseas trade shows/missions, etc.; hosting potential buyers in Trinidad and Tobago; hiring foreign sales specialists for a maximum of two years; and other similar expenses.

32 It was proposed that beginning January 1, 1988, any locally registered company with annual gross foreign-exchange earnings of at least 25 per cent of its foreign-exchange requirements be exempt from having to obtain official approval for the importation of goods directly related to its operation, "subject to a limit equal to the level of its actual annual foreign exchange earnings in the previous calendar year" (IDC, *Investment Policy*, p. 9). Companies that earn more foreign exchange than they spend are to receive an export allowance of 10 cents (in the form of a rebate on their corporation tax) for every additional dollar in hard currency they earn (companies in the petroleum industry are excluded). Finally, companies which earn all of their foreign-exchange requirements may, with Central Bank approval, maintain a foreign currency account.

33 The Aliens (Landowning) Ordinance 1962 prohibits foreigners from owning land in Trinidad and Tobago. Instead, they may only lease land for industrial purposes for periods up to 30 years, with the option to renew thereafter. The Act also proscribes the activities of foreigners in the local stock market. They may not hold shares and/or directorships in any company operating in Trinidad and Tobago unless a licence to do so is first granted by the government.

34 Senator Michael Mansoor in his contribution to the debate on the 1988 Finance Bill (Trinidad and Tobago), published in *Sunday Guardian*, May 8, 1988. Mr. Mansoor called for the repeal of the Act. The conservative *Trinidad Guardian* newspaper added its support, claiming "As it now stands, our attitude, legal and otherwise, to foreign companies wishing to invest in Trinidad and Tobago is decidedly hostile." It went on to cite some of the restrictions placed on foreign investors and rhetorically concluded, "under such conditions how can we expect them [i.e., foreign investors] to be enthusiastic" (*Trinidad Guardian*, May 10, 1988). In interviews with the author, several bureaucrats and a high-level official of the Trinidad and Tobago Manufacturers Association made similar comments. A senior official in the Ministry of Mobilization and Planning argued that whereas the Aliens (Landowning) Ordinance may have performed a useful function in the past, since its implementation (and perhaps partly because of it) sufficient progress has occurred in the localization of ownership in the economy, and Trinidadians have developed enough confidence in the management of their economic affairs, to render the restric-

tions entailed in the Act unnecessary. Indeed, it may even be detrimental to the country. Also, several years earlier, the Chamber of Commerce, in its submission to the 1985 government budget, had called for the repeal of the Act.

35 The same applies to investments in locally owned privately held companies (IDC, *Investment Policy*, p. 15). After the transaction, however, the investor is required to declare the purchase to the management of the company and the local Stock Exchange, and the management must then inform the Investment Coordinating Committee of the IDC. An Alien's Licence is still required for purchases exceeding the 20 per cent limit. This is granted at the government's discretion.

36 Such areas include property development, petroleum-related services, distributive trades, small guest houses, and the manufacture of luggage, flatgoods, and furniture.

37 Others have also been critical of the pace of liberalization of the investment climate. Local financial columnist Gale Moneypenny argues that Trinidad and Tobago has been too slow in introducing the changes needed to enable it to take advantage of the CBI and holds up the Jamaican example as one that it should follow (*Sunday Express*, February 28, 1988). In a similar vein, Senator Mansoor bemoaned the government's tardiness in implementing the IDC's investment policy statement (discussed above) which he felt was (is) "very friendly to foreign investment." See Senator Mansoor's contribution to the debate on the 1988 Finance Bill.

38 N. Girvan (1983), quoted in Watson, "The Caribbean Basin Initiative," p. 25.

39 The ratio of imports of raw materials, capital goods, and intermediate goods to value-added in the productive sectors has declined in recent years. Yet between 1983 and 1987, "fully 71 per cent of total imports have had to be allocated for these purposes" (NPC, *Restructuring for Economic Independence*, p. 65).

40 Girvan in Watson, "The Caribbean Basin Initiative," pp. 25-26.

41 Denis Pantin, "Whither Point Lisas? Lessons for the Future," in Ryan, ed., *Trinidad and Tobago*.

42 In 1988, with the exception of the Iron and Steel Company, these plants operated at over 90 per cent capacity.

43 During the third quarter of 1988, urea prices were 49 per cent higher than in the corresponding period of 1987. This improved the Urea Company's foreign earnings substantially. For the first six months of 1988, Trinidad and Tobago's nitrogenous fertilizer output and exports increased by 16.8 per cent and 23.6 per cent, respectively, over the corresponding period of 1987. Owing largely to the start up of Tringen II, total output was projected to reach a record 2 million tonnes for 1988. In the case of Methanol, the entire output for 1988 was "reportedly fully booked" and international prices were up to 49.6 per cent (US$197 per tonne f.o.b. Rotterdam) higher in the third quarter of 1988 than in the corresponding period of 1987. This increased the earnings from methanol by over 35 per cent during the same period, despite a decline of 4.3 per cent in output (*Quarterly Economic Bulletin*, 13, 2 [June 1988] and 13, 3 [September 1988]).

44 The problem becomes more striking in relation to Caribcan, the Canadian counterpart of the CBI, which has a 60 per cent value-added requirement (see C. Hyett, "Caribcan: Canada's Response to the Caribbean Basin Initiative," in this volume).

45 The Import Negative List was introduced in 1966 to offer additional protection to local manufacturers. It limits or prohibits the importation of specified commodities to the extent deemed appropriate to protect local industries. To import "listed" commodities, a special licence must first be obtained from the government.

46 Between 1983 and 1987, manufactured goods (excluding petrochemicals) accounted for only five per cent of total exports from Trinidad and Tobago, although during the last two years of that period the trend has been upwards, that is, to 7 per cent in 1986 and 8 per cent in 1987 (NPC, *Restructuring for Economic Independence*).

47 *Daily Express*, April 20, 1988.

48 Interview with Mr. Anthony Guiseppi, IDC Official, Port of Spain, Trinidad and Tobago, August 3, 1988.

49 See Ramnarine, "Political Significance."

50 The House of Representatives of the Republic of Trinidad and Tobago, *Budget Speech 1988* (Port of Spain: Government Printery, 1988). The prime minister's account is quite different from that of the CBI ombudsman, who gave the impression that CBI countries, including Trinidad and Tobago, were easily increasing the quantity of "ethnic goods" they exported to the US market (see Good, "Progress in the Caribbean Basin"). The case of ethanol is also instructive. In 1988, a US trade bill sponsored by the Democrats included provisions to increase ethanol imports from CBI countries. President Reagan vetoed the bill, claiming, among other things, that increased ethanol imports would ". . . harm US grain producers" (*Sunday Guardian*, June 19, 1988, p. 16).

51 In 1985 ISCOTT's net contribution to foreign-exchange earnings was US $-59.4 million (after debt service payments). Since 1982 Trinidad and Tobago's external debt has increased rapidly. Between 1983 and 1985 it grew at an average annual rate of 62 per cent. Obviously, ISCOTT is a major contributor to this debt (*Budget Speech 1988*).

52 *Manifesto of the National Alliance for Reconstruction 1986* (Port of Spain: National Alliance for Reconstruction, 1986, p. 16).

53 The fines were to apply to steel exported between 1984-87. As one Trinidadian official who participated in the negotiations explained, "even if ISCOTT had never exported another wire rod to the US from November [1987], it would still have had to repay duties of US $100 million for exports from 1984-87" (*Sunday Guardian*, May 15, 1988).

54 Address by Senator Sahadeo Basdeo, Minister of External Affairs and International Trade (Trinidad and Tobago), to a Special Luncheon at Caribbean Expo '88 (Port of Spain), published in the *Sunday Guardian*, April 24, 1988.

55 *Quarterly Economic Bulletin* 13, 2 (June 1988).

56 Quoted in editorial of the *Trinidad Guardian*, May 23, 1988. Centrin produces steel products (squares, flats, and rounds) from billets purchased from ISCOTT. It has a capacity of 90 000 tonnes of steel products per

annum. The company was commissioned in 1983 and represents one of the largest indigenous private manufacturing ventures in the Caribbean.

57 Editorial, *Trinidad Guardian*, May 23, 1988.

58 Ibid.

59 To its credit, Centrin has responded to this setback with enterprise and has "set its sights" on the Canadian market. In May 1988, under Caribcan arrangements, the company began selling its products in Canada, with its first shipment going to Oshawa, Ontario. It has also retained Canadian marketing specialists in an effort to expand its sales to other parts of Canada.

60 Interview with Mr. Anthony Giuseppi, IDC Official, Port of Spain, Trinidad and Tobago, August 3, 1988. Similar concerns also exist in the local private sector (see the discussion on Colourclad below).

61 Calculated from data in *Review of the Economy*, 1987.

62 In June 1987, when the ban was introduced, local producers controlled only 20 per cent of the local garment market; by year-end 1988, they had increased that share to 80 per cent of the market (*Trinidad Guardian*, December 30, 1988).

63 Ibid.

64 Employment in the garment industry has more that doubled since June 1987, amounting to about 5 000 jobs in November 1988. It was projected to climb to 10 000 by the end of 1989, in addition to which only about 500 jobs are expected to result from the "807" trade (ibid). This suggests that the relevant CBI measures have had limited effect (especially compared to domestic measures) on the revitalization of the textile and garment industry.

65 See Good, "Progress in the Caribbean Basin."

66 One IDC official (Anthony Guiseppi), in an interview with the author, was not aware of any new projects resulting from the CBI. Also, Mr. Richardson Andrews, a former General Manager of the IDC (1986-87) suggested that while there were inquiries from potential investors during his tenure, no projects have yet materialized from them. Interviews, August 3, and August 16, 1988, respectively.

67 In 1982, Melvin H. Evans, US Ambassador to Trinidad and Tobago, pointed out that although 87 per cent of the products eligible for duty-free treatment under the CBI already received similar treatment under the existing General System of Preferences, this does not affect the utility of the program because it is not current exports that should be emphasized, but the broadening of the product range over the duration of the program (*Trinidad Guardian*, March 7, 1982).

68 The suggestion came from the general manager of the Trinidad and Tobago Manufacturers Association (interview with the author, July 13, 1988). Colourclad is a relatively new company. A second company, Trincast, a joint venture between Neal and Massy (40%) and a US company, Castech (60%), has also been mentioned in connection with the CBI. However, this company appears to fall more properly under the 806.30 program. "A typical 806.30 operation would involve the export of U.S. produced metal ingots for casting in the foreign country, and returned to the United States for finishing" (The CBI Centre, Dept. of Commerce, *The Caribbean Basin Initiative 1988 Guidebook for Caribbean Basin Exports*,

Washington, DC). This description applies well to Trincast's operations. Nevertheless, according to Neal and Massy's chairman, ". . . with Trincast's shipments of bronze castings to the American market . . . ," Neal and Massy became ". . . the first company in Trinidad and Tobago to take advantage of it [i.e., the CBI]" (*Neal and Massy Holdings Limited Annual Report and Accounts 1987*, p. 5). It is pertinent to note that that statement was made after the chairman had already noted that ". . . the Caribbean Basin Initiative has not entirely come up to expectations" (ibid).

69 Interview with sales engineer of Colourclad, Port of Spain, Trinidad and Tobago, August 3, 1988. Apparently it was originally intended to entail an investment of about US $10 million, but the company has encountered difficulties obtaining the required foreign-exchange clearance from the Central Bank. This has placed the rest of the intended investment on hold and may even have jeopardized it altogether.

70 Ibid.

71 Ibid.

72 Ibid. The closed US market scenario included in the feasibility study was probably inspired by the difficulties ISCOTT was encountering in the early 1980s in entering the US market.

73 This might partly account for the company's inability (at least up to August 1988) to secure the level of foreign exchange clearance it has requested from the Central Bank.

74 Over two decades ago, when EPZs were first contemplated by a group of Trinidadian businessmen, Prime Minister Dr. Eric Williams replied that they would be allowed "over his dead body" (statement by Mr. John Rooks, chairman of the Free Zone Company in *Daily Express*, May 27, 1988). It is ironic that this is exactly how matters have transpired. The proposal had come from a group of businessmen who were interested in developing the Point Lisas area into an industrial centre with extensive port facilities. They formed a company called the Point Lisas Industrial and Port Development Company (PLIPDECO) in which the state subsequently acquired controlling interest. Today, over 20 years later, Point Lisas is the premier industrial centre in the country (though largely through state initiative) and has been selected as the site for the first EPZ in Trinidad and Tobago.

75 John Rooks, chairman of the newly created state-owned Trinidad and Tobago Free Zone Company Limited, interviewed in the *Sunday Guardian*, May 29, 1988. Mr. Rooks is also a successful businessman in the private sector. EPZs were not an issue in the 1986 general election, nor were they given much attention in the *Investment Policy of Trinidad and Tobago* published by the IDC in August 1987. So the government's conversion to the idea has been fairly sudden.

76 Phillip Rochford, managing director of the majority state-owned National Commercial Bank, writing in *Sunday Express*, July 31, 1988.

77 Senator Ken Gordon, quoted in *Trinidad Guardian*, June 16, 1988.

78 A statement from the Small Business Association noted: "The SBA is fully supportive of the EPZs, [because] the establishment of Export Processing Zones would certainly go a long way in reducing the high unemployment rate that has hit this country. Something must be done to alleviate this social disease" (*Trinidad Guardian*, July 14, 1988).

79 The other sites already selected are Point Fortin, La Brea, and Chaguaramas, all fairly evenly spaced along Trinidad's West coast. A site at Piarco, near the country's international airport, was recently cancelled. It is now to be developed as an international trade centre.

80 This sum was also to include the preparation of the Piarco site which, as noted, was subsequently cancelled (*Caribbean Business*, February 18, 1988).

81 Quoted by Denis Pantin, *Sunday Express*, May 29, 1988, section 2.

82 See John Rooks interview with the *Sunday Guardian*, May 29, 1988. Mr. Rooks has been the state's principal spokesperson on the issue.

83 *Sunday Express*, June 5, 1988. Denis Pantin is senior lecturer in economics at the University of the West Indies (St. Augustine, Trinidad and Tobago).

84 Comments by a member of Women Against Free Trade Zones, quoted in *Sunday Express*, July 31, 1988, section 2. Curiously enough, although this argument appears to be in defence of the integrity and material interests of local capitalists, the latter reject it completely. This rejection underscores what appears to be a willingness on the part of local capitalists to continue to play a subordinate role to foreign capital in the manufacturing sector.

85 The Dominican Republic has 10 Free Zones and seven more are planned; Costa Rica has eight; Haiti has five; and Jamaica has one, with others being developed. Barbados, St. Lucia, Antigua, El Salvador, and Guatemala each reportedly has at least one (John Rooks interview, *Sunday Guardian*, May 29, 1988). It was perhaps these developments which prompted an official of the Trinidad and Tobago Manufacturers Association to comment that the aim behind the CBI seems to be "to turn the entire Caribbean into an EPZ" providing cheap labour for US companies (interview with the author, July 13, 1988).

86 Good, "Progress in the Caribbean," p. 20. Many of the Free Trade Zones in the region are government run, but the pressure to privatize them is persistent. There are privately run zones in the Dominican Republic and indications are that Jamaica is beginning to move in that direction. The Export Processing Zones in Trinidad and Tobago are to be government-run, at least initially.

87 *Sunday Guardian*, May 29, 1988.

88 In December 1985, the TT$ was devalued from TT$2.4 = US$1 to TT$3.6 = US$1. In August 1988 it was further devalued to TT$4.25 = US$1. Some observers feel the TT$ is still overvalued and a further devaluation, to around TT$6 = US$1, is likely in the near future. The publication, *Business Latin America*, which at the beginning of 1988 had correctly predicted a devaluation in the TT$, expected a rate of TT$6 = US$1 by the end of that year.

89 In a promotional brochure, the San Isidro Free Zone in the Dominican Republic advertised that the legal minimum wage in the Dominican Republic was US $0.53 an hour or US $4.24 for an eight-hour day. This included all "fringe benefits." The brochure also noted that incentive pay is acceptable. This is the kind of wage against which Trinidad and Tobago must compete.

90 Rhoda Reddock, "Industrialization and the Rise of the Petty Bourgeoisie in Trinidad and Tobago," Master of Development Studies Thesis, Institute of Social Studies, The Hague, Netherlands, 1980, p. 101.

91 John Rooks statement, *Daily Express*, May 27, 1988.

92 See John Rooks interview, *Sunday Guardian*, May 29, 1988.

93 For example, the Dominican Republic is said to offer firms a "unique package." This includes "close proximity to the United States, political stability, a large supply of competent and inexpensive labour, sound infrastructure, and a positive investment climate." Article by the Investment Promotion Council of the Dominican Republic, published in the *Trinidad Guardian*, June 15, 1988.

94 See Clive Y. Thomas, *The Poor and the Powerless: Economic Policy and Change in the Caribbean* (New York: Monthly Review Press, 1988).

95 This mission was the result of discussions held in Washington earlier in the year between Prime Minister Robinson and OPIC leaders. The mission included representatives of several (reportedly 15) US companies.

96 The CBI Centre, US Department of Commerce, *The Caribbean Basin Initiative 1988 Guidebook for Caribbean Basin Exporters* (Washington, DC, 1988).

97 *Report by the U.S. Department of State on the Caribbean Basin Initiative (CBI): Progress to Date*, November 1987 (copy supplied by US embassy, Trinidad and Tobago), p. 4.

98 Even the minister responsible for the implementation of the program (Sen. Ken Gordon, Minister of Industry and Enterprise) has expressed doubts. In a debate on the issue on national television, he commented that Trinidadians are under the illusion that foreign investors are poised to pounce on their country to exploit it for their own benefit, when in fact there in no evidence of a queue of interested foreign investors (*Issues Live*, Trinidad and Tobago Television, August 1988).

99 See, for example, Charles Ford, "Wages, Hours and Working Conditions in Asian Free Trade Zones," *Development and Peace* 5, 2 (Autumn 1984).

100 A senior government official remarked to me that the CBI was nothing more than a Reagan administration effort to channel funds to the Contras and US-supported regimes in Central America. We have seen earlier also that an IDC official characterized the program as being "ridiculous," while a senior TTMA official has characterized it as a device designed to benefit US capital more than the stated "beneficiary" countries.

101 In this context it should be noted that, of all the Caricom countries (with the possible exception of Guyana), Trinidad and Tobago was the least supportive of the US intervention in Grenada in 1983.

Chapter 8

1 *Treaty Establishing the Caribbean Community*, Chaguaramas, 1973, Caribbean Community Secretariat (hereinafter CARICOM Secretariat) 1973.

2 The member states of CARICOM are Antigua and Barbuda, The Bahamas, Barbados, Belize, Dominica, Grenada, Guyana, Jamaica, Saint Lucia, St. Kitts-Nevis, St. Vincent and the Grenadines, Montserrat, and Trinidad and Tobago.

3 CARIBCOM Secretariat, "Pattern of Intra-regional Trade," *CARIBCOM Bulletin* 3 (1982): 14.

4 Communiqué: The Saint Lucia Meeting of Heads of Government of Commonwealth Western Hemisphere Countries, February 20-21, 1983, CARICOM Secretariat, p. 16.

5 Kenneth Hall, "The Management of External Relations in CARICOM," *Ten Years of CARICOM* (Washington: Inter America Development Bank, 1984), p. 171.

6 Marie Freckleton, "Balance of Payments Policies in the Caribbean Community," *CARICOM Bulletin* 3 (1982): 3.

7 Alistair McIntyre, "Adjustments of Caribbean Economies," *CARICOM Bulletin* 3 (1982): 3.

8 Freckleton, "Balance of Payments Policies," p. 21.

9 Report by a Group of Caribbean Experts, *The Caribbean Community in the 1980's*, Caribbean Community Secretariat, 1981, p. 3.

10 G. Lewis, "Historical and Cultural Background of CARICOM" in Hall, *Ten Years of CARICOM*, p. 53.

11 *The Caribbean Community in the 1980's*, p. 25.

12 Hall, "The Management of External Relations in CARICOM," p. 169.

13 *Communiqué of the Ninth Meeting of the Standing Committee of Ministers Responsible for Foreign Affairs*, Grenada, 1981, CARICOM Secretariat, 1981.

14 See, for example, the *Communiqué of the Ninth Meeting of the SCMFA*, the *Ocho Rios Declaration*, the *Communiqué of the Third Conference of the Heads of Government of the Caribbean Community*, Ocho Rios 1982, and the "Communiqué of the Fourth Conference of the Heads of Government of the Caribbean Community," Port of Spain, 1983 (unpublished).

15 Kari Levitt, "The Origins and Implication of the Caribbean Basin Initiative, Mortgaging Sovereignty?" *International Journal* 40, 2 (Spring 1985): 264.

16 The private sector development bank was never created, but the administration chose to reduce financing of the Caribbean Development Bank and to channel such resources through a private sector institution, the Caribbean Association of Industry and Commerce.

17 *Communiqué of the Third Conference of the Heads of Government*.

18 The Governments of Antigua and Barbuda, Barbados, St. Kitts-Nevis, Saint Lucia, and Saint Vincent and the Grenadines were co-signatories of the Memorandum.

19 "Communiqué of the Fourth Conference of Heads of Government."

20 Report by a Commonwealth Consultative Group, *Vulnerability, Small States in the Global Society* (London: Commonwealth Secretariat, 1986).

Selected Bibliography

The research conducted for the articles in this collection was based on extensive consultation of government documents in Washington, DC; Ottawa; London; and the Caribbean; a wide selection of published books, articles, and working papers; and extensive interviews with policy-makers and policy-analysts. The selected bibliography provides articles and books which are both readily available and accessible to a wide readership.

Articles

Berger, Peter L. "Can the Caribbean Learn from East Asia? The Case of Jamaica." *Caribbean Review* 13, 2.

Beruff, Jorge Rodriguez. "Puerto Rico and the Militarization of the Caribbean, 1979-1984." *Contemporary Marxism* 10 (1985).

Black, George. "Central America: Crisis in the Backyard." *New Left Review* 135 (September-October 1982).

Bolin, William H. "Central America: Real Economic Help Is Workable Now." *Foreign Affairs* 62, 5 (Summer 1984).

Brenner, Philip. "Waging Ideological War: Anti-Communism and US Foreign Policy in Central America." *Socialist Register* (1974).

Dam, Kenneth W. "Economic Growth and US Policy in Central America." *Current Policy* 509. US Department of State (September 14, 1983).

_____. "The Caribbean Basin Initiative and Central America," *Current Policy* 529. US Department of State (November 29, 1983).

Dominguez, J.I. "The United States and Its Regional Security Interests: The Caribbean, Central and South America." *Daedalus* 109, 4 (Fall 1980).

Feinberg, Richard E., and Richard S. Newfarmer. "The Caribbean Basin Initiative: A Bilateralist Gamble." *Foreign Policy* 47 (Summer 1982).

Gonzalez, Heliodoro. "The Caribbean Basin Initiative: Toward a Permanent Dole." *Journal of Interamerican Studies and World Affairs* 36 (Summer 1982).

Halliday, Fred. "Cold War in the Caribbean." *New Left Review* 141 (September-October 1983).

LaFeber, Walter. "The Reagan Administration and Revolutions in Central America." *Political Science Quarterly* 99 (Spring 1984).

Leo Grande, William M. "A Splendid Little War: Drawing the Line in El Salvador." *International Security* 6, 1 (Summer 1981).

Lowenthal, Abraham F. "Changing Patterns in Inter-American Relations." *Washington Quarterly* 4, 1 (Winter 1981).

_____. "The Caribbean Basin Initiative: Misplaced Emphasis." *Foreign Policy* 47 (1982).

Manning, Robert. "Reagan: Sights on a New Order." *South* (September 1983).

McColm, R. Bruce. "Central America and the Caribbean: The Larger Scenario." *Strategic Review* 11, 3 (Summer 1983).

Middendorf II, J. William. "The Private Sector's Role in Latin American Development." *Current Policy* 609. US Department of State (August 30, 1984).

Newfarmer, Richard. "Economic Policy Toward the Caribbean Basin: The Balance Sheet." *Journal of Interamerican Studies and World Affairs* 27, 1 (1985).

Ortiz-Buonafina. "The CBI Is Not Enough: The Case of Honduras." *Caribbean Review* 14, 2 (Spring 1985).

Pantojas-Garcia, Emilio. "The US Caribbean Basin Initiative and the Puerto Rican Experience: Some Parallels and Lessons." *Latin American Perspectives* 12, 4 (Fall 1985).

Pastor, Robert. "Sinking in the Caribbean Basin." *Foreign Affairs* 60, 5 (Summer 1982).

Phillips, Dion E. "Caribbean Militarization: A Response to the Crisis." *Contemporary Marxism* 10 (1985).

Ramsarran, Ramesh. "The Caribbean Basin Initiative." *The World Today* 38, 11 (1982).

Riding, Alan. "The Central American Quagmire." *Foreign Affairs* 61, 3 (1983).

Schoultz, Lars. "US Policy and Human Rights Violations in Latin America: A Comparative Analysis of Foreign Aid Distribution." *Comparative Politics* 13, 2 (January 1981).

Watson, Hilbourne A. "The Caribbean Basin Initiative: Consolidating American Hegemony." *Trans-Africa Forum* 1, 1 (Winter 1982).

_____. "The Caribbean Basin Initiative and Caribbean Development: A Critical Analysis." *Contemporary Marxism* 10 (1985).

Weintraub, Sydney. "The Caribbean Basin Initiative: A Flawed Model." *Foreign Policy* 47 (Summer 1982).

Books

Ambursley, Fitzroy, and Robin Cohen, eds. *Crisis in the Caribbean*. New York: Monthly Review, 1983.

America's Watch. *Human Rights in Nicaragua: Reagan Rhetoric and Reality, July 1985*. New York: America's Watch, 1985.

Barry, Tom. *Dollars and Dictators: A Guide to Central America*. New York: Grove Press, 1983.

Boodhoo, Kenneth. "The Economic Dimension of US Caribbean Policy." In H. Michael Erisman, ed., *The Caribbean Challenge: US Policy in a Volatile Region*. Boulder, CO: Westview Press, 1984.

Development Group for Alternative Policies (The Development Gap). *Supporting Central American and Caribbean Development: A Critique of the Caribbean Basin Initiative and an Alternative Regional Assistance Plan*. Washington, DC: The Development Gap, August 1983.

_____. *Prospects and Reality: The CBI Revisited*. Washington, DC: The Development Gap, November 1985.

Erisman, H. Michael, ed. *The Caribbean Challenge: US Policy in a Volatile Region*. Boulder, CO: Westview Press, 1984.

Erisman, Michael, and John D. Martz. *Colossus Challenged: The Struggle for Caribbean Influence*. Boulder, CO: Westview Press, 1982.

—————. *Forging Peace: The Challenge of Central America*. New York: Basil Blackwell, 1987.

Fagg, John Edwin. *Pan Americanism*. Florida: Robert and Krieger Publishing, 1982.

Feinberg, Richard E., ed. *Central America: International Dimensions of the Crisis*. New York: Holmes and Meir, 1982.

Hayes, Margaret Daly. *Latin America and the US National Interest: A Basis for Foreign Policy*. Boulder, CO: Westview Press, 1984.

Jonas, Susanne. "An Overview: 50 Years of Revolution and Intervention in Central America." In Marlene Dixon and Susanne Jonas, eds., *Revolution and Intervention in Central America*. San Francisco: Synthesis, 1983.

Kissinger, H. et al. *The Report of the National Bipartisan Commission on Central America*. Washington, DC: US Government Printing Office, January 1984.

—————. *Appendix to the Report of the National Bipartisan Commission on Central America*. Washington, DC: Government Printing Office, March 1984.

Kornbluh, Peter. *Nicaragua: The Price of Intervention*. Washington, DC: Institute of Policy Studies, 1987.

—————. *Inevitable Revolutions: The United States in Central America*. New York and London: W.W. Norton, 1984.

Lafeber, Louis, and Liisa L. North, eds. *Democracy and Development in Latin America: Studies in Political Economy, Society and Culture of Latin America and the Caribbean*, vol. 1. Downsview, ON: Centre for Research on Latin America and the Caribbean, 1980.

Langley, Lester D. *The United States and the Caribbean in the Twentieth Century*. Athens: University of Georgia Press, 1982.

Latin American Bureau. *The European Challenge: Europe's New Role in Latin America*. London: Latin American Bureau, 1982.

Latin American Research Unit (LARU). *Central America: A Contemporary Crisis*. Toronto: LARU Studies, 1982.

Leo Grande, William. *Central America and the Polls*. Washington, DC: Washington Office on Latin America, March 1987.

Lewis, Gordon K. *The Growth of the Modern West Indies*. New York: Monthly Review Press, 1968.

Palmer, R.W. *Caribbean Dependence on the US Economy*. New York: Praeger Special Studies, 1979.

Pastor, Robert. "US Policy Toward the Caribbean: Continuity and Change." In Peter M. Dunn and Bruce W. Watson, eds., *American Intervention in Grenada: The Implications of Operation "Urgent Fury."* Boulder and London: Westview Press, 1985.

Payne, Anthony, and Paul Sutton, eds. *Dependency Under Challenge: The Political Economy of the Commonwealth Caribbean*. Dover, NH: Manchester University Press, 1984.

Pearce, Jenny. *Under the Eagle: US Intervention in Central America and the Caribbean*. Boston: South End Press, 1982.

Pelzman, J., and D. Rousslang. *Effects on US Trade and Employment of Tariff Eliminations among the Countries of North America and the Caribbean Basin*. Washington, DC: US Department of Labour, January 1982.

White, Richard Alan. *The Morass: United States Intervention in Central America*. New York: Harper & Row, 1984.

Wiarda, Howard J., ed. *Rift and Revolution: The Central American Imbroglio*. Washington, DC: American Enterprise Institute, 1984.

_____. *The Continuing Struggle for Democracy in Central America*. Boulder, CO: Westview Press, 1980.

Index